Copyright 2008 191847011
ISBN# 978-1-4276-3445-0

Publisher......Robert Daugherty
Book Cover......Melvin Parker Jr.
Editors...Alice Daugherty,
Robyn Winslow, Sheila Cothran Word

COMENTARYS

I highly recommend this book, which gives the testimony of Robert Daugherty. I know it will encourage the reader to understand that God will bring us out of every difficult situation in our lives. Reverend Aubrey Kishna, Pastor-Jubilee Worship Center, St. Louis Missouri. I have personally known and worked with Robert for twenty years. He presently serves as an associate minister at Jubilee Worship Center and is involved in several areas of ministry. Included are: Praise and worship, preaching, and outreach ministry. He is faithful in his ministry for the Lord. I know he has shared his heart in this book that will encourage you to find God's purpose for your life.

Vimla Kishna, First Lady -Jubilee Worship Center
Recently, I went back to Kinloch, and stood in the place where my house used to be. I was immediately flooded with memories of home, and family. The houses are all gone now, along with all of the wonderful things that marked the trail to Robert's house. In this book of memories, Robert rebuilds all of those houses and places from our past and teaches that every moment of life is truly a miracle.

My dear friend Robert, continues to be a constant source of inspiration and true friendship. His life's journey from page to page, reveals a light within that will never be dimmed. He has always asked the hard questions. Who are we? What is the nature of the universe? How do we get to the Light? In every story and anecdote, we can feel his search for what is good and just. From the beginning, he doesn't tip-toe around. He let's us know that Jesus is the answer. With Jesus, comes joy, and our destiny is to reconnect with him. With my eyes clearly focused on Robert's "Highway to Heaven", I look forward to the next "chapter" of his life. John Cothran Jr. Actor, and friend. Los Angeles California.

My attention was fully captured as I listened to some of the life stories that are in Robert's book. I am sure that the readers will be captivated as well. People hear what you say, but learn from experience what and who you are. He imparts his life into his work.

It was definitely the hand of God! Pastor Thelma Parker Overcomer's Christian Church, St. Louis, Missouri.

It was the wisdom and spiritual insight of Mr. Daugherty that helped us as THE TRAK STARZ Producers realize our success. For many years, Mr. Daugherty has given us advice, guidance, and encouraging words. My partner Sham has been blessed to grow up with it and I've been blessed to have access to Mr. Daugherty. Now the world will get a chance by reading his book.
 Alonzo "Zo" Lee of the TRAK STARZ

{Shamtrakstarz} Grammy award winning producers. My father taught me how to be a winner. He told me to have faith, and trust in God no matter how dark it gets, and He will pull you through when you take His advice. I've sold millions of records and won two Grammys. "Words of Wisdom"
Shamar Daugherty, {Sham-Trak Starz}

Copyright 2008......... ISBN#................1	
COMENTARYS..2	
ROBERT'S STORY 6	
FROM DEATH UNTO LIFE 6	
ABOUT THE AUTHORS 7	
Danielle 7	
Robert 8	
THANKS AND ACKNOWLEDGEMENTS 9	
CHAPTER ONE 10	
THE EARLY YEARS..10	
CHAPTER TWO 17	
GRADE SCHOOL DAYS 17	
CHAPTER THREE 24	
HIGH SCHOOL DAYS 24	
CHAPTER FOUR 44	
TRADE SCHOOL AND LIFE AFTER HIGH SCHOOL 44	
CHAPTER FIVE 58	
ROBERT JOINS THE NAVY 58	
CHAPTER SIX...71	
ROBERT GOES HOME----AND HOSPITAL, SCHOOL ...71	
CHAPTER SEVEN 76	
PATUXENT RIVER MARYLAND----NAVAL AIR STATION........76	
CHAPTER EIGHT 87	
FMF- SCHOOL-----CAMP PENDLETON CALIFORNIA 87	
CHAPTER NINE..91	
GRADUATION FROM FMF SCHOOL & DOC BECOMES A PLATOON MEDIC 91	
CHAPTER TEN 104	
ROBERT AND THE 5TH MARINE DIVISION HEAD FOR VIETNAM...104	
CHAPTER ELEVEN..109	
ARRIVAL IN VIET NAM..109	
CHAPTER TWELVE...117	
ROBERT IS INJURED BY A LAND MINE 117	
CHAPTER THIRTEEN..126	
ROBERT IS FLOWN TO A HOSPITAL IN JAPAN 126	
CHAPTER FOURTEEN 135	
ROBERT RETURNS TO THE STATES 135	
LIFE AT SCOTT AIR FORCE BASE....................................135	
CHAPTER FIFTEEN 138	
ROBERT ARRIVES AT SCOTT AIR FORCE BASE 138	
CHAPTER SIXTEEN...145	
ROBERT FINALLY LOOKS AT HIS WOUNDS................145	
CHAPTER SEVENTEEN 148	

ROBERT IS MOVED TO AN OPEN WARD 148
CHAPTER EIGHTEEN 151
   ROBERT'S FIRST TRIP BACK HOME 151
CHAPTER NINETEEN 155
   DEPRESSION SETS IN ON ROBERT.......................................155
CHAPTER TWENTY 160
   ROBERT RETURNS TO GREAT LAKES..................................160
CHAPTER TWENTY- ONE..169
   ROBERT IS RETIRED FROM THE NAVY 169
   AND RETURNS HOME TO ST. LOUIS....................................169
CHAPTER TWENTY- TWO..174
ROBERT MOVES OUT ON HIS OWN....................................174
CHAPTER TWENTY- THREE 178
   ROBERT'S CLOSE CALL WITH DEATH..................................178
CHAPTER TWENTY-FOUR 182
   THE VA FINALLY COMES THROUGH 182
CHAPTER TWENTY- FIVE 185
   THE CHICAGO INCIDENT 185
CHAPTER TWENTY- SIX...190
   ROBERT MOVES IN WITH HIS SISTER 190
CHAPTER TWENTY- SEVEN 193
   ROBERT BUYS HIS FIRST HOUSE 193
CHAPTER TWENTY - EIGHT 196
   ROBERT GETS MARRIED...196
CHAPTER TWENTY- NINE 203
   ROBERT AND THE FAMILY MOVE TO NORH COUNTY..........203
CHAPTER THIRTY 207
   ROBERT'S MOTHER PASSES AWAY 207
CHAPTER THIRTY - ONE..210
   ROBERT'S SEARCH FOR KNOWLEDGE AND TRUTH............210
CHAPTER THIRTY - TWO 215
   ROBERT GETS BAPTIZED IN THE HOLY SPIRIT...................215
CHAPTER THIRTY - THREE 219
   ROBERT'S STRUGGLES AND VICTORIES, AND GROWING AS A CHRISTIAN..219
CHAPTER THIRTY - FOUR..222
   A NEW CHURCH ENVIRONMENT 222

ROBERT'S STORY

FROM DEATH UNTO LIFE

ROBERT DAUGHERTY

US NAVY HOSPITAL CORPSMAN

BY DANIELLE MORRISON & ROBERT DAUGHERTY

ABOUT THE AUTHORS

Danielle

I was born on December 26th, 1988, to David and Valerie Morrison, in St. Louis Missouri. I graduated in May of 2008 from Hazelwood East High School in North County of St. Louis. I grew up listening to my family tell interesting stories about some of the events in their lives. After listening to so many interesting and fascinating stories about Uncle Robert's life, I asked him if I could do a biography on his life. He told me to go right ahead. I took the challenge, and started to pursue the project. I plan to do more writing, as I continue my education in college, and find my place in society.

Robert

Over the course of time, many people would often say, *"You ought to write a book."* I would never take them seriously because I figured that only important people wrote books about their lives. I considered myself as someone who had a few hard times, and was just trying to survive the everyday trials of life. Even though I would talk about some things, I never wanted to go back into a lot of the details, that I was trying hard to forget. I knew that it would be very painful to relive some of the darkest times of my life. But as usual, God has the final say so. When God put it on her heart to accomplish His will, Danielle, nor I, knew that it would involve so much work. After many months, and hours of putting the book together, it was a welcome, but pleasant relief when it was finished. It proves once again, that God is looking for someone who will just say yes. I could see the hand of Satan, from the start to the finish, trying to do everything he could to spoil and stop the project. I am very grateful to everyone for putting up with my mood swings during the project. I am also thankful to my wife, Rosemary, (Tracy) for being so supportive. It took more prayer and endurance, than the normal eye could see. But most of all, I thank God for sending Jesus to provide me with everything I would need. This book is truly dedicated to Him, who is able, and enables me to highlight all of His goodness and mercy through the testimonies in this book. I realize that this book is a testimony about Him, more so than me.

THANKS AND ACKNOWLEDGEMENTS

Rosemary (Tracy) Daugherty. My wife, who supports and inspires By trusting me to do what needs to be done.
Alice, Linda, Lisa, Allen, (Knuckles) Patrick & Shamar, (Sham) ---MY KIDS
All of my brothers and sisters,.........Med, Florence, Ruth, Rose, Mary, Barbara, Claudette, Dianne, & James
The Grandchildren, Cousins, Aunts, Uncles, Nieces, Nephews & Friends
Valerie Morrison,.........Her inspiring words, "Keep on writing."
Gladson David,...Kept the computer working, & Pre edited.
Sheila Cothran,Word.............Helped edit, even through illness
Pastors Aubrey /Vimla Kishna...Jubilee Worship Center St. Louis
The Entire Jubilee Worship Center, Church Family
Bishop Melvin Dunn..................St. Louis
Pastor Winston Larry..................Springfield Mo.
Pastor Sam Ramphal...................Kansas City Mo.
Pastor Greg Bruce.......................St. Louis
Reverend Larry Rice....................New Life Evangelistic Center, St. Louis
Hayden E. A. Goodwin...St. Louis VA, Protestant Staff Chaplain
Assemblies of God N.B.F. Central Region
Miss Jamesetta Roach.................Helped to start the project
Pastor Thelma Parker ....Overcomers Christian Church, St. Louis
Barbara Taylor...My sister. A surviving cancer patient...Support and inspiration
Special acknowledgements to Bishop Melvin S. Dunn, My spiritual father in the Lord. Pastor Greg Bruce, and the Bruce family for seven years of experience and growth at Hope Church. Special thoughts go out to Pastor Melvin Parker Sr., and Pastor James Bruce, who have gone to be with the Lord.

CHAPTER ONE
THE EARLY YEARS

Robert was born to Vennie, {Emma} and Med Louis Daugherty, on February 24, 1946. Med moved to St Louis from Memphis, Tennessee, and Vennie moved to St Louis from Sunflower, Mississippi. Ten children were born to them during their marriage. They had seven girls and three boys, with Robert being the ninth of ten children.

From age two, yes, age two, Robert recalls his father putting him in their blue Dodge car. When he pushed the horn, it made a funny sound. (UGGA- UGGA) He would drive him from their home, which was a building behind the old drug store in Kinloch Park, where his parents had settled. There he built the house that would be the home to the Daugherty family.

The small all Black community was right by the airport. At that time the whole area was called Kinloch Park. Many families from different parts of the South came there with high expectations. They settled there and built their own homes after purchasing a plot of land. They built schools, churches, and businesses. They went through an era, where they raised their families, and started businesses.

After arriving at the new house site, Robert's dad would meet with a friend of his, and both of them would work on the house. Robert remembers when his dad started the foundation digging. The foundation was poured from a cement truck, and after the cement dried, he remembers seeing the frame of the house gradually being put into place. Over many months, he saw the progress of the frames turning in to walls that turned in to rooms. Robert's oldest brother would also help his dad build, while he and his other brother would play, and try to stay out of the way. Soon the roof was finished and Robert thought that the house was finished, but his father told him that the inside had to be finished too.

He remembers the thrill of riding his tricycle around the house after the cement was poured and dry. After many months of hard work and sweat, the Daugherty family finally moved into their new house built by their father. The family settled in their five- room house, which was rather small. But compared to their old living quarters, this was a mansion. About a year later, all the joy turned into sadness. It was a sunny afternoon when the phone rang while Robert and his brother who was a few years older were at the sitter's house. The phone rang, and before anyone answered it, something inside of Robert said, your father is dead. At the age of three, he wasn't quite sure what that meant, but he kind of knew that he wouldn't see his father alive again. After that, the lady with a sad look on her face came to Robert and his brother and told them that their father had just died while at his job. Robert told her that he already knew. She asked how did he know? He told her that he didn't know, he just did. She went to console his brother who was having a hard time dealing with the bad news. Robert understands now that his heavenly father was consoling him at an early age as he would through all of his many pains and trials that he would have through out his life.

Everyone was all dressed up, and Robert didn't know he was going to the wake. He thought they were going to a party or somewhere to have some fun. When they got out of the car and went into the funeral parlor, he knew from the tears and sadness that it was not going to be fun. At what he now knows to be a wake, the people were passing by his father's casket and crying. Robert was too little, and couldn't see his father in the casket. His family wasn't going to let him look at his father lying in the casket, so he was trying to pull himself up to see what was going on. A lady that he knew saw him struggling, and picked him up so he could see his father for the last time. As Robert looked at his dad's lifeless body, he noticed something that seemed to be out of place. He called out to his mother, and asked her where the rest of his father was. She told him the rest of him was under the lower part of the casket. The casket was half closed, and Robert thought they had cut his dad in half. He was ready to go home but he had to wait until everything was over, which for him couldn't have been too soon. Robert was tired, and had felt the pain of losing his father for the very first time.

He remembered arriving at the cemetery where his father was to be buried. After getting out of the car and walking to the gravesite, Robert saw his mother, who was dressed in a black dress with a veil over her face, sobbing and crying. Robert went to her and tried to comfort her, seeing that she was in a lot of pain. After that, in a child's way of thinking, and even now, it seemed like a long time had passed since his family lost their dad. They needed some manly help in a lot of areas that was previously taken for granted when their father was alive. One of the things left unfinished was the toilet facility, or "out house" as it was called. Bubba, as he was called, had built a cesspool and left an opening for the wooden structure to sit on. Everyone had to endure the inconvenience of using the white bucket, called the potty. The potty was kept in the corner of one of the rooms in the back of the house. When the pot was almost full, his two older brothers had the chore of taking the pot out, and dumping the contents into the hole in the concrete cesspool. The task was extra hard in the winter months.

On one sunny afternoon of the following year the Daugherty's miracle arrived. Robert remembers very clearly the glorious day that everyone was looking forward to with great anticipation. After many days of watching and waiting, the time had come. Robert and one of his brothers saw a truck pulling into the driveway. They had sounded quite a few false alarms previously, so they had to make sure that this one was the real thing. They saw proof on the back of the truck, but just to make sure, his brother asked the driver if it was theirs. The driver, a volunteer Kinloch fireman, like their dad, confirmed it was theirs. That was all they needed to hear. They told everyone in the house that it was here. Everyone was waving and cheering as their newly built outhouse was unloaded and placed squarely on the opening of the cesspool that their dad had left. That was indeed a victorious and happy day for the Daugherty family.

He still has fresh and vivid memories of the three years that he had with his father. He remembers climbing onto the running board of Bubba's blue Dodge car, and sitting in the spacious back seat as he drove the family to a picnic. There was a convoy of about three or four cars headed for what he now knows as Forest Park. He remembers hearing the whistling sound of the wind as they passed other cars coming in the opposite direction, and wondering why the other cars were doing that to them.

He also recalls a bright sunny morning when his dad was getting ready to go fishing. Robert had never been fishing and didn't know what fishing was. All he knew was that he and his brothers were going fishing with their dad to have some fun. Everyone was ready to go when his dad noticed that Robert didn't have his suspenders on to hold up his pants. He had a rope around his pants trying to keep his pants up. He told his dad that his suspenders had fallen into one of his paint buckets and was soaked with paint. He gave Robert a few minutes to get his suspenders together or they would have to leave him. His orange and black suspenders were now orange, black, and brown. There was so much paint on them that Robert and his mom couldn't get the paint out that quickly. They needed to be soaked in turpentine to get the paint out. His time was up and Robert's heart was broken as he watched his dad and two brothers load the fishing poles and bait into the trunk of the car and drive off without him. That was one of his last bitter, sweet memories of his dad before he died. There were bits and pieces of remembering his father saying grace at the table before meals. He remembered him being very strict with his children. He didn't believe in "sparing the rod" and spoiling the child. He also remembers his dad with his big lunch box as he went to work in the morning. One of his fondest memories was seeing him dressed in his fireman's uniform, the same uniform he was buried in. Looking back, Robert did not realize that he was that young when all these things were taking place. Robert was with his dad for the first three years of his life, but they seemed much longer than three years. Although he missed his earthly father, he knows that his heavenly father has picked up the slack and has taken very good care of him. During all his pains and trials as he walks this planet called earth, he knows that he has a heavenly home waiting for him for all eternity.

Robert had only been around for three years and his life was already filled with seemingly unending bitter, sweet memories. He recalled an incident in their new outhouse. The two-seat outhouse was too tall for him to reach by himself, so someone had to sit him on the stool and take him down when he was finished. When he was done he would call out as loud as he could, *"I'm Thu"*. Well one night, he was taken to the outhouse by one of his sisters. When he had finished his business, he started his usual chant of *"I'm Thu"*. He had to be out there for over half an hour in the pitch- black darkness of the night, with the toilet door closed. It was a good thing that he was on the shallow side instead of the deep seat of the cesspool, because if he had fallen in, he would have been a goner. After losing his voice and growing weary of singing the famous *"I'm Thu"* song, he just gave up. There was nothing he could do but wait and be rescued from what could have been the infamous outhouse. He couldn't get down and was trapped alone in the dark outhouse. Finally, he heard the kitchen door slam. He started to chant again as loud as he could. One of his sisters opened the door to the outhouse, and rescued their little brother. Robert asked her in an angry voice "why didn't you come and get me, I told you that I was Thu." When he got in the house, they were gathered around the nine- inch TV screen. They all apologized to him and tried to make it up to him by hugging and kissing him on the face.

. They begged him not to tell momma so they wouldn't get into any trouble. He agreed not to tell if they gave him some ice cream. Robert tried to think positive about the situation since the late night singing of his famous anthem. It may have helped develop his lungs for singing and running track in high school.

By the time he turned four, he decided it was time to grow up. On his fourth birthday, he made up his mind to learn how to tie his shoes. One of his sisters had showed him what to do, so he went to work. It was a warm day in February and Robert knelt in front of the house on the sidewalk and didn't come in until he could effectively tie his own shoes strings. There was a lot of trials and error but after over half an hour, he had passed the test. When his brothers and sisters came home from school, he proudly showed them his new art of tying shoe tying. They were happy for him, especially since he no longer had to track them down to tie his shoes.

As time went by, he would take part in other work around the house. His brother taught him how to chop wood that they used in their potbelly stove that was situated in the corner of their living room. The stove would get red hot as the smoke rose up the chimney through the flue in the attic and out of the chimney that was on the roof of the house. Looking back, it took a major miracle for eleven family members, and sometimes relatives and friends to live together in that very small house. The necessary closeness brought out the best and sometimes the worst in every one of them.

He remembers when he was about five years old, one of his brothers had him in tears. For some reason, he chose to harass Robert the whole morning. One of his sisters tried to get him to stop, but he got worse. She told Robert to go the police station to report his brother, Robert thought she was joking or trying to scare their brother into stopping what he was doing. His brother also thought she was bluffing until she went and got Robert's jacket and gave him a note to give to the police. The station was a short distance from the house and Robert had passed it many times, but never by himself. Robert reluctantly took the note from his sister and headed out the back door, through a path in the field behind the house. He was almost at the police station when his brother caught up with him and made a bargain with him. He told Robert that if he gave him the note and not go to the police, he would not bother him any more. Robert made him promise or he would go to the police on his own the next time. Robert agreed and gave him the note, which he tore up. Robert went home and told his sister that the police said they would arrest his brother if they had any more trouble out of him. Robert and his sister didn't have any more problems from their brother.

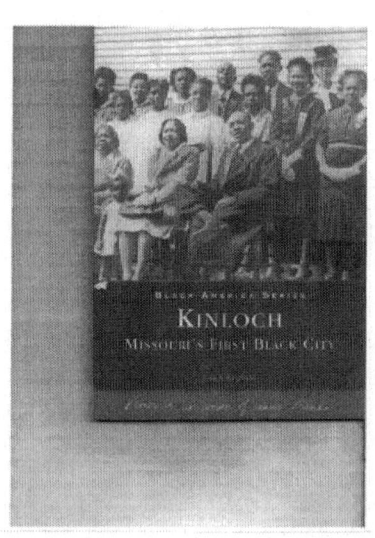

CHAPTER TWO

GRADE SCHOOL DAYS

At the age of six, Robert started the first grade at Holy Angels School. Even though it seemed a lot further to Robert, it was only about ten minutes of walking from their home. He was very glad to be reunited with his brother and some of his sisters at what he thought of as a big show, which was only grade school. Elementary school was going to be quite an experience for Robert as he began to learn more about life and about himself. While his mom was raised Methodist, the family was recruited and raised in the Catholic Church. They were allowed a tuition break that enabled all the children to attend and graduate at Holy Angels grade school in Kinloch. The school was run by an order of Nuns from Baltimore, Maryland called the Oblate Sisters of Providence. They were the first and only black order of Nuns in the Catholic Church. They were sent to Kinloch, an all black community to teach, educate and indoctrinate at the Holy Angels School and church. The Nuns were excellent teachers and excelled in fundamentals. They inspired the children to learn and got the most out of the students. The students learned life skills and were taught music, art, drama and dance. As a child, Robert was a quick learner in most subjects and he didn't realize that he was being slowly indoctrinated in the Catholic religion. They were taught the fear of the Lord, but somehow got mixed up with the fear of some of the Nuns. Every morning, they had to go to mass before going to classes, Sunday mass and Holy days of obligation were a must that students attend. It was considered a mortal sin if they missed Sunday mass without a legitimate excuse, and if you didn't have one, you had to go to confession and get the sin off your soul before you died, or you would face the punishment of hell.

Robert remembers missing Sunday mass when he was in the fifth grade. He spent the weekend at his older brother's house with a promise that someone would take him to mass. Sunday came and no one would take him to mass. Robert felt bad, but he had no choice in the matter. The next day, he had to report to the principal's office. If a student's envelope wasn't counted, they knew the student wasn't at the Sunday mass. Everyone had to give account, but Robert wasn't worried because he thought he had a good excuse. As he stood in the absentee line waiting to see the Reverend Mother, he started to get a little nervous because students that were coming out of her office said she wasn't cutting anyone any slack. Robert was ready to take whatever punishment Mother was going to dish out but was not prepared to stay after school for a week and clean and scrub the bathrooms. He valued his freedom and that was just too much to handle. He was next and had to come up with something fast. He was listening to the student that was in the office before him who said they were at mass but lost their envelope. The Reverend Mother asked him what the Sunday sermon was about, so he told her and he was home free. Robert jumped on it right away. He did not hear the student's answer about the sermon, but he knew that the Monday morning sermon that the priest gave was always the same as the Sunday morning sermon. Robert had started out ready tell the truth, but after hearing the Reverend Mother hand out harsh punishments for the offenders, he decided to play it differently. Robert told her that he was at Sunday mass but had lost his envelope as the other student had done. When asked to prove it, he told the Reverend Mother what the sermon was about based on the Monday morning mass. Robert was excused. He had beaten the Reverend Mother. He was glad that he wouldn't have to stay after school and clean toilets, but he still felt terrible that he had lied over such an innocent thing; he couldn't even tell the priest what he had done in the confession booth. It took years for Robert to forgive himself for lying to the Reverend Mother. Only after he learned about the forgiveness of God was he able to finally let it go.

Over all, his family was treated fairly well by the staff. After seeing some of their homemade lunches, the nuns got together and put them on the "free lunch" program. Sometimes Robert wouldn't eat lunch at all; he would sometimes give his smashed up sandwich to a guy they called "Piggy". He was worse off than Robert and he would eat anything. Before, Robert could only smell and watch the other students enjoy a hot meal that was freshly cooked in the school cafeteria. Now he was able to exchange his lunch ticket for a nice hot meal.

Robert never looked at himself as being poor, but in comparison to some of his friends and other students, financially they might have been. But he never saw himself as poor since his mom did the best she could for her ten children with what she could afford. The house that their father built was on very good and fertile ground. The house withstood rain, sleet, snow and storms, including a tornado that came through the neighborhood. The front yard was spacious but the rear of the property ended at the sidewalk behind the house. Even though the property ended there, the field behind the house was like the Garden of Eden. The field was heavily weeded, but was surrounded by flowers and fruit trees.. There were two large apple trees, a blue plumb tree, a tree with red plumbs and a mulberry tree.

The front yard also had a red plum tree. The next-door neighbors also had a lot of apple trees and a peach tree. The yard had a big chain fence so Robert and his brother and some of their friends sometimes raided their trees at night. Even the vicious watch dogs didn't stop them from their mission.. Robert, his brothers and their friends would put a board across the fence that rested on a shed in their yard and carry out the night raids and sometimes daylight raids on the overloaded fruit trees. The field was open to anyone and there was plenty of fruit to go around. The field did not belong to anyone that they knew, so whoever was closer to any particular tree laid claim on it as if it was their own.

When Robert was in the third or fourth grade, he had an unforgettable experience in the field, as they called it. One afternoon after school, he decided to go to the far end of the field to pick some apples on his own. This was a dangerous move since one of the notorious families had laid claim to that particular tree since it was closer to their house. They did not have anything personal against Robert. Anyone outside of their family or group was considered fair game. When Robert got to the tree, no one was in sight, so he thought he would climb to the top of the tree and shake some apples to the ground, and take his haul home in a bag that he left on the ground. Robert was up in the tree for a few minutes when all of a sudden some of the boys came right under the tree and started to pick some apples off the ground. A few of the older boys were considered to be more dangerous. Robert tried to be still and quiet, hoping that they would leave before he was spotted. They were just about to leave when one of the younger brothers looked up and saw

Robert on the top limb of the tree. The leaves on the tree had provided him with cover but he was spotted, and now dead meat. One of the older brothers told Robert that he had ten seconds to come down out of their tree or they are coming up after him. Robert was scared and didn't know what they were going to do to him. They told him that they were going to beat his you no what. He started to count: one, and before he got to two, Robert jumped down from the limb and landed in the middle of the bunch of would be pursuers. They were shocked to see him jump from the high limb. As he landed on his feet, he was already in a running position. As soon as he touched the ground he took off running. He dashed between the dazed and shocked bullies without so much as a pause. By the time they realized what had just happened, Robert was half way to his house before they started to chase him. The tree was about a hundred yards or so from his house and he made it home safely leaving the bewildered and stunned brothers in their tracks. He told his big brother what had happened, but by the time he had rounded up some of his friends and went to the field, the boys were gone. For the time being the battle was over.

    Some time later, Robert had an incident with the same group. It was a sunny day after school. Robert's mom had sent him to the store to buy a stick of margarine. He had to keep his eyes open because he had to pass through enemy territory. The trip to the store went well. He was almost home when one of the brothers spotted him while riding his bike. Robert thought that he was gone, until he came back with about four of his brothers. He shouted out "There he is, let's get him". He was blocked from his path to his house, so Robert dropped the bag with the butter in it and started running as fast as he could in the opposite direction from his home. He figured he could lose them and come back home another way. He ran down some back trails that he knew and ran through some wooded areas and jumped a creek. He thought that he had lost them since two of them were on bikes and wouldn't be able to cross the creek. Robert's house was in the middle of Kinloch and he was headed for what was called "the bottom". Robert ran as far as he could until he ran out of territory. He was at the very end of Kinloch and was headed for the town of Berkeley, which was unfamiliar territory for him. He had run out of ground to run on and had no choice but to surrender. They grabbed him by the arm and marched him back up the hill. One of the boys told him that he was going to get a double beating because he had broken his bike while crossing one of the creeks during the chase. They were passing a house where a girl from his class was playing in the back yard. She didn't know that Robert was in trouble as she called out "Hi Robert Daugherty", as she waved at him. One of them told her that "he won't be no Robert Daugherty when we get through with him". Robert had no idea what they were going to do to him, but he knew that they didn't mind beating up people or terrorizing them with their dogs that they had groomed to be mean and vicious. If an unsuspecting kid came down their street with a bike, scooter, wagon or anything else that they wanted, they would send their dogs on them and take their goods. If they didn't fully cooperate, they would take their goods and beat them up. Robert didn't know what his fate was going to be. By the time they reached the place where the chase started, which was right around the corner from their house, He got some unexpected help. There was a man walking on the other side of the street across from them. He was dressed in a long brown coat and a brown dress hat. Robert had never seen the man before or after that day. As they were about to turn up their street, the man came to a stop and looked over at the boys who were holding Robert. The man said three words in a very authoritative voice, "Let Him Go" The thugs immediately let Robert go and went their way without saying a word. Robert went home, relieved and tired. Robert's mother saw him and said that it took him long enough, where's the butter?

Robert had forgotten what he had left home for in the first place after all the action that he had just went through. He told his mother that he was going to bring it to her in a minute. He didn't want to get a whipping, so he dashed out of the house with no one seeing him and headed back to the place where he had dropped the bag with the margarine in it. He didn't tell his mother or anyone else because he didn't think that anyone would believe a story like that. He decided to take his chances, figuring that the coast would be clear. He got to the spot where he dropped it and spotted the bag. There it was, but it was flat and didn't look like anything was in the bag. He picked the bag up and opened it. The butter was there, but someone had stepped on it and smashed it during the chase. Robert took the stick of butter and shaped it back to its original form. It was still in the plastic wrap and was in good shape. He took the butter back home and gave it to his mother. She didn't notice anything wrong as she took the butter and used it for her cooking project. Looking back, Robert wonders about the stranger who rescued him. He wonders if the man who showed up at just the right time could have been heaven sent. Since his heavenly father has always been watching over him, he wouldn't doubt it.

    During that same time period, Robert was becoming very frustrated and disillusioned about life as he was experiencing it. He couldn't understand why a young boy, who wanted nothing more than a simple peaceful life, had to spend most of his time running and dodging other people just to make it to the store and back. He had questions for God that he needed answers to. He knelt on his knees one night with his hands folded, and asked God a very sincere heartfelt question. He asked God was life going to always be this hard? Having to fight all the time just to get through life seemed to him to be the only option. Not that every day was a struggle, but having to keep your guard up all the time and not be able to just enjoy a simple walk down the street. After saying thank you Lord and Amen, Robert climbed to the top of their bunk bed and went to sleep. Robert had a dream that night that would strengthen him and give him a totally different outlook on his life, as tough as it would get.
    In the dream, Robert was walking down the main street in Kinloch, headed toward the post office, which was located in the bottom part of city. As he was walking on the right side of the street, he looked to his left and noticed someone walking right beside him. It was Jesus. Jesus looked him in the eyes and told him not to worry or fear anyone or anything. He told Robert that he would always be with him as he held his hand. Robert woke up the next morning refreshed and with a new sense of boldness, He went to school that morning feeling good about what he had seen and heard. He knew without a doubt that it was the Lord Jesus Christ. He didn't need anyone to convince him otherwise, so he didn't bother telling anyone. At the time, Robert didn't know that those words were right out of the Bible: Deut. 31-8, Matt. 28-20, Heb. 13-5. Those were encouraging and eternal words that would carry him through the rest of his life, especially the Vietnam war, even though he would endure hardship, pain, and tribulation.

Robert's home life was hardly ever simple, though it was lived with simplicity. His large family had to share one outhouse until the inside bathroom was built. Even then, having to share that one bathroom with seven sisters and their friends was not an easy matter. Having one television meant that everyone had to watch the same program together, if they were going to watch it at all. It was a family time that everyone accepted and learned to enjoy. Even when Robert watched Superman, some of the family joined in. Saturday night was bath night at the Daugherty house. The whole family used the same metal tub at different times. Hot water had to be heated on the top of the cooking stove in pots and pans. When they finally got their new bathroom; it was like a gift from heaven. As Robert grew older, eight or nine years old, he had to take his turn in the kitchen which meant washing and scrubbing pots and pans for a whole week.

Robert would always hang around the kitchen watching his mom cook. He learned how to make biscuits, pancakes, and bakery cakes from scratch. There were no instant pancake or cake mixes, so every thing had to be measured just right. Robert baked his own birthday cake for his tenth birthday party. One day, Robert's mom told him that no woman was going to starve him. Robert asked her what she meant by that? She told him that he would find out one day. He still enjoys cooking and barbecuing. Robert's mom always gave her children plenty of room to grow and express themselves as best as she could. Looking back, he can see how hard it had to be and how simple she made it trying to raise ten, sometimes hardheaded and stubborn children, as well as some of their friends. Day by day, and step by step, they were being groomed and nourished for the life they were living and the life that lay ahead of them.

Robert is very aware of the fact that his family and experiences cannot be compared to any typical or atypical family in America or anywhere else. He just wants to tell his story as he experienced it. He is thankful to God for giving him the inspiration and opportunity to share it with someone else. He is hopeful that someone will be encouraged, inspired and strengthened by the story of a not so average, everyday person that normally goes unnoticed and forgotten. And at times, even misunderstood by society and even family and friends.

CHAPTER THREE

HIGH SCHOOL DAYS

Robert's grade school days were ending as the sixties came around. Civil unrest was rapidly unfolding as the Vietnam War was beginning. After eight years at Holy Angels grade school, it was time for Robert to enter high school. Only two of Robert's older sisters had gone to Catholic high schools and he was not expecting to follow in their footsteps. He knew that that there was no way that his mom could afford tuition at a private school. The rest of his brothers and sisters had gone to Kinloch High and he was expected to go there as well. The staff at Holy Angels worked out a grant from the Archdiocese of St. Louis that would enable him to go to the new Catholic school for free. St Thomas Aquinas High School had been open for only one year, and had only one other Black in attendance. He was reluctant about going there since he would be only the second black person in the new all white school. The other black person was a girl from Holy Angels who had gone there the year before. The nuns talked him into trying it out, especially since he didn't have to pay a dime. The classrooms at Holy Angels were small and close knit. They had two grades in one classroom, so this was going to be a new cultural experience for Robert.

Robert thought that the fact that it was going to be a Christian school would be a positive motive in getting along with the other students. He was sure that the one bond of faith in Jesus would override any negative influence that might come about. The first day and week went by well, or as well as he could have expected. The uniform was the same as his days at Holy Angels, which was a white shirt and blue pants. Inspection was held every morning. One morning, he was targeted for being out of uniform for not having a belt that he forgot to put on before he left home. He was given four hours of Saturday detention. One of his sisters gave him a ride to detention session but he had to walk the almost three miles back home. Robert didn't think that it was fair since other students had done the same thing and just got a warning. However, he made sure he never forgot his belt again, no matter how big a hurry that he was.

Math was never one of Robert's strong suits, so Algebra 1 presented him with a minor challenge. For once, he really had to study, which was something he wasn't used to doing. He passed the class with a D+, but he could have and should have done better. His best classes were Religion and English Literature out of the seven classes that he had. Overall, the students and teachers were easy to get along with. Even though he was in the definite minority status, he believes that it was harder for them to adjust to him than it was for him to adjust to them. All he could do was to just be himself. It may not seem like much, but as a kid he remembers a cartoon character encouraging the kids to be themselves no matter what the circumstance.

The little cricket taught Robert a little wisdom that he never forgot. Being a major minority in any condition could be a trying ordeal. The only time he saw a black face was in the lunch line when he would see his former classmate: the girl from Holy Angels School in Kinloch.

Sometimes, while waiting in the lunch line, he could hear some of the students say some ignorant and dumb things. One of the favorite sayings was "hey nigger, why don't you go back to your shack in Kinloch". Some of the other students encouraged Robert not to pay them any attention, and he didn't. He knew that there were rude and ignorant people everywhere, and it had nothing to do with the color of their skin. He was just a little disappointed in the fact that he thought that being in a Christian environment would be a major plus, but he knew that his learning experience would involve more than his schoolbooks could provide.

Robert's only up close and personal experience with white people were when he was very young, and with the priest at Holy Angels Church where he was an altar boy. As a very young boy, one of Robert's sisters used to baby sit for a white lady. Sometimes she would bring the boy and girl to their house to spend the night while their mother was at work. They were about the same age as Robert and his brother and would be treated like part of the family. They played together, got in trouble together and even shared the same bed. Robert remembers one night during the Christmas season when the two kids spent the night. Robert and his brother and the two kids were lying on the floor on a blanket where they were going to sleep that night. They were in the kitchen looking through the door to the living room where the Christmas tree was lit and decorated. They dared each other to raid the tree and take some of the gingerbread cookies that dangled from the tree limbs. Robert and his brother persuaded the boy to go and get some cookies from the tree while the rest of them stood watch. The boy bravely and stupidly dashed in the room and grabbed enough cookies for all to snack on during the night. The next morning, Robert's sister noticed that the tree had been raided and gingerbread cookies were missing. Since everyone covered for each other and no one took the blame, all of them got a nice and painful spanking. Robert realized that as children, they didn't see each other as black or white. They just enjoyed each other and had fun playing together. Their parents felt the same way, when they would come to pick their kids up, they would always be friendly and leave something with Robert and his brother. He was also impressed with his sister because the other family trusted her enough to leave their two children with her and her family time after time.

Every day was an adventure for him on the way from school. The bus that he rode picked him up and dropped him off in a neighborhood in Berkeley. Berkeley was an all white community, just north of his home in Kinloch. He had to take the fifteen- minute walk through the neighborhood, back and forth to his home. He would often get called names and sometimes just get stared down. The children and adults would say things like, "there goes that nigger again". He would just ignore them and keep on walking and singing to himself. There was another route that was longer, where he could have avoided the hassle, but he chose the shorter route so he could get home sooner after a long day at school.

One day as he was passing a particular house, something a little different took place. He thought he would get a free pass since there were only two small kids playing in the yard. One of the kids, who was about four years, old came walking down the long yard towards him.

He braced himself for some more name calling, when something happened that he didn't expect. The little boy asked him a deep question. He said, "Hey mister, do you mind if we call you nigger?" He saw that the little boy was sincere, and wanted an honest answer to his question. No one sent the boy to ask the question, so he thought he owed the boy a good answer. He didn't have long, because he knew that his family would be coming to his rescue at any moment.

He remembered when he turned four years old, and had taught himself to tie his shoes on his birthday. He thought he was getting older and should know how to do something for himself. Since the boy was about the same age as he was then, he knew he understood what he was doing. He told the little boy that God had made both of them, and the only difference between them was the color of their skin. He told the boy that he shouldn't call anyone nigger or any other name that might hurt them. Especially if he didn't even know what it meant. By this time, the boy's parent's and older brothers and sisters came out of the house. They yelled at him to get away from that nigger. The boy said goodbye and waved as he walked back towards his parents. Robert started walking away from the house, which wasn't that far from the safe borders of Kinloch.

He remembered the lesson that the little boy taught him and hoped that the boy remembered as well. He was shown that racism and ignorance was taught and passed on by adults who don't know any better than to teach their children prejudice and hate. This goes for all races of people. He also realized that talking with the boy was not by chance, but was designed and orchestrated by God. Even so, he felt that the time had come for him to no longer take that route any more. It was springtime, and school was almost out, so he figured he didn't need any more drama the last few weeks of school. Today, that same neighborhood has changed: it is now predominately Black.

He tried to finish his freshman year at Aquinas with as little fanfare as possible. He loved sports, but could only watch and be a cheerleader. The only time he could participate was during gym and playing a game of "keep away" ball at lunch break. The track coach saw some potential in his ability during gym and asked him to try out for the track team. He thanked the coach, but told him he wouldn't have a way home after practice. He would have had to walk all the way home, which would have taken about an hour. He would have been too tired to do his homework and very little time to relax before preparing for the next day of school.

Having no time for after school activities would play a major role in his decision to transfer for his sophomore year. He had to make up his mind about what he was going to do as the school year was coming to an end. He had to put everything into perspective in order to see just where he stood. He remembered his classmates talk about their summer vacations to places he had only seen on television and some places he had never heard of. It was real disheartening when the teacher would ask the students where they had been for summer vacation and the only place he had been was to Wellston, which was a bus ride from the city limits of Kinloch. He didn't even entertain the thought of a vacation to anywhere. That is why to this day, he tries to take his family and relatives on vacations as time and finances allow. He also considered some of the staff's attitude towards him, which at times wasn't very supportive. But the major reason he gave to the principal why he wouldn't return to Aquinas High was that he couldn't participate in any after school activities because he had no transportation back home. She thought that some of the things he had to endure during the year were his main reasons for transferring. He assured her that even though it was no picnic, he would be back if there was transportation for him to get home after practices and other activities.

The principal gave him up to the last day of school to change his mind, but his mind was made up and he wasn't going to change it. Aquinas was going to be in the history books for him, but he had helped pave the way for the Black students who would follow him. He told the other girl from Holy Angels of his decision, and she completely understood. She went on to graduate from Aquinas High along with many other Black students from Kinloch, and other schools who came after her. St. Thomas Aquinas High has since merged with another Catholic school because of low enrollment.

School was out, and he spent the summer enjoying family and friends, and playing baseball in a YMCA league. He could play every position except catcher, only because he really didn't like it.

He had played on a neighborhood team before, but this was the first time he had a real uniform to wear. He considered himself to be an average player, but really enjoyed playing baseball a lot. When he wasn't playing or practicing, he would always find a game of Indian Ball or a good cork ball game. When he wasn't playing baseball, there was always someone playing basketball on a homemade hoop. He even tried his hand at pitching horseshoes. He developed a pretty good flip that he could depend on for ringers.

By the fall of the year, he was ready to enroll at Kinloch High. He was joining a brother and sister who were still there. The school was less than a fifteen- minute walk from his home. That was much closer than the walk to the bus stop when he was going to Aquinas. He started his three-year journey at Kinloch High with no expectations other than finally being able to enjoy going to school again, to participate in sports, to graduate and get his diploma.

Even though he was now in familiar territory, he still had a cultural adjustment to make. The previous year, he was in an all White school. Now he would find himself in an all Black school again. Even though he grew up in the community with the students, there were still a lot of them that he didn't personally know. Likewise, he had to adjust to students who didn't know him. Kinloch was divided into sections, and the some of the people never crossed paths with each other. He had spent eight years at Holy Angels grade school, and most of the students attended Dunbar or Vernon public schools. His first day of school was an adventure in itself. He spent the entire morning trying to get his schedule straight and maneuvering his way through the crowded hallways looking for the right classroom. The principal was a little short lady with thick eye- glasses and a very loud voice. She seemed to strike fear and respect in the biggest and toughest of the Kinloch students. He would eventually find out that underneath her shield and armor was a very lovable nice lady.

The first bell had rung, and he was still trying to find his locker. After he found his locker, he couldn't find his homeroom. He found himself checking classrooms to find out if he was supposed to be there. After having no success, and wandering the hallways, he had no choice but to go to the office and face the boss lady principal.

She was already chewing out some students for being late, and he was a little nervous. When he got his turn to face the boisterous lady, she immediately started to scold him for being late. After explaining his situation, she got one of her aides to take him to his homeroom class.

When he went into the class, which was already in progress, he made a negative impression on his teacher and counselor. She didn't tolerate anyone being late for her class no matter what the reason. Out of all the classes he had, he got the lowest grades in hers. Other than his geometry class, her class was the worst as far as grades were concerned, in his three years at Kinloch High. Since he was sure that she never really understood him, he didn't take her attitude towards him personally.

He was adjusting well to his new environment as time went by. He only had to change classrooms, where before, he was sometimes changing buildings when he was at Aquinas. Other than geometry, most of the classes were relatively easy. Geometry was different from Algebra, and required him to have to think more than he was use to doing. Typing and English Literature were his favorite classes. Physical Education was more like recess, but still had to be approached with effort. His track and baseball coach always gave him excellent grades. He also offered him a track scholarship to a small college.

Cross Country track would be his first opportunity to participate in sports. It was a three-mile course over sometimes rough and hilly terrain. He looked forward to the competition as the coach got the team into shape with some hard training. They did stretching and other workouts to go along with jogging around the track. Later they would run around the hilly streets of Kinloch to test their stamina. That was easy for him, since he could finally run around Kinloch with no one chasing after him. He got advice and pointers from some of the runners who had experience in competition. There was one upper classman who went beyond the regular practice routine. He wore ankle weights to jog around the track. Then would come inside, and jog up and down, and around the bleachers in the gym. He was so impressed with the runner that he thought he might not measure up to the task. He told Robert that it helped build up his muscles, and he could run a lot easier when he took them off.

It was time for the first track meet, and the best runner wasn't able to compete. The runner who had trained extra hard, had pulled a muscle in his leg by training too hard. All the hard work he put in was for nothing. He was done for the entire Cross Country season. The coach told the rest of the team to pick up the slack for the absent star runner.

When the race started, he was feeling pretty good. He kept up with the pack and was breathing okay. He didn't know what to expect, so he stayed close to the more experienced runners. About half way through the course, he began to feel the pressure of the race. The pace that the runners had set began to have an affect on his breathing. He thought seriously about giving up because he couldn't breathe. Then he remembered what the coach had said about a second wind kicking in. He had no idea what that meant since this was his first race. He decided to keep running and see what would happen. As he tried to relax, his second wind kicked in, and he felt a lot better. He was just going to try to finish the race so he could at least help the team gain some points. To his and everyone's surprise, he not only finished the race, he came in first for his team. A few of the upper classmen were a little jealous, and said he was just lucky that time. His coach and some of the other teammates congratulated him and were glad for him.

He would learn a lot in his first competitive race. He went on to run Cross Country races for the three years he attended Kinloch High. He loved the competition; especially the district meets, when hundreds of runners from around the state would compete. He finished 54th out of over 300 runners in his second district meet over a very rough course. In his final district meet, he finished 26th out of almost 400 runners from around the state. The races gave him an insight about himself that he never would have known. It gave him a better perspective on being mentally and physically prepared when he had to endure hardships and obstacles in life. He also knew that he gave all he had, but could have given even more if he had it to give by being in better shape.

When spring track came around, he was ready to compete. He practiced all of the events until he found out which ones he would be more successful with. He settled for the half- mile run, the 440- relay, and the broad jump. Even though he enjoyed all the events, his most successful was the half- mile run. He knew he could have been better in the broad jump, mainly because of a practice jump he took in his baseball spikes. During a baseball practice, his track coach wanted him to get a practice jump in. He ran up to the pit and took a casual jump. After the coach measured the jump, it was 24 feet and 7 inches. He measured it twice to make sure it was the right measurement. It was the right measurement, but he was only able to jump no more than 19 feet since the incredible practice jump. But he knew that if he did it once, he could have at least come close to the big jump again.

He had a good junior year when he qualified for state in the half mile. He qualified by finishing third in the district meet, and beating out some of the best half milers in the area. The runners from Riverview Gardens had been getting all the press, and blistering all the competition. They were expected to sweep the district meet and send three runners to Jefferson City for the state finals. Robert and his teammate from Kinloch didn't get any notoriety even though they had finished first and second in all of their races. His teammate always took first while he took second. The track coach asked him why he always settled for second while his teammate took first. He told the coach that as long as the team got credit for first and second place, it didn't matter who finished first.

The two Kinloch runners planned on how they could at least beat out one of the Riverview runners. When the gun sounded, they started the pace faster than they had ever done before. Since the Riverview runners were use to setting the pace, they wanted to confuse the favorite runners. When they reached the final 220 yards, the three Riverview runners and the two Kinloch runners were the only ones still in contention. Only the first three runners would qualify for state, and Riverview was right where they were use to being at that stage of the race. What they didn't realize was that the two Kinloch runners were in a comfortable position as well.

Since Robert had set the fast pace for his buddy, he didn't know if he would have anything left coming down the stretch. He saw that his buddy was about to take first place away from the Riverview runner. He also noticed that the other two Riverview runners had passed him while he was rooting for his buddy. The two runners thought that he was done, and would coast in for third and fourth place. When he saw that they were no longer paying any attention to him, he suddenly put on a burst of speed and kicked past the stunned runners and nicked them at the tape, and taking the final qualifying spot for state. They both were stunned and upset with themselves as well as the Riverview cheering section. They had come to district expecting to send three runners to state, and could only send one. That was a truly a gratifying victory for the lowly underdog track team from Kinloch High.

.   The sad thing about it for Riverview was that Robert didn't even go to state. Just so happen, the baseball team had a home game, the same day as the state meet. He had a choice to make, and he chose to stay home and play baseball before the home crowd. Since very few, if any body went to the track meets, they would surely turn out for a home baseball game at Kinloch High. Needless to say, the track coach wasn't pleased, but Robert had made his decision.

The Kinloch Braves lost the game, and he didn't play that well, but he was satisfied with his decision. His buddy didn't medal at state, but he represented as well as he could without his running buddy. His high school days proved to be an ongoing learning experience. The wins and losses in sports, the As, Bs, Cs, and Ds, and the one F he made in geometry one quarter were all a part of his highs and lows. He was learning about his abilities, potentials, and inabilities. Together with his fears and strengths, he was trying to put his life in a proper perspective. He took a good look at other people who seemed to have a personal mission of making other people's life miserable.

He sometimes reflected on his life as far back as he could to help him in his present state of mind. Some things were more relevant than others, but they all served a purpose. He recalls one of his fears of watching a movie before he started grade school. He remembers walking to the Lincoln movie theater in Kinloch with one of his aunts. Just before they got to the movie, they had to cross a bridge with holes in it. There was a creek underneath the bridge, but it seemed like a river to him. His aunt had to convince him that the bridge was safe enough to walk on, but he didn't believe her. She had to pick him up and carry him across the bridge every time they went to the movies.

That was just the beginning of his fears. When they got into the theater, his aunt would buy him popcorn, soda, and milk duds. He would watch the cartoons with no trouble. But when the feature started with real people, he would never look at the screen. He would close his eyes and sometimes peek through his fingers to pretend he was watching the movie. It was just too much for him to see all those big people on the big white screen. When the movie was over, she always asked him did he enjoy the movie. He always said yes, because he didn't want to take the chance of not being able to go with her again and miss out on all the good refreshments, which was the only reason he wanted to go. He never told her that he never was able to look at the movie. But somehow, he thinks she might have known all the time.

He had pretty much adjusted to life at Kinloch High by his junior year. He picked up on some inside tips from some of his friends that helped him survive in his new environment. He never looked for or got any favors from any of his teachers. However, his gym teacher and baseball and cross country coach would sometimes give a free pass to some of his players to some of the high school dances at the school.

He made friends pretty easily because of his outgoing personality. He also made some enemies pretty easily as well. Some people just didn't like him for their own personal reasons, and some enemies he created all by himself. He had an aggravating ability of giving nicknames to those who he felt deserved them. They never did him any physical harm because they could never catch him. He also had pranks pulled on him sometimes. His school locker would sometimes be broken into. He never found out who did it, and no one ever took the credit.

There were some who didn't like him and would try to prove their superiority. He never backed down from any body. But when the odds were against him, he did what he had to do to even the odds. He would use baseball bats, bricks, rocks, or whatever was available.

Robert was not very big in stature, being only five feet seven and one half inches tall. The most he ever weighed in high school was one hundred and eighteen pounds. There were several bullies who would try to beat him up at every opportunity. Because of his size and mild mannerism, he seemed to be easy pickings to his challengers. He wasn't going to beat anyone with force and strength so he had to out quick and out smart his opponents. He also took comfort in the dream that he had as a young boy with Jesus telling him not to be afraid of anyone.

Robert recalls a sandlot pick up football game that they often played on the high school field. He was basically picked just so he could fill out the team. The full tackle games were played without and pads or equipment. There was a play where one of the opposing team's biggest players had broken into the open field and was headed for the goal line. There was no first and ten rule. This was fourth down, and he was stiff- arming and running over everyone on his way to the winning touchdown. The only thing that stood in his way was Robert. He was licking his chops as he approached little old Robert. He figured that all he had to do was to run around or over Robert and the game was over. These games were taken very seriously and Robert didn't want to let his team down. As he got closer to Robert, he had his arm out ready to stiff- arm him and run over him. Robert could see in his eyes that he meant business. Even so, Robert knew that the big man had to be brought down. Robert got an angle on him and dipped his shoulders and hit him just below the knees. The big man came tumbling to the ground as Robert wrapped him up and gave his team a chance to win the game. They went on and scored the winning touchdown with Robert also catching a key leaping pass from their quarterback. His team was inspired by the game saving tackle by Robert. They drove the ball down the field with a renewed confidence and scored the winning touchdown.

These seemingly insignificant experiences meant more to Robert than just winning or losing. They earned him a certain amount of respect from his peers as well as help build his character and confidence that he would use in other areas of his life. As Robert looks back at all the fights and different distractions that he faced, he is sure that those trials helped him in even tougher times.

School days weren't always about conflict, competition, and stress. There were school plays, dances, and other events that didn't involve pressure and danger. And even though there were chores to do at home, there was still time to relax and have some fun. After homework, it was off to find a pick up basketball game or baseball game, depending on the weather. Basketball was an all year round event in Kinloch. There was always a hoop to be found in someone's yard or on a vacant lot. If the weather was cold, a fire would be built to keep warm while they waited their turn for the next game.

Kinloch had many hills and valleys where they could sleigh ride and roller skate down. There was a hill behind Robert's house that they could roller skate and sleigh ride down on a peaceful day.

Robert remembers a scary event when he was about ten years old. He was roller- skating down the hill behind his house one day after school. He was flying down the hill by himself, when he a saw a man at the bottom of the hill. Robert was at peak speed when he reached the bottom of the hill when the man stood at the edge of the street with a whiskey bottle in his hand and laughing like a mad man. Robert didn't think that he would be a problem since he knew the man and was about to pass by him. As Robert got to where the man was, the man suddenly threw the whiskey bottle at Robert's feet. He tried to swerve, but it was too late. The bottle hit his skates and broke into pieces. Robert went down hard on the hard street and rolled over several times. He was bruised and hurt as he got to his feet. He picked up his broken skates and went to the man and asked him why he did such a mean thing. The man just kept laughing in a drunken stupor. Robert even went to the man's wife, who saw the whole thing and asked her if they could at least pay for his skates that were beyond repair. She said that if she interfered that she would be beaten up, so it was best that she stayed out of it.

Robert was dejected and bruised as he took his broken skates and walked home. He had scratches on his arms and a bruise on his right ankle that would take a long time to heal because he tried to doctor on it himself. It became infected and ugly and stuck to his socks as blood and pus would ooze through his sock. To Robert this was a small wound that got worse, but in time, it would heal under Doctor Robert's treatment and some good advice from one of his sisters..

Adversity would prove to be a painful partner that would follow Robert throughout his life. But in happier times during high school, Robert would often find himself over friends and neighbor's homes listening to music and trying to croon with his partners as they listened to some of their favorite artists. Singing was one of Robert's and his family's most enjoyable past times. They thought that they were sounding good, but it really didn't matter. They just had fun, and singing was relaxing and meaningful. When Robert was smaller, his family would sit out in the front yard in the summer time, with a bucket of burning rags that produced enough smoke to ward of the mosquitoes, and sing until they got tired. The Daugherty house was on the bus route, and it would pass right by their house. They would wave at the bus drivers as they sat in their yard and sang at night, with the stars and moon being the only source of light.

They had made friends with one of the late night bus drivers. The middle age White man would always bring them candy on his last route at night, and Robert's sisters would always have a pitcher of lemonade waiting for him. They kept up the routine until the man's route changed, but they never forgot about the nice man whom they considered to be their friend.

Robert's older brother played the drums and was in a band that would practice at their house once a week. The band had a saxophone player, a large base fiddle player, a guitar player and his brother on drums. Robert loved to listen in on their practices and jam sessions. His brother has since moved to California and is on the California musician's board. His sisters always had something going on with their social clubs. With all of the family and friends, the Daugherty house always had plenty of company. The Daugherty house was one of the many of what was called a Kool- Aid house. The name speaks for itself, and yes, Kool- Aid was usually served.

Kinloch high was often an extension of the home life of most Kinloch students. Kinloch has produced a variety of contributions to the world at large. Kinloch has produced educators, singers, musicians, movie actors, preachers, as well as everyday people that are a vital part in being contributors to their community. Even some of what was considered tough guys and girls found their place in life. But tragically there was some who didn't make it at all. They were often victims of petty crimes that would sometimes end up in tragedy. There were no Bloods and Crypts then, but there were pockets of groups who were seeking to make a name. They had to be dealt with, and the dealings usually ended up with trouble for someone else.

Robert remembers a high school gang that would terrorize other unsuspecting students. They didn't usually have any thing personal against the students that they picked; it just came down to the luck or unlucky draw of the name from a hat. They would write the names of other students who weren't in their group and put them all in one of their big hats. Sometime during the day, they would randomly draw a name from the hat. Whoever name that came out that day had an unexpected beating coming from the entire gang after school. One day after the final bell had rung, one of Robert's baseball teammates came hysterically running up to him. He told Robert that he had found out that his name was pulled from the hat and he was in trouble. Robert asked him why he was telling him since he thought that he was pretty cool with some of the dudes who were in the group. He said that he was scared and that Robert had to do something to help him out.

Robert asked him what he expected him to do against fifteen or so mean dudes with baseball bats, brass knuckles, and probably knives and more things. Robert told him to go and talk to the principal or some of the teachers because he wasn't crazy enough to try and take on a mob, especially since it wasn't his fight. He told Robert that if they didn't get him today, that they would get him the next day or some other time. Robert felt sorry for him and told him to call home and get some of his brothers, because he had a lot of them. He told him to do whatever he had to do, but he wasn't going to try and get himself killed too. Robert tried to get away from him. However, he grabbed hold of him and would not let him go. The boy was terrified. Robert made one last attempt to get away from him by telling him that for all he knew, his name could be in the hat too and they could just jump both of them at the same time. He was still begging and persisted that Robert had to help him. Robert couldn't understand why he came to him out of all the people that he knew in the school. Robert finally gave in. He figured that the most that could happens, was that they would put up a good fight and get beat down. Then if he survived, he would go and get his brother and some of his friends who were considered bad and dangerous, and go and find the mob and get even with them. Robert told his friend that he didn't know what was going to happen, but he would walk with him as far as he could. When Robert and his friend walked out the front door, the gang was on the other side of the street.

Robert told him that it might be safer if they went down the main street since they were waiting in the back of the building as well. Robert and his friend starting walking down the street as the gang started walking and taunting them and promising bodily harm to his friend. Robert told him to just keep walking and not to look across the street at the mob. Robert told him that once they crossed the street and started to attack, that he was on his own and to start making tracks as fast as he could. As they continued down the hill towards home, they began to curse Robert and his friend, saying that they were going to beat both of them down. They didn't know how long it would be before the gang crossed the street and go into their beating mode that they were known for. As Robert reached the corner where he would turn to go to his house, he told his friend that he had reached the point where he told him that he would have to leave him if by some miracle they would make it that far. He pleaded with Robert not to leave him since the gang was still across the street and ready for some action.

Robert reluctantly agreed to go a little farther since their luck seemed to be holding. He figured that if they were going to do something, that he and his friend would be toast by now. Robert hoped that his gamble would payoff, but they continued to taunt and threaten them. After over fifteen minutes, they were getting closer to his friend's house. When they were minutes away from his home, the gang began to break up and fade away. Robert had called their hand and had come out on top so far. When they got to his friend's house, they were relieved and rested for a while. His mom asked them how they were doing, and they told her that they were doing okay. These battles were considered personal, and weren't shared with parents. It was the survival of the fittest, because you had to face your peers again and again. But Robert had a big problem. He still had to make the ten to fifteen- minute-walk to his house by himself.

He told his friend that he would be okay. He felt that he could out run them and get to a safe place if he had to, Robert started walking back home, but was ready to start running at any moment.

On the way back home, he ran into several of the guys who were in the gang. They told Robert that his friend was lucky that the leaders in the gang decided that it was better to let them go. They said that if Robert had not been with him, that his friend would have been beaten to a pulp. They also said that the rule was that if anyone made it past them without getting beat up, that they had to eliminate them from further confrontations. Robert was relieved and called his friend when he got home, who was also very glad to hear the good news. Robert was never sure why they allowed them to pass since that wasn't their style. He didn't bother to ask them either, but kind of thought they might have been thinking along with him about the fallout that might occur with Robert's brother and some of his friends who were known for beating and hurting people just for fun. Anyhow, Robert was glad to have that ordeal end up with no bloodshed, especially his own. He still never knew if his name was folded up in one of the big black hats and never bothered to ask.

Looking back on the four years of high school seems like a blur to him now. But while it was going on, it seemed like a very long period of time. In between schoolwork, sports, relationships, good and not so good, life seemed to be moving in slow motion. The memories of teachers and all the in between events, were an education in themselves. He watched his brothers and sisters grow into adults, and wondered what the future would hold for him.

There was a place aside from school and home that was a welcome sanctuary for a lot of Kinlochians. It was a confectionery hangout for teenagers and young adults, or anyone else that just wanted to enjoy the kosher and relaxed mood. The confectionery was just down the street from Robert's house and was operated by a man and his wife. Everyone who knew them called them aunt and uncle. They were both pillars in the small community as they instilled positive and spiritual values to anyone that would listen. They sold everything from cornflakes to root beer floats. But what they were most famous for as far as Robert was concerned was their hamburgers, chili, and frank sandwiches. Their Big Time candy bars and big Stage Plank cookies with strawberry icing on them weren't so bad either. As soon as you walked in the place you could hear the pinball machine clattering and the jukebox playing the latest hits. There was plenty of jazz on the jukebox as well as gospel music. The dance floor would be crowded with people practicing and dancing their smooth moves. The two owners were good Christians and were always telling the young people to stay out of trouble and go to church on Sunday. They have since passed on and left a permanent and positive legacy.   They were both loved and respected by all who knew them. They would sometimes let Robert work behind the counter and wait on customers, while giving him and others a chance to make a little spending change. They also let him do other chores like cleaning up the store after closing time. Another thing they were famous for was giving out dinners, free of charge, every Thanksgiving to anyone who came to their house. They did the hard work of cooking the turkey and ham and potato salad and pumpkins pies with the help of a few of their neighbors.

They passed out hundreds of dinners before they would stop later on in the day. They didn't have any children, but they had adopted as many that would come through their friendly doors every day and night.

They were givers, teachers, preachers, and parents to all. They were counselors, and whatever they needed to be for everyone in the community. Robert still remembers their wide smiles, and words of wisdom. The short but forceful, gentle little lady was known for her literal rod of correction that she didn't mind using on anyone who got out of hand. They were by far two of the most impressionable people in the community that Robert would ever know.

With Kinloch High being a small school, Robert's graduation class consisted of only twenty- six students. The senior class had more, but some didn't graduate with their class. Robert was sixth in his class academically, but knows that he could have done better with a little more effort on his part. Never the less, he was thankful that he got his diploma, and marched with his class. Robert had never thought about not graduating on time, even though one of his teachers gave him a brief scare. For an unknown, but suspecting reason, the teacher threatened to hold up his last credit that he needed to graduate because of a report that suddenly came up missing and was considered late. The teacher gave Robert two days to turn in the lengthy report that he had already turned in, or he wouldn't graduate. Robert had two free periods in his senior year, and used that time as well as home time to turn in the twenty plus page report. The teacher had tacked on some extra work because it was considered late. After finishing the report, he turned it in to the teacher before the deadline. The teacher quickly flipped through the thick pages that Robert took a lot of time to make sure that the assignment was accurate and correct. After taking less than one minute to look at the papers that took Robert two days to do, the teacher looked at him and said, "You passed". Robert was disappointed at the teacher's dismal response to all the hard work that he had put into the bogus assignment, but he didn't make any objections. He was just glad that he could finally get the credit that he needed to graduate. Robert had nightmares about not graduating for a long time because of that one teacher.

Nevertheless, his senior year had a lot of fun times. His track coach had offered him a scholarship to a local college but he wasn't really focused on his future just yet. He just wanted to exhale for just a little while, because he knew that whatever he would do would be another time consuming challenge. He wanted to enjoy life just for a little while before he made the leap into adulthood. While still a senior, Robert would often to go watch the Cardinals play at Busch Stadium. He would sometimes take the bus and go by himself.

He never encountered any problems with anyone during his trips to the ballpark. Nevertheless, on a senior trip to Forest Park and the Highland amusement park, Robert would have an unexpected negative experience. After picnicking and visiting the zoo, Robert and his classmates went to the amusement park later in the day. The park was just across the street from the picnic area. Robert and his friends were together riding some of the rides and playing some of the games. They were taking a break while watching some of the other people try to win some prizes. While Robert was watching and trying to decide if he wanted to play this particular game, a big policeman with a German shepherd dog on a leash, came up to where they were waiting. The policeman shouted to them to move on. Robert and his friends couldn't understand what the policeman meant, since they were waiting to play a game. They moved on anyway to another game area. They weren't there five minutes, when the same policeman showed up again. This time, he was just singling out Robert. He told him, "1 thought I told you to move on nigger." He was swinging his night- stick at Robert, while the big dog was barking and growling at his leg. The big fat policeman was overly aggressive while he was shouting and foaming at the mouth telling him to get out of the park. Robert had no choice but to head for the exit. Robert wasn't moving fast enough for the angry officer, so he used his German -Shepherd dog to help speed him along. As Robert was leaving out the gate, the policeman was still shouting and the dog was still at Robert's heels. When Robert finally got out, the policeman chased him from the entrance of the park and told him not to come back or else. He didn't have to worry; Robert wasn't going back in there for anything.

When Robert got a little further from the entrance, he noticed a Black man in a suit. No he wasn't an angel. He was a police detective walking his beat. Robert felt a momentary relief, thinking that he might get a little help. Robert asked him if he saw what just happened to him? He said that he saw the end of it. Robert told him that he was there with his senior class and hadn't done anything wrong. He told the policeman that he and some friends were just waiting to play some games when the policeman hit him with his Billy club, put his dog on him, and then chased him out of the park. Robert asked him that if he could help him, or at least call someone and report the other police officer to his superiors. He told Robert that there was nothing that he could do and that he was sorry. He told Robert that he had better leave the area before the other policeman came back. Robert told him that he was a sorry excuse for a policeman as he left the area.

Robert's classmates were still in the amusement park having fun. They didn't even miss him. He had to go back to the picnic area where the cars were parked that they had come to park in. He had to wait on a picnic bench for almost two hours in the dark until his classmates finally came out. All he could do was wait, and hope that nothing else happened before he got back home. When they came to where Robert was, he asked the people that he was with, why they didn't tell everyone else what happened.

They told him that they did, but they had to finish their time and couldn't leave out until everyone else was ready. They said that they knew that he would be okay because they knew that he could take care or himself. They said that they didn't have any trouble with the police so there was no need for them to leave early.

Robert told them that he couldn't understand why he was the only one to be thrown out of the park. They just laughed and teased him and said that's what he get for being so noticeable. Robert was tired and angry and didn't see the humor in it at all. Robert didn't trust or respect policemen for a long time after that, Black or White. He was puzzled about why he was targeted by the bully policeman and his dog, and not anyone else in his class. All he could do was to let it rest and try to learn whatever lesson he could from the incident. Because for Robert, many more challenges would lie ahead. The particular problem that he had on that day would seem small in comparison to what would lie ahead for him.

CHAPTER FOUR

TRADE SCHOOL AND LIFE AFTER HIGH SCHOOL

Shortly after graduation, it was time for Robert to register with the Selective Service. Robert was eighteen, and eligible to be drafted into the military at any time. Robert didn't have any type of military draft exemption, so going to war was a very likely possibility in his near future. The Vietnam War was in full swing with men dying, but Robert wasn't thinking that far ahead just yet. Robert remembers a very close friend of one of his sister's who would come to their home to visit her. He eventually was drafted into the Army, and would come by the house in his Army uniform. He was a very nice and polite young man and Robert was very impressed with him. Then, after a short while later, his sister received the news that her friend had been killed in action in the war in Vietnam. His sister was devastated and heartbroken, as was his family.

Robert was trying to grasp the cruel reality of someone that he knew and admired to have his life taken away at such an early age. His death affected Robert in a way that he didn't have words to explain. But this would only be the beginning of the tragic effect that the Vietnam War would have on the families of the small community of Kinloch. There would be an all too often announcement of another person that Robert grew up with and knew had been killed in Vietnam. Times were very uneasy and depressing, and no young man could relax for long.

He had very little time to decide what he was going to do with his life after high school. One thing that he knew was that he needed a break, no matter how short it might be. He was tired of school, and the pressure of the war was staring him right in the face. Some of his friends went to college, which would give them a temporary deferment from the draft. Even though Robert was offered a track scholarship, he didn't have any incentive to attend college at that time. It was a short time later when a new government program was offered to young men that he took a long look at. The only problem for Robert was that it started less than two months after he had graduated, and had no draft deferment plan. There was civil unrest everywhere and the Vietnam War was leaving very little room or time to try and make a positive and rational decision about life.

No matter what decision he would make, he knew that it would only be short term. All he could do was to follow his heart and believe that God would be with him in whatever he decided to do.

After thinking things over, he decided to go to the free government program and learn a trade. He had to say goodbye to his summer vacation and hello to school once again. O'Fallon Trade School was a three bus and one hour ride from his house in Kinloch. The program offered a once a week check of twenty dollars for transportation. The twenty dollars had to be tightly budgeted. Robert was interested in electricity, and took it as his primary course. The technical school also had courses in woodwork and metal work. The program ran for a year without any break in the classes. They were expected to maintain good attendance and work hard toward completing and graduating the prescribed courses. The program was made up of young men from different backgrounds from all over the St. Louis area. There were high school dropouts as well as graduates. There were even some young men with some college experience looking to learn a meaningful and skillful trade. Every one had to take preliminary courses in all of the classes before going on to their major course. Robert survived the woodwork and sheet metal classes with some minor injuries from some of the sharp tools they had to use in their projects. They were all good lessons and projects that helped him prepare for his basic electricity class. Basic electricity started with theory, before moving on to circuit breakdown and then application of all that was learned.

Working with electrical circuits involved a lot of concentration and patience. However, impatience on one of Robert's projects would almost cost him his life. He had to hook up a large 220 Volts neon light circuit board for one of his final grades. It was a Friday, and Robert was the last one to work on the project for the day. The board was located in the balcony of the classroom away from everything else. Class was almost over for the day and the weekend, and Robert wanted to get his project done before the weekend was over. He had a short time to hook up the parallel neon light project. He knew that if he had to wait for the previous classmate to take his project totally down, that he wouldn't have enough time to complete his project. So he told the classmate to leave his foundation up and he would connect his wiring to his classmates. Robert figured that all he had to do was follow the color code and make a few adjustments, and things would work out fine. Robert finished his wiring before the bell rang and was ready to have his project tested. He was sure that he had wired the big board up properly and told the shop steward to turn on the voltage. He was leaning over the balcony so that he could see his neon lights flashing when the power came on. As soon as the switch was turned on, there was a hissing sound of burning wire. Suddenly the whole balcony area was filled with smoke. There was total silence on the floor below as the rest of the class waited for the smoke to clear. When the smoke finally cleared, the shop steward called up to where Robert was and asked was he okay? Even though he was leaning over the board when it went up in smoke, he immediately jumped back and hit the floor at the very first spark. He knew he had to get back and down as quickly as possible or he would be toast. After being stunned and almost shocked to death, Robert slowly stood up, waved, and said that he was all right. He came back down the stairs to the floor feeling bad that his project went up in smoke, but glad to be alive. The shop steward was also glad that Robert was all right and relieved. He just told Robert to come back Monday and try it again. Robert knew that he should have waited in the first place, and learned a valuable lesson about being patient when it came to working with such a powerful and lethal force as electricity. Robert came back Monday and started his project from scratch. He hooked up the neon lights on the big board and they came on flashing with no problem. He got his passing grade plus a very valuable lesson: *"Patience!!!!"*

The year went by relatively quick with the help of a winter sports program at the Page Park YMCA gym. Robert would take two buses to the gym, and the van provided by the school program would take the boys to the school. The students would arrive at the gym two hours before classes started to workout and play basketball. Robert loved to shoot hoops and wouldn't miss any days of the pre school activities. While he was there, he would meet some of the other students from the school and developed a closer association with some of them. Some of the boys were from some of the more notorious areas of the city. During the ride back to the school, the students would often exchange stories about happenings in their neighborhoods. Robert just listened and never talked about any of his experiences for specific reasons. Some of the dudes were pretty tough and had some bad reputations. After about a month, they noticed that Robert never talked much. One of the dudes finally asked Robert what part of the city he was from. He told them that he wasn't from the city. With a big gulp in his throat, he reluctantly told them that he was from Kinloch. Robert waited for their reaction, because he knew that Kinloch wasn't a favorite place for some city dwellers because it had a bad reputation of it's own with some people. After he said the name Kinloch, one of the real tough dudes said, "Kinloch? Man, if we had known you were from Kinloch before we got to know you, we would have beaten your butt." Actually the words weren't really that kind. He told Robert that he had a good game on the court and was a pretty cool dude. He told him that nobody was going to mess with him now that they knew him. He shook hands with Robert and told him to stay cool. Robert was never afraid, but was relieved. He had proceeded in that particular situation very cautiously.

During the entire year, almost everyone laid aside whatever petty differences they might have had and focused on why they were there: to learn an employable skill. In fact, in spite of racial and cultural differences, everyone pulled together and helped each other to get through the school year. After surviving the summer heat and the winter cold at the bus stops, Robert had an early springtime adventure. One night after having to stay at school and finish a project, he missed his first bus connection by less than a minute. He could see his bus pulling off as he tried to run down the sidewalk to catch the bus before it was too late. The next bus wasn't due for another hour and there was nothing to do but wait on the bridge for the next bus. After waiting for a few minutes, Robert decided to start walking until the next bus caught up with him. It was after nine o'clock and no one else was at the Southside bus stop. It was a warm night, and Robert kept walking with his little transistor radio for company. He walked several miles to his next connection point but he had just missed the bus. It would be another hour before the next bus came, so he started to walk from the Kingshighway bus stop to the Wellston loop where his last bus would take him home. He had to get there before the last bus left the depot before midnight. He got there a little before midnight, but the last bus to Kinloch had already left. He didn't have near enough money for cab fare, so he left the Wellston depot headed for home. He would have been home over an hour ago on his normal schedule, but this night was totally different. Robert kept walking and singing to the tunes that came from his small radio. He kept walking north until he finally reached the Highway. He was still over an hour away from his home as he continued down the dark stretch of Highway 70. As he approached Bermuda road, which was a little closer to his exit, but still quite a ways from his destination, a car that had just passed him by, pulled to the side of the highway and waited for Robert to get to the car. He didn't know who it was until he got close enough to recognize the car. The driver just happened to be from Kinloch who had dropped Robert off close to his school earlier that afternoon. He had gotten off from his midnight shift and happened to recognize Robert walking down the highway. He was surprised to see Robert and he told him to get in the car and explain to him why he was walking down a dark highway well after midnight. Robert told him the story about his missed buses as his driver just shook his head in amazement. He dropped Robert off in front of his house where he had picked him up earlier in the day. Robert thanked him as his friend gave him his work number in case he ever missed his bus again. Robert never missed his bus again, and of course he didn't bother to mention the event to his family.

Robert went on to complete the courses and receive his completion certificate. He completed 1,530 out of 1,560 clock hours in shop classes and basic electricity and electronics. With school now behind him, Robert went about town putting in applications hoping to land a good paying job. The Vietnam War was in full swing, so the job opportunities were wide open.

Robert was thinking that even when he got a job, it wouldn't be long before he would no longer be a civilian. The war was on every young man's mind, and with good reason. Nevertheless, he kept looking for employment. Robert took the test for a job with a large corporation. He passed the test and the interview. All he needed was to take and pass a physical, and the job was his. Robert passed the physical, but due to a typo or a misunderstanding on the physical print out, he was held up. By the time the error was figured out, time had expired and the job was no longer open for him. He still wonders what his fate would have been had things turned out differently and he would have gotten that job. However, he accepts it as being a part of God's plan for his life.

Robert continued to look until he found a job. He found one that didn't pay as much as the one that he was close to getting earlier. It was also more demanding and challenging. This job would test and stress him in ways that he had never experienced. It was a manufacturing company in the downtown area and a three bus ride from his home in Kinloch. Robert worked in the metal area of the plant that produced trash cans and tubs. He had worked previously for a brief time loading and unloading trucks on the loading dock. He also spent a short time stacking unfolded boxes that came in on the truck loading dock. Most of the workers in the plant consisted of southern White gentlemen whose secondary purpose after collecting a paycheck was to drive off Black workers as fast as they could. Robert was taken on a tour of the plant the first day he arrived. During the tour, one of the few long time Black workers in the plant told Robert not to expect to be there very long. Robert asked him what he meant by that? He told him that he would find out and that he might not make it through the day. When the tour was over, he was taken to his post. On the way, he saw a young Black man headed for the exits. Robert asked him where was he going so early in the morning. He told Robert that he had been there for two days and he had enough and was quitting. That didn't look very encouraging at all to Robert. He knew that he would have to brace himself for the worse.

His first day was not as bad as he expected it to be. In fact, the first couple of weeks were not so bad, the workers in that particular area were not overly friendly, but they managed to hold their insults to mainly stares and gestures.

Robert could live with that and thought that it wouldn't be as bad as he imagined. He was eventually transferred to the metal plant where the trash cans and tubs were made. One of the Black workers told him that the fun was about to begin. Robert didn't quite know how to take that statement, but he prepared himself for the worse just in case. This would be the crew that would test Robert to the limit. They welcomed him with a new name. He was called, "Buckwheat", a character in a television series. Since Robert was use to giving people nicknames himself, that didn't affect him like they thought it would. He didn't like it but he didn't let them get to him. Every day would be more of the same with a new twist here and there.

Every morning, Robert would rise up early, take the long bus ride downtown, and clock in on time for work. He never knew what to expect, so he braced himself for any and everything. He asked God for the strength to make it through each day. He was determined not to let them drive him off as they had done so many before him. He was going to leave on his own terms. They intensified the name- calling while making his job as hard they could. While working on the assembly line, they would slow his line down, leaving stacks of cans for Robert to catch up on. He would sometimes miss his breaks and have little time for lunch trying to catch up on his work. Complaining to the foreman made no difference at all. He would just tell Robert to do his job. Seeing that he had no options, he just toughed it out and did his work while whistling and singing. One of the lead workers, who was named after his home state of Tennessee, would gather the other workers together and plot new ways to get to Robert and force him to quit, but Robert wasn't as easy to drive off as some of the others. He would sometimes bring a sack lunch and eat it on the docks by himself. Other times, he would eat a hot lunch that was served at one of the dinners near the plant. One other Black worker who had been there for years would ask Robert to come there and eat with him. He eventually went and had lunch with him from time to time. Before long, he would go there without the other man whenever he had enough money and felt like listening to country music that was played on the jukebox.

Robert had a near fatal experience one day while on another job assignment. He and another worker, who was a full-blooded American Indian, were transferring trash cans to another floor on one of the freight elevators. After the last load was done, Robert and the other worker was looking in the space in the back of the elevator while standing on one of the wooden dollies to see what was in the open space between the floors. They were on the fifth floor when Robert was still looking in the space while his whole head hung over the gate at the rear of the elevator. The only thing between Robert's head and the gate that he was hanging over was a brick wall. The other worker didn't know that Robert still had his head hanging over the metal gate in the elevator. He went to the elevator button and pushed it. The elevator started upward to the next floor. It took less than one second for Robert's head to meet the immovable wall with his neck still on the elevator's gate like a guillotine. Robert instantly

50

felt a thud on his head and knew right a way what had happened. He thought it was all over for him. He was wearing a nylon bebop cap on his head that might have helped save his life. Miraculously, Robert's head slid out of open trap while his cap dropped five floors to the bottom of the elevator shaft. The other worker stopped the elevator, but the damage was already done. Robert turned to the hysterical worker while holding his bleeding neck and trying to talk. He couldn't speak and only made choking sounds. A huge lump had risen on the top of his head. The other worker took the elevator down to the first floor and ran out of the elevator shouting, "Get the nurse, Daugherty got his head caught in the elevator!!" He thought that he had killed Robert and was shaking like a leaf as he came back to the elevator with some help. They carried Robert to the nurse's station and laid him on the medical bed and treated him. They stopped the bleeding on his neck and wrapped it and put an ice pack on the top of his swollen head. He wasn't able to talk, but he was sure that they would take him to a hospital and get him some emergency treatment. He didn't know if he would ever be able to talk and thought that he was in worse shape than he was. Considering what had happened, he couldn't understand why he wasn't taken to a hospital.

    After about an hour, the nurse and doctor who had come in asked Robert how he felt. He was afraid to open his mouth, because all he was able to do was make sounds but not say any words. Surprisingly he was able to talk and tell them that other than a headache, he felt all right. He asked them what this neck looked like since it was wrapped up. They told him that it didn't look that bad and he would be all right. He stood up and walked around the room without any dizziness or any noticeable side effects. Robert was glad to be talking and walking, because he knew that he had miraculously escaped the jaws of death. The whistle blew, and it was quitting time. They asked Robert if he could make it home by himself. He told them that he felt that he could. As he walked from the nurse's station, he ran into the worker who was on the elevator with him. He told Robert that he thought that he had killed him and was glad to see that he was all right. Robert had bought an old long back green Chevy from a friend, and had driven to work. Once he started driving in the rush hour traffic, he began to get a little nervous just thinking about what he had just been through. He had to make a few adjustments and focus on making it home safely. After getting home, Robert told his mom and family what had happened to him after he took a short nap and composed himself. By now, things didn't look as bad as before. He still had a hickey on the top of his head, and after nervously taking the wrapping from his neck, where he was spitting up blood, and not able to talk earlier, he seemed only to have a few scratch wounds on his throat area. Robert was amazed, and thankful that things turned out so well.

They thought that Robert was being overly dramatic in his description of his near death experience. Nevertheless, his mom suggested that he go to the hospital the next day and get checked out by a doctor. Robert told her that he would not go to work and go to the hospital the next day. Robert felt a lot better and went to be with some of his friends. He told them the story of what had happened and showed them the knot that was still on the top of his head. They joked around and thought that it was funny with his newly arranged head shape. They went around telling everybody that Robert's head was so hard that he broke an elevator. He took no amusement in their joking about something that was so serious. Robert knew that if God hadn't performed a miracle, no one would be laughing. Nevertheless, he just let them have their fun at his almost fatal mishap.

The next day, Robert went to see the doctor at the company's expense. They ran test and took x-rays and examined his reflexes. All the test and x-rays came out negative. It was a company doctor, and he told Robert that he could return to work anytime. Robert was glad to hear the good report, but he knew that he needed an adjustment period before he could return to work. They took out money from his check for his union dues and now it was time for him to cash in with a little rest period. His job would call every day trying to get him to come back to work, but Robert was taking a week off. He wanted to make sure that he felt one hundred percent ready before he went back into that lion's den to face those southern gentlemen. The following week, Tennessee, Alabama, Arkansas, and the rest of the crew, welcomed Robert back with more test and trials.

Even though Robert's near fatal mishap was a legitimate misfortune, his scheming work partners were starting to wonder what it was going to take to get rid of him. Robert had far exceeded their expected time for him. They got together to come up with what they thought would be the final curtain for Robert. Their next plot caught Robert totally by surprise and almost worked. One day after the whistle sounded announcing quitting time, Robert closed up his job site and headed for his locker as usual to get his belongings and head for home. This particular day would be a little different from the others. He noticed that his pad lock was loose, but thought that he might have left it unlocked by mistake. He opened the locker door but there was nothing unusual that he could see. He put his jacket on, then took his favorite black Knox hat from the top shelf. He noticed that everyone was looking at him as if they were expecting something to happen. Robert didn't pay them any attention as usual and proceeded to put his hat on his head. As he did, he noticed the smell of paste that was used to seal the metal cans that they made. He didn't know where the smell was coming from so continued to get dressed. As he lifted the hat to put on his head, he smelled the paste again. He put the hat on his head, and instantly realized what the problem was. As quickly as he had put his hat on his head he took it off even faster. He looked inside his hat and saw the silver paste, lining the inside of his favorite hat. He had gotten some of the paste on his head and started to get it off before it got into his eyes. By now, the entertained onlookers were rolling in laughter. They had the show they had expected at Robert's expense. Robert realized what some of his co-workers had done, and was as hot as he could be. His first thoughts were about how he could get even with those dudes. He thought about rounding up some of his partners and jumping those dudes. He knew that reporting them to their superiors would be a waste of time, because they were the major part of the problem at the plant. They were literally holding their bellies in laughter as others watched and waited for Robert to explode in anger. Robert suddenly realized that he couldn't control the part of their devilish plan that was already over, but he could take control from there on. He had put up with name-calling, bad working conditions and all that they could think of to torment him in order to get him to quit.

After calming down, he wasn't going to give them the ending to their plot that they wanted. With the entire work crew, as well as the foreman looking on, Robert slowly reached into his pocket and took out his handkerchief from his pocket, and began to wipe the smelly silver paste from his head. After using his entire handkerchief, he looked into his locker for a rag to wipe his hat. He found a small rag that wasn't big enough. About that time, a sympathetic co-worker gave Robert his handkerchief and found another rag for him to use. The now stunned attentive crowd continued to watch as Robert calmly cleaned his hat out as good as he could. After he finished, he slowly reshaped his hat, put it on his head, and walked through the crowd without saying a word and went to his car. The worker who gave Robert the rag walked to his car with him and told Robert that even though he knew what they had planned, that he had nothing to do with it. He told Robert that he was sorry and hoped he understood. Robert told him that it was okay because he never gave him any trouble. In fact, Robert thanked him for being the only one that would eat lunch with him and treat him like a friend. Robert thanked God for giving him the peace and wisdom that he needed to get through that situation. Robert didn't look at that as some small hurdle. He knew that he could put up with a lot, but growing up not having much, he treasured what he had. He took a lot during his short but challenging life, and messing with his clothes would almost guarantee a fight. He showed up for work the next day and acted as if nothing had happened even though the smell of the paste was still present in his favorite hat. And oh yeah, he didn't breathe a word about it to his family or anyone else.

    Robert had no idea how long it would take before he left that job. He only knew that he wasn't leaving until he was ready to. After about four months at the downtown plant, Robert felt that it was time to start looking elsewhere for employment. He had put several applications in for jobs and was waiting for a response. After he got home one evening, his mom gave him a letter from McDonnell Aircraft. He had put in an application there earlier. He went there and took some test and waited for a response. After a couple of weeks, he got a call telling him that he could report for work the next week. There was only one big problem, the plant was on a wildcat strike and he would have to cross a picket line filled with angry Union workers. After pondering the situation and asking about what problems he would face, he decided to take the job.

    Robert's days at the downtown plant were finally over. He notified the personnel office that he was leaving after picking up his check on pay day Friday. The personnel lady knew of the ongoing tradition of chasing off Black workers and asked Robert what his real reason was for leaving, thinking that the workers had finally succeeded in their evil task. Robert told her that the real reason was that he had found a better job, and that it was time for him to go. She wished him well and told him that his final check would be mailed to him. He wished her well because he knew that she was just doing her job and had no power at that time to do anything about the problems except report them to her superiors which Robert made sure that she did. Robert was back to catching the bus now because his car had thrown a rod while driving down the highway, and walked to the stop with the one person whom he considered a friend and told him that he got a job at McDonnell Aircraft and that was his last day there. He wished Robert the best as Robert did him also. They shook hands and went their separate ways. Robert felt sorry for him because he was a high school dropout and was stuck there with all the others. Robert encouraged him to get his GED so that he could get a better job. But as for Robert, the time of his challenging education was over for now and he felt like he had passed the course.

Robert got on the bus and headed for home. On the way back, he decided to take his time and enjoy the scenery. He felt a tremendous relief, knowing that he would never have to see that manufacturing plant ever again. He took a different route home so that he could stop and look at some cars that he might buy. He got out on Natural Bridge road where a lot of car lots were. He walked down the sidewalk, stopping at different car lots. In between lots, a patrol car pulled him over and put him in the back of the car and interrogated him. He told them that he was on his way home from work, and just looking at some cars. After calling in his name and ID card that he had, they let him go and told him not to get into any trouble. Robert was tired and just went home to rest and have some fun. During the ride home, he thought deeply about his past and his future. After about a week, Robert started his new job at McDonnell Aircraft. There was no bus line going to the plant, so one of his sisters took him to work on the first day. After he was dropped off at the gate, he saw the picketing Wildcat strikers intimidating anyone who would dare cross their picket line. Robert and the replacement workers were not union, so they could work without any union threats. Robert didn't mind their taunting since he had more pressing issues on his mind.

He worked on the assembly line, so he was use to the work. The only difference was there was no game playing. He ended up working with a friend that he went to grade school with. He gave him a ride home and picked Robert up on his way to work. His friend had been there for a while and had no trouble when he was a little late. However, Robert would be reprimanded for being late since he had just started. Because of the strike, the delivery trucks that supplied the plane parts didn't cross the picket line at times, so the work was sometimes slow and there was nothing to do except look for some work to do in other departments.

As time went by, it became harder for Robert to look busy when there wasn't that much to do. Robert was also late for work sometimes because his ride would show up late. His friend didn't seem to worry that much about being late since he had been there a long time. But for Robert, the combination of not looking busy enough and being late would cost him his job. After about three months on the job, Robert was fired. He didn't take it that hard since it was hard to focus on any thing any way. He knew that at any time, he could be drafted into the Army and sent off to war.

It wasn't long after that when he and some of his fellow Kinlochians were called by the Selective Service draft board to go to the Federal building for a physical and full examination. A few of the dudes purposely failed the written test, and some played a little crazy on the mental part of the examination. It just wasn't in Robert to purposely fail the testing, so he passed the entire test and was eligible for the draft along with many of the other young men who had been tested. Robert didn't look down on the ones that he knew flunked some of the test on purpose. He knew that this was a life and death decision and not everyone was ready to face that possibility. After a couple of months of collecting unemployment checks, Robert knew that his time was running out. People were getting drafted, and people were dying in the war everyday. Robert and a buddy of his had been thinking about joining the Air Force or Navy so they wouldn't be drafted into the Army. They visited an Air Force recruiter and a Navy recruiter. They both were four year enlisted tours, while the army was only two years: if you survived them. After talking it over with each other, they decided to join the Navy. They told their family what they had decided to do. Robert's family didn't agree with his decision for fear of him being killed. He tried to assure them that the Navy would be a lot safer than waiting to be drafted into the Army. They reluctantly accepted his decision and supported him in it. At least he got to cerebrate his last Christmas as a civilian for a while. February of the following year was their scheduled time of departure.

When January came around, Robert and his friend threw a big going away party. Since he wasn't going to be around for his birthday, they combined the two. Robert's friends were somewhat skeptical since this was his second going away party in two years. Robert's first going away party was shortly after he graduated from high school. He was going to move to San Jose, California to live with his older brother. His brother had convinced him that he would be happy and successful in sunny California while helping him with his business. The going away party was a blast. However, a short while later, Robert changed his mind.   After thinking about it for while, he decided he couldn't leave his family and friends. He decided to stay in St. Louis and see what was in store for him. His friends teased him and didn't believe he was going anywhere. They told him that if he wanted to just have a party, he didn't have to say that he was going anywhere. Robert and his friend assured everyone that it was a done deal and they would be leaving for the United States Navy in early February.

CHAPTER FIVE

ROBERT JOINS THE NAVY

    Robert's days as a civilian would end when early February came around. Robert and his friend was driven to Union Station by family and friends where the train was scheduled to leave early that evening. They boarded the train along with other area Navy recruits. They waved goodbye to their family and friends as the train left St. Louis headed for Chicago, which was their first stop on the way to Great Lakes Naval Training Base. There was nothing to do but sleep on the five hour journey to Chicago. Everyone was tired after getting all the fun time in that they could before boarding the train. There was a two hour lay over after arriving in Chicago. The Navy officer that was assigned to the new recruits told everyone to hang around the Union Station train depot in Chicago and visit the USO club that was in the train station. He told everyone to make sure that they were at the gate a half an hour ahead of time so that they wouldn't miss their connection. If no one realized it before, it finally sunk in that they were now the property of the United States government. Everyone boarded the train for their final leg to the base where they would begin their boot camp training. It was dark and there was nothing to see out of the windows of the train. This was their last chance to contemplate what was left behind and what lay ahead for them.

    They arrived at the base with nothing but the clothes on their back to the sound of another Navy officer barking out orders to the new recruits. After departing the train, they boarded waiting buses that took them to a building where they would start their first stage of Navy life.

    All of the new recruits got off the buses and entered the building where they were screened and given their military clothing in exchange for their civilian clothes. Even though it was almost midnight, everyone had to take their first military shower. No one minded the late night shower except the fact that there was no hot water. Everyone had to take the icy cold shower whether they wanted to or not. This was their first direct order and introduction into what would be known as the Navy way of doing things. After a short night's sleep, everyone was awakened to a six o'clock bugle call. A drill instructor was yelling out "REVELEE" at the top of his voice. They all got dressed and were marched to the chow hall for breakfast. Afterwards, they were taken to a building where they were giving shots. The rest of the day, they got their personal care packages and the rest of their military clothing issued.

The next day, everyone was taken to the barber shop where they all got their first military haircut. All of the civilian long hair was reduced to almost a clean shave. The entire first week of boot camp mainly dealt with orientation and processing the recruits into the military system. Once their Navy ID card with their picture and service number on it was issued, the recruits were as official as they were going to get.

Boot Camp was going to be a new challenge for Robert as well as the new Navy recruits. Every morning started at six o'clock with the bugle blast and the call of REVELEE by the company officer. After a shower and shaving, the bunks had to be made, the Navy way. The clothes had to be folded a certain way in their drawers, and the dirty clothes bag, which was called a "ditty bag", had to be tied and hung from the bunk bed. Everything had to be perfect and in order. Their clothing that they wore had to be worn a certain way, and their boots had to be spit shined. After everything was done, everyone had to stand in front of their bunk as the company commander passed by one bunk at a time and held an inspection of everything, including the men. They were inspected from the top of their heads to the sole of their boots. Anything that was found out of order was a hit on each person that added up and affected the whole company. Anything found in their pockets, including lint, was considered gear drift, therefore was a personal hit. Everyone stood at attention with their right thumb holding out the neck of their tee shirt that was inspected for dirt around the rim of the shirt. There was no way to hide anything from the crafty inspectors. Anyone who had more than their allotted hits would be penalized with different chores such as extra clean up assignments, or guard duty. Men with excessive hits would have to go to a place called, "Mickey Mouse". It wasn't as funny as it sounded as Robert found out one day. They had to go to a drill hall where they had to perform an hour of hard physical exercise. The place was always packed with recruits who didn't quite meet the satisfactory eyes of their inspectors. It only took Robert one trip to Mickey Mouse to convince him that he didn't want to go back.

After inspection, the company was marched to the mess hall for breakfast. The new recruits on the base had to always do double time. This meant they had to practically jog everywhere they went on the base. This had to be done all the way up to graduation. That was a total of seven weeks. The breakfast menu wasn't anything to write home about, but hunger cured all the shortcomings. After getting to the mess hall, the newer companies had to wait outside until the advanced companies had finished their meal. The first month was sometimes cold and snowy and was a little uncomfortable to deal with. But everyone had to suck it up and gut it out. This was the same procedure for all three meals and everyone just got use to it.

Every week of Boot Camp had a different theme project. One week was called, Service Week. Each class had to spend a whole week working in different areas of the base serving the other recruits. Robert spent his service week working in the mess hall. He spent the week peeling potatoes, washing dishes, serving on the chow line and cleaning the mess hall. It was hard and tedious work, but felt rewarding serving the other recruits.

Physical exercise and marching drills were an everyday part of Boot Camp. All of the recruits were issued an M-16 rifle that was used in most of the drills. The rifle had to be broken down every day and kept clean.. The 16 and twenty- six count manual drill was a standard drill for Navy boot camp. The drill practice was carried out in any and all kind of weather. Every day all of the companies would meet in the main drill hall for inspection as well as being judged on their marching and drill skills. Each company consisted of over sixty men and there were well over thirty companies in every graduating class. The top brass would be the inspectors and judges in the huge drill hall that was filled with Navy recruits. Every company and battalion did the exact same drill at the same time. It was a sight to behold. The results of intense precision training were very impressive when all of the drill teams and companies came together. The drills and marching events really turned out to be competition that would result in flags that would be given to the companies who were more efficient in their drills as well as their personal and company inspections. The leader of the company led them out of the drill hall, who was also a recruit. They followed their company commander, as they passed the reviewing stand where each company commander would salute the brass with an eyes right, while the company commander gave a hand salute. They were judged on every movement that was made. After leaving the drill hall, all of the companies were marched back to their barracks and prepared for the rest of the events of the day.

The drill hall exercise and the inspections were over, but as they headed back to the barracks, everyone was still aware of the inspection that was taking place at the barracks. While they were in the drill hall, teams of inspectors were inspecting the inside and the outside of the barracks where the laundry was hanging on the cloth lines drying from the night wash. There were no washers and dryers so everything had to be washed and rung out by hand. Everything had to be hung, rather tied, in a special way. The ropes used for hanging had to be tied in a perfect square knot, and every item had to be exactly two fingers apart from each other. And of course cleanliness was the first and foremost order of the day. Anything that was out of order would be a hit on the person as well as the entire company that would add up and cause points to be lost in the competition with the other companies. Even the grounds were gone over with a fine tooth-comb. Nothing was left unchecked by the sharp eyes of the inspectors.

By the time everyone got a little rest and prepared for the next event of the day, they were made aware of who was guilty of personal hits as well as anything else that they may have been responsible for. They knew that there would be a price to pay, one way or the other. But it was too late to worry or do anything about it except to find out what went wrong so it wouldn't happen again.

Robert and some of the other men would sing to break the monotony while washing their clothes in the company laundry room. It brought some consolation, especially while they helped each other ring out some of the larger items such as sheets and blankets. One of the recruits from Los Angeles who use to sing in a group would teach Robert and a few others harmonizing parts. He taught them an upbeat version of Old Man River that sounded pretty good. So good, that they caught the attention of one of the top Brass who could hear them singing through the walls of the office where he was working at night. But it wasn't until after they had their orders that he approached them with the offer of possibly using their talent to sing with the USO to help entertain the troops. But since they already had their orders, it was too late to get them changed. Had he talked to them a week earlier, it would have changed their job description as well as their lives. But for Robert, he sometimes thought that time or anything else was not on his side.

Boot camp was doing it's job of molding all the young boys into men. Well almost all of them. There was always a few who had a harder time adjusting to military life than others. Every company had at least one of what was called a company scrounge. No matter how hard they tried, they couldn't or wouldn't conform to the Navy way. Class work and note taking was an ongoing activity for the boot camp recruits. A notebook was literally part of their wardrobe. It was kept in their leggings, which were strapped over their spit shined boots with their dungaree blue jeans neatly tucked into them. Everything that they wore had a purpose and a special way of fitting.

After a week of learning about gasses and the proper use of a gas mask, there was a major test. Everyone had a chance to experience how to put on a gas mask. They had to put the gas mask on in a room where gas was being released. It had to be done correctly and in a given amount of time. Robert passed the first time around and didn't have to go back a second or third time as some others did. The next test was a little more difficult. The classes ahead of them would warn them about George. They would never say what or who George was, but would only say that it was hard. Robert and some of the others figured that the gas room was the hardest thing that they would face, and George was just a lot of hype. It was a rainy day when company 150 was marched to where George was situated. Nobody knew what to expect except the company aide who was in charge. When they got there, all they saw was a brick building in the middle a field. There was a company just leaving the site and telling them that they just had a terrible experience. Robert's company waited while some of the workers were building a fire with wood, inside a part of the brick building. When the fire was ready, the aide gave instructions to the waiting recruits. They were told to go into the building and not to come out until three minutes were up. He said that if anyone came out before it was time, that they would have to go back in until they got it right. Robert went in with the first group of about twenty men. The first minute was easy.

Then the smoke started to fill the room. Robert had a plan to start counting until three minutes were up to be sure that he wouldn't have to do it again. He was up to the two- minute mark when the smoke got thicker and thicker. After two minutes, all that could be seen and smelled was smoke. However there was plenty to be heard. Robert could hear people coughing and gagging. Robert was inhaling the oxygen from his wet rain gear after he had held his breath for as long as he could. He had his eyes closed and was counting down the time. He was doing okay until he heard someone calling out for their mother. He started to laugh and inhaled some smoke for the first time. The last thirty or forty seconds seemed like it would never end and Robert was almost ready to panic. But he knew that he was close to the time limit and wasn't about to risk having to go back into the smoke house again. When the door to George finally opened, some came running out, which was a mistake. They were instructed to walk with their arms raised in the air. If anyone came out running, they would not pass the test. Robert made sure that he came out the right way. He had passed the test and never wanted to see George again. Robert later had a son who went to Navy boot camp who told him that George was no longer in operation. Robert told him that he was glad that he missed what he considered to be the worst experience that he had at boot camp.

The easiest and safest class was the rope tying class. They learned to tie every kind of knot that was used in the Navy. They were already using some of the knots everyday in their barracks tying up their clothes and other gear. The water survival classes were easy up to a point. The final test had to be passed before they could graduate. The first test was in the shallow end of the pool. It involved their white hat, their shirt and pants, which were all floatation devices. They had to jump into the water with their clothes on and take them off while under the water. Then they had to tie the ends of the shirt and pants, and float between the legs of the pants. The white hat was also used to stay afloat as it was held onto, while an air pocket was created. Robert would have passed had it ended with those tests. But the final test involved a little more swimming, which Robert was not equipped to handle.

They had to swim around the deep end of the Olympic size pool any way they chose, just as long as they made it back to the starting point. There was no reason for Robert to even start the test since he knew that he couldn't finish. Robert could hold his breath under water but he had never taken one stroke. He and three of his classmates were set aside and were giving swimming classes after regular duty hours. They joined the group of other non- qualified swimmers. NQS. They had four days to pass the class, or risk being set back a week to another graduating class or until they passed the test. Some of the men were sent back two or three weeks from their original date, for one reason or another. The class didn't really teach them how to swim. It was all about survival. They had to stand on the diving board with their hands folded across their chest, and jump feet first into sixteen feet of water. After coming back up, they had to float on their back all the way around the deep end until they got back to where they started from, and then climb out of the water. Robert had four days to pass the test. The first three days were all the same. Robert was pulled out of the water with the long rescue pole and sent back to the barracks. He only would make it half way, then down he would go. The company commander tried to encourage him and the others but nothing seemed to work. Two of the men passed the test on the third day. One of them was seemingly the most unlikely one to pass. Robert watched the tall frail classmate who was scared of the water, float all the way around the deep end on his back and finish the course. Robert had one more day to pass the test or he would be set back. Robert stood on the diving board knowing what he had to do. He jumped into the pool and came up on his back. He heard the instructor say the same thing he had been saying for three days. He told him to just relax. This time it finally sank in. Robert stroked around the pool on his back in total relaxation. He could have gone around the entire pool but was very content to get back to the starting point and climb out of the pool. He thanked the instructor and happily went back to the barracks and told everyone the good news.

 Even though Robert passed the survival test and was no longer an NQS, he still wouldn't learn how to really swim until later on in life. The weeks of Boot Camp seemed to drag except for some of the more fun times. The week of sports competition that went on between companies was one of the lighter sides of training. It would have been even better had Robert not pulled a calf muscle during one of the qualifying races. He was one of the fastest runners in the competition until he pulled up lame in a qualifying win, but was now on the mend. He was in a lot of pain and could hardly walk.

The same day of the injury, Robert asked the company clerk, who was in charge of clerical matters, for a pass to go to sick bay to have his leg checked out. The clerk was a recruit just as he was, but was a little power hungry. He denied Robert's request and told him that he would feel better in the morning. The company commander and his staff were off duty, and he had no choice but to wait until morning.

Even though he was in unbearable pain, he had to wait until the next morning when the company aide came in. Robert practically begged the company clerk for a pass to go to sick bay. When the company Aide came in, he had the clerk to write Robert a pass, and to assist him to the hospital dispensary. He and another recruit helped Robert as he hobbled to the dispensary. After being examined by the Navy corpsmen, they asked him how long he had the injury. Robert told them that it happened the day before during the racing meets. They asked him why he didn't come in right away, seeing how much pain he was in and the severity of the injury. He told the senior medic that the company clerk denied him a pass and told him that it wasn't that bad. They asked Robert where the clerk was and what his name was. He told him the clerk's name and told him that he was in the waiting room. He knew that justice was about to be served on the power hungry clerk. When the clerk came into the room, the senior medic chewed him out unmercifully. He told him that he had no authority to keep someone from coming to sickbay. They told him that this had better be the last and only time that something like that happened. The clerk was in tears as he humbly left with a better understanding of authority and his position as the company clerk. Robert was wrapped up with ace bandages and given something for pain as he went back to the barracks. He was given a cane to walk with and placed on light duty for a couple of days. He would need a major miracle for his injured leg to heal in time for the final competition.

.

He was on the basketball team as well as the track team, so he would need a miracle healing if he was going to compete. His company commander told him that the company needed him to be ready to run if he could. His recovery was delayed because of the power hungry company clerk. He couldn't drill with his company or participate in any other activities that he needed to be at full strength in. After the three day lay off, Robert wasn't at full strength, but he decided to give it a try. The basketball competition was the first test. He had to see if he could compete at a normal or close to normal level. The semifinal game was not that hard because the team that they were playing was not that good, but the finals, which was played a few hours later, was harder because the competition was better and he really needed more time to recover from his injury. His company put up a good fight, but could not beat the better team. Robert was nowhere near his full capacity, but gave it all he had.

He didn't want to play too hard because he knew that he still had the track competition the next day. His team still took the second place flag for company 150. All of the events were held in a huge drill hall, which served as a gymnasium. The track competition started the next day with Robert running the 100- yard dash. He was only about 70 percent healthy but was going to give his best. Robert had never run the 100 yards dash in high school, so this was new for him. He smoked the qualifying field previously before his injury. This was a better field than the one before. The field was made up of runners from their high school teams. One was even a state champion from Pennsylvania who Robert beat in the qualifying races. When the gun sounded Robert ran hard but cautiously. He wanted to finish the race without doing any further damaged to his partially healed leg. He ran just well enough to finish third which still gave his company a flag. He also had to run in a relay shortly afterward which his team finished second. Even though he couldn't compete at full strength, he was satisfied with his performance. He would find out later in his life that he would never be at full strength and would have to do the best he could with what he had.

As the weeks and days were dwindling down, Robert and the other guys were getting excited about seeing civilian life and their loved ones again. However there was one more stumbling block in the way. It was the aptitude test that involved everything that was learned in classes as well as training exercises that went on throughout the weeks of boot camp. Every recruit had to focus and recall specific details on practically everything that was taught and learned from their instructors. The three and a half hour exam was by no means easy. Especially the math, which had problems that he had never seen before. The test had to be passed, because failure meant being sent back a week, or however long it took before they could graduate from boot camp. Just like the swimming test, it took some men a week to three weeks for some to finally pass the test. Robert had family, who had already made plans to attend his graduation exercise on the scheduled completion date, so he didn't want to disappoint them by being sent back a week. The day of the test had come and Robert said a prayer and went into the exam room with the rest of his company. After over three hours of intense concentration, he turned in his papers and hoped for the best. He felt good about everything except the advanced math, which was always his weakest subject. The test was taken in the morning, but the results would not be known until later in the afternoon. Everyone waited anxiously in the barracks for the results to come back. When they finally arrived, the company aide read the results of everyone who had passed. Over half of the company was called out and Robert was sweating bullets thinking that maybe his name wouldn't be called. Finally his name was called with those who had passed. He could breathe again and was relieved to know that he would be graduating on time. His family was driving up to Great Lakes the next weekend and had made hotel reservations and taken off from their jobs and they didn't have to change their plans. They didn't know how close it was that Robert could possibly not have graduated on schedule.

After the final exam, the recruits finally got a week of rest and what was considered leisure time. There was no more double timing all over the base. They could walk around like normal people. They didn't have to salute anyone who wasn't a ranking officer any more. Some recruits saluted him, thinking that he was an officer. As a recruit, they were told to salute anyone if you were in doubt. Of course, Robert couldn't salute them back, but it made him feel important after being looked down on for all those weeks of boot camp. That was also career week when everyone got their job assignments and duty station. Robert tried to get into an electrical field since he had a year of trade school training. The field was already filled so he had to choose another one. He tried a clerical field but it was also filled. The smooth talking career officer told Robert that the next best thing to a clerical field would be working in a hospital. He told Robert that the hospital corps field was wide open. He told Robert the truth but what he didn't tell him wouldn't come to light until later on. He chose the hospital corps, thinking that he would be doing a lot of clerical work.

Robert left the career session feeling confident that he had made a good choice, given what was available. When everyone got back to the barracks, they were sharing with each other what field they had chosen. Robert told them that he was going to be a hospital corpsman. One of the men asked him if he knew what a corpsman was. Robert told him that the officer told him that he would be working in a hospital and doing a lot of clerical work. He told Robert that most corpsmen would end up in Vietnam. Robert didn't believe him because he was told that he would be able to use his typing skills in a hospital. Robert found out that his hospital work was only temporary and a part of the training that would eventually take him to the frontline of the war in Vietnam.

Robert was given his orders to report to hospital corps school, which was on the main side of the base at the Great Lakes, Naval Training Center. He had his orders, and all he could do was follow them and see where they would lead him. Not even the Brass, who had heard them singing in the laundry room, could have his orders changed. He was the only one in the singing group who was going to hospital corps school and eventually Vietnam. He had chosen one of the most dangerous jobs in the Navy after dodging the Army, which was a guarantee of being sent to the frontline. Instead, he would end up with the Marines, who are under the department of the Navy.

Spring had come and graduation day had arrived. It was a beautiful spring day and everything was picture perfect. Robert's family was there to see him graduate from basic training and he couldn't wait to see them. However, he wouldn't see them until all of the ceremonies were over later that afternoon. Since it was a nice sunny day, the graduation ceremonies would take place outdoors on the large drill field where they routinely practiced. Robert and the other graduates would wear their dressed white uniforms for the very first time. It was a sight to behold for the family members and the guest in attendance. Over a thousand sailors doing the same drills at the same time was quite a spectacle. No one dared miss a count or step on such an important day as this. Everyone knew that their family was in the audience, but no one dared to try and spot them during the exercises. Total focus and attention had to be on what they were supposed to be doing. The drills and exercises were flawless and the special drill teams put on a magnificent show for the crowd and the Brass. They had drilled and practiced in good and bad weather, so this day was perfect in every way.

After all of the ceremonies and speeches, the time had come that everyone was waiting for. After the base commander gave his speech and wished everyone well, the air was filled with white hats as they were tossed into the air. There was a joyous shout as the recruits had finished the boot camp training, and were now ready for duty. They were marched back to their perspective barracks, changed into their casual dungaree dress, and waited to see their families and friends. The area wasn't that large so everyone had to wait their turn before they could see their loved ones. After over an hour, Robert finally got a chance to see his family. Robert hugged his mom and family as if he had been gone for a year instead of weeks. After their brief reunion, Robert went back to the barracks. Later that day, they met in the main cafeteria for dinner and some more time of getting together and chatting. After things had settled down, his family returned to their hotel where they would spend the night. The next morning, they drove back to St. Louis and waited for Robert to come home.

Robert graduated on a Friday, but wouldn't be processed out until Monday morning. All that was left to do was to clean out lockers and a few other things in the barracks. However, the other details would take place over the next few days. Monday morning came, and Robert and the other graduates finished their checkout details and went to the final staging area where they would pick up their orders and pay check which included their travel pay to their next duty station. Robert spent most of the morning sitting on his duffle bag waiting for his name to be called. It was afternoon when Robert's name was finally called. He had already said his goodbyes to most of his buddies who had gotten their orders and left for the train station. It was a joyous as well as a sad occasion. After getting to know so many people, he knew that he would never see them again. The only ones that he would see were the two others from his company who would come back to hospital corps school with him. After saying his goodbyes, Robert put his heavy duffle bag on his shoulder and headed off the base to the train station. The train would take him to Chicago's Union Station where he would have a two hour layover before departing for St. Louis. Robert went to the USO club where he ate snacks and shot pool. The time had come to board his train for St. Louis. As the train departed the station, Robert looked back at the Chicago skyline, knowing that he would be returning there in fifteen days when his leave was up, to attend hospital corps school at the Great Lakes Naval base.

CHAPTER SIX

ROBERT GOES HOME----AND HOSPITAL, SCHOOL

After an early morning of activities and waiting, Robert was tired. He slept almost the whole train ride back to St. Louis. As the train approached downtown St. Louis, he could see the Gateway Arch on the horizon. The huge silver arch seemed to be saying, "Welcome home". The Arch had a symbolic meaning for Robert since he watched it being constructed from the very first day. He would walk past the work site every day as he went to his job where he once worked. His friends were waiting at the St. Louis Union Station to pick him up and take him home to his family. It was a joyous homecoming for Robert and his family and friends.

The partying didn't start until his buddy came home from boot camp the following week. He had to wait a week to graduate but they quickly made up for lost time.

This would be the only time that they would spend time together on leave, so they made sure that they did all that they could to enjoy themselves. When Robert's leave was up, he headed back to Great Lakes for hospital corps school, while his friend would spend his tour on a ship as a Boatswain mate. They went their separate ways and said their goodbyes to their family and friends once again. This would be a pattern that Robert had to get use to while being the property of Uncle Sam. This time around, he flew to Chicago on a military standby flight from St. Louis because he only had to pay half the price of a plane ticket. It was only a forty-five minute flight if he could get a flight out in time. He landed at Chicago's Midway airport where one of his uncles who lived in the windy city was waiting to pick him up. He had left a day early and had some time to spend with some of his relatives in Chicago. He only had a short time to visit some of his cousins, uncles, and aunts, but would have a little more time in the near future. After spending the day with them, they took him to Union Station where he boarded his train that took him to the naval base. He arrived at the base late that evening, reported for duty, and checked in on time for morning muster. This would be his home for the next six months while attending hospital corps school. After muster, Robert and the rest to the incoming class of corpsmen were assigned barracks where they would sleep, relax and study for the next six months. He would meet new friends and associates who had the same thing in common. Everyone's number one concern would be what would the future hold with the Vietnam War? It was a number one priority. However, the focus for the time being was to be on the schoolwork, which would prepare them for their next challenge. Later that day, they were taken on a tour of the main side base and the school where they would be studying. They were shown the classrooms, introduced to the instructors, and assigned their classrooms and teachers.

    The next day, the students reported for their first day of classes. All of the classes were made up of students who didn't know each other. The teacher introduced herself as a no nonsense instructor, but easy to get along with as long as the students cooperated and did their best. The first session was a getting acquainted period. The teacher, who was also a Navy nurse, had everyone fill out a personal profile form. It had questions about hobbies, favorite foods, where they were from, and other questions. Robert put down chili and pancakes for some of his favorite foods. For hobbies, he put down certain sports, and singing. After filling out the forms, they were given to the instructor. She would then have each student stand as she called their name and then read the comments from their forms. No one knew any body's name, or anything about them until their bio was read after they stood up. After reading Robert's profile, which was sports and singing, she made the comment, "I see we have an Irish tenor in the class". Out of about thirty students in the class, there were only two Black students, and Robert was one of them. With his last name being Daugherty, she didn't count on Robert being one of the black students. After she finished her comments, she asked Robert to stand up. Robert knew that she was expecting a red haired, freckled face White dude to stand up, as was the rest of the class. Robert paused for a moment, feeling a little embarrassed for the assuming teacher. There was complete silence as she called his name again with everyone waiting for the Irish tenor to stand up. Robert slowly got up from his desk as the entire class erupted in joyful laughter. The nurse's face turned as red as a peach. She realized that her assumption was way off base. She apologized to Robert and the class for assuming something. This was a violation of the number one rule in the study of medicine. Robert told her that it was all right because it could happen to anybody, and it just happened to be her. One good thing came out of the mistake. Up until that time, there was solid tension and apprehension, but now the ice was broken. The atmosphere was a lot more relaxed, and would stay that way, but the instructor reminded everyone that there was still not going to be any nonsense in her class. Everyone understood, as they entered their first course in the study of anatomy and physiology, the study of the body and its structures.

Some of the practical work involved identifying and dispensing medicines. Oranges were used to practice giving shots and the art of sewing and removing sutures. They also learned about patient care and making beds with the use of hospital corners on the sheets and blankets. The regular duty hours were from eight to four thirty, but there were clean up details after hours at times. The weekends were free when there was no extra duty work. Robert would often go to Chicago to visit relatives who lived on the West and South side. They would also take him to visit another uncle who lived in Gary Indiana. After Robert learned his way around the city, he would catch the bus and the L train to get around. When money would run a little low, he would stay on the base and go to the gym to shoot hoops or play some pool. He would also sometimes go to Waukegan, which was a small town, a few miles from the base. There wasn't much to do there, but it was a break from life on the base. The months of Corps School was also a time of reflection. He knew that the peaceful atmosphere would have to eventually come to an end. The Navy Waves, [women] were also aware of the Viet Nam War. Some of them had lost friends in the war and were very sympathetic to the men who would have to go to war. As the weeks went by, the reality of the war would hit the men in different ways. Some of them had to make a decision to stay the coarse in school, or flunk out and look for a duty chore that was less hazardous than a field medic. They knew the war would be their ultimate destiny. Robert wasn't very knowledgeable of the bible, but he decided to put his life in God's hands and see where he would lead him.

The final weeks of schooling were spent working in the base hospital as aides to the nurses. After that, they were tested with written test and graded as they were observed while handling their hospital chores. Robert passed the course and received his certificate after the graduation exercise. He returned home for a week's leave before reporting to his next duty station.

75

CHAPTER SEVEN

PATUXENT RIVER MARYLAND----NAVAL AIR STATION

After his week of fun and relaxation, Robert took a flight from St. Louis to Baltimore to Washington, DC. From the Washington airport, he took a Greyhound bus for the fifty mile ride to the Naval Air Station at Patuxent River, Maryland. He would spend the next year, working at the hospital dispensary in preparation for his next duty challenge. It was night time when he arrived at the base and couldn't see much of anything. When morning came around, he got his first look at the base and smelled the fresh Maryland air. After a moment of peaceful reflection, he quickly zoned in on what he was there for. This wasn't going to be a picnic or a vacation, but another necessary step on the path to the road of war. Robert reported to the hospital dispensary for duty and was given his hospital wardrobe and his first assignment: which would be working in the hospital pharmacy department.

Robert was introduced to the Chief Petty Officer in charge of the pharmacy. He was a no nonsense guy and he let the new workers know who was in charge. He was a short, balding, eyeglass wearing Chief Petty officer, who knew his job inside and out. He had an experienced staff that would help train the new workers as wells as make sure that the patients were supplied with the proper medication that was prescribed by the doctors. Robert spent the first couple of weeks typing labels for the medicine bottles. This was an easy job since Robert was a good typist from his high school days. Robert remembered what the career officer told him in Boot Camp about the possibility of clerical work as a hospital corpsman, but he knew that this would be very minor in comparison for what lay ahead for him. As simple as the job was, it was also very important, as were all of the jobs. The prescription had to be typed just as the doctor had written it. The name of the medicine, the dosage, and the instructions had to be one hundred percent accurate. Sometimes the doctor's handwriting was hard to interpret. That's when the staff would help, and even sometimes had to call the doctor to clear things up so that there wouldn't be any mistakes that could cause problems for the patients.

He was quickly adjusting to his new surroundings, the people, his job and the military. He was still very conscience of his temporary leisure duty, so he tried to make the best of it during duty hours and after duty hours. Robert often went to the gym to play basketball with some of the other men from different parts of the base. Then there was the service club where music and happy hour literally soaked up a lot of his time. Washington DC was only a half an hour's Greyhound bus ride from the base that was also an option for a lot of the servicemen. The strip outside of the base had its share of restaurants and nightclubs that was frequently visited by most of the service men and women as well. One of the pitfalls of going off base was the abundance of slot machines and other gambling devices. Everywhere you went, restaurants, clubs, and even the bus depot had pinball and slot machines with a chance to win or lose your money. The pinball machine was attractive in the sense that Robert used to play them for fun at the local confectionery back home. He had promised himself that he would only play, or lose a very minimum amount of money, and then quit. One evening after payday, Robert was taught a very valuable lesson. He had won twenty-five dollars on the slot machines. He took his winnings and bought dinner for himself. A couple or multiple beers later, he decided to try his luck again. He played all of the machines, and had gone in the hole. He was over his limit that he had set for himself. The more he tried to get back to even, the deeper he went into his paycheck. After almost two hours of hit and miss, the machines had taken all but fifty dollars of his paycheck. His next payday was a month away.

He knew that he had to quit while he still had something left. He was so angry with himself for letting those machines get the best of him. He had to put himself on a budget that would allow him to stretch his now limited funds. He vowed to himself, never to lose his money on gambling again, whether it was playing cards or the one arm bandits. He would now have to eat breakfast, lunch and dinner in the base cafeteria. There was no going into town for a night out. Happy hour was his only option, and the gym was his recreation. Poker for money was out, and so was any other means of giving his money away. The three and a half month duty in the pharmacy would be the easiest and less stressful of the three jobs that he would have at the Naval Air Station.. The hardest part was making cough syrup in a large vat that had to be bottled and labeled and ready to be distributed. He had to fill prescriptions and pass them on to the patients, which took a lot of focus, because of the big responsibility for accuracy. At the end of his stint in the pharmacy, the Chief gave Robert an average evaluation. He told Robert that he was too nonchalant and didn't show enough enthusiasm therefore he couldn't recommend him for Pharmacy school. He also told Robert that he was too cool, based on his tinted shades that he wore after duty hours. He had read Robert's report that stated that his only brush with the law was a ticket that he got at home in a village called Cool Valley. He associated the name of the city with little ole cool Robert. Robert didn't agree with his negative evaluation because he didn't think that it was based on his performance, which he thought was pretty good. Some of the other workers often asked Robert for help and advice. Even so, their evaluation was better than his. Robert realized that people's judgments could sometimes be short sighted, miscued, and biased.

Robert's next job would be the most challenging of the three that he had at the naval air station. He would spend the next three and a half months working in the emergency room. He would see and do things that he had only seen on television. They would also help train him for duty in combat. They involved everything from the common cold to car accidents to plane crash victims. With the base being a naval air station, there was always danger of jets crashing on and around the base area. Whenever the loud crash alarm would sound, whoever was on duty, whether they were at lunch or on break, would have to stop what they were doing and grab the emergency medical kit. Then, they would run to the emergency ambulance and head for the airstrip. There were times when their assistance was not needed, but there were also times when some of the jets and the pilots would be in serious trouble. More often than not, the alarm would go off when Robert was on duty. He can still remember the loud sound of the alarm bell in his head today. Jets were always being tested, and the reality of danger was ever present. A lot of the jets were from McDonnell Aircraft in St. Louis where Robert worked for a short time. One day while on duty, Robert answered the phone as he usually did. The call was from McDonnell Aircraft in St. Louis. Robert jokingly took it as a personal call from home. They had the wrong extension and Robert quickly put them in contact with the right people. Nevertheless, it was good to hear from home, even if it was official business. While Robert was on duty one night, he had his first encounter with death. Two pilots were brought in who had crashed in the bay not too far from the base. Their ejection button didn't work, and they were trapped in their jet. They still had their helmets on when they were brought in. Robert had to assist the medical examiner as he prepared the bodies to be taken to the morgue, which was right behind the emergency room. That experience left a lasting impression on Robert, and gave him a stronger sense of the reality of death. He also realized what the Navy had in mind, as he and others were being prepared for other duty chores.

The job in the ER had no specific description. Whatever needed to be done was always standard procedure. However the things that needed to be done, was what they were trained for and being trained to do in the future. Taking vital signs was always the first thing to do when patients checked into the ER. He was responsible for giving tetanus shots and rabies vaccine. He would also do minor suturing, preliminary diagnosis and many more chores.

Robert's first suturing job would come at an unsuspecting moment. He had always assisted but never had sewn any body up by himself. He was just about to get off duty for the day, when a man was brought in with a lacerated scalp from a swimming pool accident. Robert cleaned the wide wound, did the paper work and took it to the doctor to finish the job of sewing him up. The doctor read the report, and looked at the patient's lacerated scalp. After a short pause, he gave the report back to Robert and told him to sew him up. Robert was sure that he was talking to someone else but there was no one on duty but him. He didn't dare tell the doctor that he couldn't or wouldn't do the job because he knew that he had to do what was expected of him. He had been over a month in the ER, and he had to take on the responsibility of carrying out the doctor's orders. Robert went back to the patient and began to prepare him for minor surgery. He shaved the area to be sutured, cleansed it thoroughly and gave him a shot of Novocain to deaden the area. He got the needle and threaded it with 5.0 silk suture thread. He knew that was the correct suture to be used for scalp injuries. After putting eight stitches into his very cooperative patient, who knew that this was Robert's first solo job, he called the doctor in to inspect his work before putting the finishing touches on the job. The doctor came in with another doctor whom he was conferring with earlier. The first doctor looked at the job and said it was good work, and to finish it off. The second doctor who out ranked the first doctor asked what grade of suture he had used? Robert told him that he used 5.0 Silk. The first doctor said that it was okay. The second doctor disagreed and said that he should have used 6.0. After a brief conference with each other, the out ranking doctor won out. After Robert's first solo job, which he thought was a done deal, they told him to take the stitches out and use the other grade. Robert's patient told him not to worry about it because he wasn't in any hurry. It also helped that his patient wasn't feeling too much pain when he came in. He had maybe one too many beers at happy hour and was feeling pretty good. Robert reversed the procedure and started all over. This time, the doctors accepted the results and Robert sealed the sutures and sent the man on his way with orders to return in seven days to have his sutures removed. He also told him to come back in a few days to check on his sutures. His practice on oranges in corps school and his attention as an assistant had paid off. Experience proved to be the best teacher at this particular time.

Robert recalls a hectic Friday evening at the ER. Weekend duty was always the busiest and bloodiest time of the week. A lot of the accidents were alcohol related and this night wasn't any different. A man and his wife were brought in and were in pretty bad shape. They were civilians who lived not far from the base. The man, who was the driver, had a lot of cuts and bruises and was in bad shape. His wife was in worse shape; as she had major cuts and bruises as well as a few fractured limbs. The most significant wound was a severe laceration to one side of her face. Her face was sliced from the top of her head almost to her chin. It was so bad that the doctor on duty went into a panic mode and Robert and the other corpsman on duty had to take over until he calmed down so that he could do his job. After cleaning and stabilizing the lady, she was taken into the OR for emergency surgery. After over four hours and over a hundred stitches to close all of her wounds, she was taken to a ward where her husband had already been admitted. Robert wouldn't see them again until the next day after he came on duty. Robert and his friend who had treated them in the ER would keep in touch with them until they left the hospital. They both made a full recovery and the lady's face seemed miraculously cured. There was a visible scar, but compared to the way she came in, it was a miracle that they not only survived the accident, but made a full recovery surgically as well. The doctors did a real masterful job on both of them.

After the couple got home, they invited Robert and his friend for dinner one weekend to show their appreciation for their initial and ongoing support. Robert's friend was White and the couple was Black. Color was no issue for any of them. They fixed a nice dinner for them and served refreshments afterwards. Robert and his friend said their goodbyes and left in the borrowed car that his friend was driving. They never saw the couple again. They were glad they didn't have to see them in the emergency room again. Robert and his friend would sometimes go to restaurants and clubs outside of the base. Robert would sometimes take him to the Black clubs, but the White bars and clubs wouldn't allow Robert to come in because of his color. His friend told them that if Robert couldn't be served, that he would leave with him. This was not the deep south, but the East coast, and right outside of the military base, and only fifty miles from Washington DC. The Vice President of the United States was the former governor of Maryland and there were still segregated restaurants and nightclubs. There were establishments where signs read one side for Black, and the other side for White. Robert and his friend didn't see color nor did the couple that they had helped on their road to recovery. Robert's three and a half months in the ER seemed to never end. Nevertheless it was a time of maturing and growing as a military person and a human being. Once again he had to remember that all of the on the job training was still a tune up for his ultimate destiny: Vietnam.

After life in the ER, Robert spent the next four months or so working on the hospital ward. It was between the ward and the laboratory where he would spend most of his time. The lab work consisted of taking sample cultures and drawing blood. Locating good veins was the hardest part of the lab work. The medical ward work involved patient care, dispensing medicine, giving shots, prepping for surgery and whatever else was needed. The patients' charts had to be kept in order so the doctors could keep up with their progress. The standard rule for passing out medication and starting "IV'S" was that if you were not sure, you had better ask somebody who knows. The night shift was the easiest, yet more demanding. The main job of the night corpsman was to make sure that the patient made it through the night .Bed checks and IV checks had to made every hour. Night medications had to also be given. Robert worked all of the shifts at one time or another. One of the other duties the hospital staff had to do was the night watch because the whole hospital dispensary had to be patrolled all through the night. Weekend watch was the most inconvenient because some of the men would want to go home or somewhere else for the weekend. The men would help each other out by exchanging watches or paying someone to take their watch. Most of the enlisted staff stayed in the hospital barracks, where the watch started. The men slept in bunk beds and kept the area clean.

Robert recalls an incident in the barracks one morning after he had just finished night duty on the ward. He was resting on his top bunk when trouble came knocking. There was a new corpsman in the barracks that had recently been released from the Brigg in Fort Leavenworth Kansas. He was an imposing and menacing figure. He was a big Brother, who stood about six feet four inches, with muscles bulging from every part of his body. He had gotten in top shape while lifting weights in the Kansas prison, and he had a huge ego, which he would use to get his way. When he came in the barracks, he would pick a bunk that was already occupied and demand that the occupant get up so that he could have the bunk. The person in the bunk would always give in to his request to avoid any trouble with the not so gentle giant.

Robert would sometimes eat meals with him in the hospital cafeteria and had never had any problem with him nor did he expect any. Robert lay in his top bunk waiting for him to finish his usual antics so that he could go to sleep. As he walked the floor with bunks on each side of the barracks, he slowly made his way to where Robert was bunked. Robert didn't expect any trouble from his acquaintance, but just in case, he decided to act as if he was sleep. He got to where Robert was and shook him, and told him that he wanted his rack. Robert told him that there were empty racks everywhere and he should get one of them. He turned over to go to sleep. He wasn't even thinking about giving up his bunk for him or anyone else.

Everyone was watching to see what was going to happen. This was the first time that the bully had been turned down and he didn't like it. He had an image to uphold, so he snatched Robert from his top bunk and threw him to the floor. That didn't take much since

Robert was five feet seven and one & a half inches, and one hundred thirty pounds at the most. What the bully didn't count on was Robert's Kinloch toughness, and the experience he got from watching wrestling at the Chase in St. Louis. Even though most of the professional matches were rigged, the holds and moves were real and effective. When Robert got off the deck where he had been thrown, he collected himself and told the bully that it was on. Robert started off swinging with everything that he had, but the dude was too tall. Therefore, Robert tricked him by swinging for his head and catching him off balance. He went for his knees and brought him down. Robert went from one hold to another, but the big man broke them all. Robert nevertheless kept him on the floor, knowing that he couldn't let him get back to his feet. He finally got a head lock on the big man and wouldn't let go. The big man carried Robert all over the barracks but Robert didn't let his neck go. The big man finally got tired and fell back to the deck. Robert continued to apply pressure to his neck as the big man's face began to turn red. He was loosing oxygen and was about to pass out. He told Robert that he couldn't breathe and to let him go. Robert thought that he might be trying to trick him so he squeezed even tighter. After over fifteen minutes of battle, Robert finally wore the big man down. Realizing that the big man was at his mercy, Robert made him promise not to ever mess with him or anyone in the barracks ever again. With every one around watching, the big man's ego wouldn't let him do it. So Robert applied the pressure to his neck once again. After he couldn't take any more, the big man finally spoke out loud the words that Robert gave him to say. Robert told him once again to promise not to bother anyone ever again. With the big man gasping for air, Robert let him go. He got back in his bunk and went to sleep, as did every one else. There was no more trouble from him and everyone lived in peace again. By the time Robert got up from rest, the news had spread around the hospital how he had brought down the bullying giant. Robert didn't think anything about it. He just wasn't going to let some bully, no matter how big he was, take his bed. He grew up with over ten people in a small house in Kinloch, and it just wasn't an option of giving in to some bully. He would have had to fight Robert every day if that was what it took.

    Robert knew that his time was winding down before he got his orders for Fleet Marine Force Training (FMF). However, it was getting close to Christmas. Robert had never spent Christmas away from home and was getting a little nervous. He didn't have enough money for a flight, and flying military standby would be too much of a risk for such a short time. He had a five day pass but no way to get home. He had told his family that he probably wouldn't make it home for the holidays. He had all but given up, when he got a break. Robert was talking to one of the Dental Technicians who was about to drive home for the holidays. They stayed in the same barracks and talked many times together. Robert asked him where he was headed, and he told him that he was going to Missouri. Robert told him that he was from Missouri, too. Nothing connected until he told Robert that he was from Wentzville, [the home of Chuck Berry]. Robert knew that he would practically pass his house in Kinloch as he drove west on highway 70. He told Robert that he had one other rider who was going to dropped off in Ohio, and he could ride with them. This was very good news for Robert. He had two days to get ready for the ride home. He kept it a secret from his family and wanted to surprise them. He bought small gifts for everyone, which was only a token of the real gift, which would be to have him home for the holidays.

    They left early in the morning on Christmas Eve. They arrived in St. Louis later that night and made the exit off the highway that was about five minutes from Robert's house. There was a light snow as he pulled into Robert's driveway where he unloaded his things along with the bag of gifts that he had bought for his family. Robert thanked his friend and gave him the simple directions back to the interstate that would take him the final thirty miles to his home in Wentzville. His friend left and told him that he would pick him up on the way back to the base in Maryland. His surprise was still intact and no one knew that there was anyone outdoors because they had dimmed the lights as they pulled into the driveway. Robert dragged his bags up to the kitchen door and knocked as if he was a visitor. He could hear them inside asking each other who that could be at the door so late. Someone asked the familiar question, "Who is it?" Robert didn't answer but kept knocking, because he wanted them to be totally surprised. Finally, one of his sisters peeked through the curtain and shouted, "It's Robert!!", as she quickly opened the door. Other family members that were in the living room and elsewhere, thought that she was joking and didn't even bother to move. As Robert entered the house, he was greeted by hugs and kisses from his family. His surprise was in effect and working beautifully. His youngest sister who was very close to him, was especially excited. She ran up to him and gave him a big hug.

When all of the excitement of seeing their brother and son was over, Robert went back outdoors and brought in his personal bag along with the bag of gifts that he had bought for everyone in his family. They were all excited as they un-wrapped their small but appreciative gifts. All of the family members, who were there, truly had witnessed a miracle on that Christmas Eve night. Those who didn't see him that night got a chance to see him first thing in the morning. That was truly a blessed Christmas for Robert and the Daugherty household. With the few days that he had, he enjoyed his family and friends until it was time to leave. His friend picked him up in time for them to report back for duty at the base in Maryland. After they got back, it was work as usual. Robert could look back on his miraculous surprise visit as a wonderful and meaningful time, even though it was only a few days. Robert thanked his friend for providing him the opportunity to visit his family for the holidays.

The winter months in Maryland were not as bad as Robert had anticipated. The deepest snow was about eight inches, which quickly melted away. It was less snow than he was use to seeing. He would have liked to see a little more snow, which would have reminded him of home. He was starting to hope that they had forgotten about his orders for FMF School. It was now over a year since he had been in Maryland and he knew that he would have to soon give up another group of friends. He had even met a girl who he thought about marrying. But he knew that he was going to war and probably would have a very short future. Military towns were hotbeds for potential hookups. A lot of the local girls were looking for a way out of town and the military men were just looking.

Sometimes even the parents of the girls would be more than encouraging. Robert was on duty one evening at the hospital during visiting hours. A man and his daughter were visiting a relative as Robert was just going about his business. After visiting hours were over, the man came up to Robert and asked him a strange question. He asked him why he didn't try to talk to his daughter. Robert was stunned at the man's bold imposition and didn't quite know how to answer him. He told the man with his very nice looking daughter standing there, that he was very flattered, but he was dating a girl already. The man said that he understood, and told Robert that it didn't matter and he could arrange a meeting with her anyway. Robert told him that it wasn't necessary. The man left his phone number and told him to call if he changed his mind. Robert thought to himself that the man had to be really desperate to get rid of his daughter; but he did tell Robert that he was a good judge of character, and thought that he would be good for his daughter. Robert considered that to be a pleasant distraction from the reality of what lay in store for him.

As springtime came around, it was getting real close for his tour at the Naval base to be over. He would try to enjoy the remaining days not knowing when his orders would come in. True to form, his orders came in just before summer. The Navy had an agenda, and Robert was a part of it. He was to report to Camp Pendleton Marine Corps base in California for field medical school training. The base was sandwiched between San Diego and Los Angeles, but closer to San Diego.

CHAPTER EIGHT

FMF- SCHOOL-----CAMP PENDLETON CALIFORNIA

Robert once again said his goodbyes to his friends and acquaintances and took the Greyhound bus to Washington DC, for a long bus ride to St. Louis. He had thirty days leave, and wasn't in any hurry. He was going to take the full thirty days which was the whole year's worth, because he didn't know just how things would go once he got to California. He wasn't sure if he would ever see home again. When he got home with all of his Navy gear, his family had a hard time understanding why he was going to be with the Marines, when he had joined the Navy. He tried to explain the best he could that the Marines was under the Department of the Navy, and all of their medical care came from the Navy. He told them that as a Navy corpsman, he was going to train as field medic, and be a part of a Marine unit, with full Marine Corps gear. They still didn't quite understand what he meant, and he didn't really tell them that he would end up in Vietnam. He told them that they would understand eventually, but for now just enjoy the time that they had with him. He wanted to enjoy his time at home, and knew that no one would be able to if they knew the danger that he was going to be in.

The trees and flowers were in full bloom, and Robert never appreciated his home more than he did now. St. Louis, and especially the small community of Kinloch where he grew up gave him a sense of pride and a deeper appreciation of the simple things in life. He didn't know how those before him felt before they left home not knowing for sure if it was going to be the last time they were going to see it.

However, for him it was like being in the final act of a play, and he wanted everyone to believe that somehow everything was going to be alright, no matter how it ended. Robert's thirty days as a civilian seemed to go by in a flash. He packed his civvies, [civilian clothes] loaded his Navy sea bag in the trunk of the car of one of his family members, and headed for the airport. As the plane took off and headed west, he realized that he was finally going to sunny California, but it wasn't exactly how he thought it would be. It was later that evening when the plane landed in San Diego that reality once again began to sink in. He took a greyhound bus from there to Ocean Side, a small town outside of the Camp Pendleton Marine Corps base. When he got off the bus, he looked around, and all he was able to see was darkness around the borders of the town. The weather was also not what he expected. It was very cool, and almost cold. He didn't pack any jackets or long sleeve clothes because he thought that it was going to be all short sleeve weather. Robert got to a phone, and called home and told his brother to pack some warm clothes and he would tell them where to send them as soon as he had an address. After over a half an hour, he boarded a shuttle bus with some other men that took them to the main gate of the Marine Corps base. Robert showed the guard his orders and was taken by bus to the barracks of the field medical school, where he would spend the next three months in training.

The next morning he woke up to a whole new world. He now realized why everything looked so dark.. The huge mountains provided a background for one side of the town, while the other side was boarded by the Pacific Ocean. This was the first time that he had seen mountains up close and personal. He was impressed at the sight, but would become more impressed when he realized that he would soon be climbing every one of them at one time or another.

The three months of training was filled with classroom work as well as field training. All of the Navy corpsmen, short, tall, and small, had to endure the same rigorous training. Everyone was issued a full supply of Marine Corps green, along with everything else needed for a combat medic. All of the Navy corpsmen were issued a forty-five pistol, which they had to learn to disassemble and put back together with their eyes closed. It would be the same weapon that they would carry with them in combat. Robert and the rest of the corpsmen had to get use to saluting the officers as they passed them by. This was a big adjustment since they hadn't saluted anyone since boot camp. The Navy didn't require saluting on the base. The Marine Corps also didn't allow facial hair of any kind. Robert had grown a mustache and had to be threatened before he finally parted with his well- groomed mustache that he had for over a year. He had to come to the understanding that there was a Navy way, and now a Marine Corps way. He and the other Navy corpsmen had to quickly make the necessary adjustments.

All of the classes had their own Marine drill sergeant. They trained together, lived together, and hung out together. Robert would become acquainted with yet another group of friends and associates. He had made one special friend from North Carolina. Robert would let him wear some of his clothes when they went out on the town. He showed Robert a picture of his wife and his two little children. He had hoped to be reunited with them when his tour of duty was over, but realistically, they both knew that their chances of coming out alive were very slim. They would often check the Navy Times paper and see that corpsmen was at the top of the list in casualties. Sea deaths and wounded in action was a common thing for Hospital Corpsmen. The combat tour of duty was one year, but hospital corpsmen became casualties within weeks of entering the combat arena. The picture was not very pretty. Between the lectures and the simulated battlefield training, the corpsmen got a clear picture of what to expect in the fields of Vietnam.

Most of the casualties were caused by booby traps and anti personnel land mines. Robert's company drill instructor was a Vietnam veteran who had served a tour of duty in Vietnam. He was a tall blonde dude from Indiana. He slept with the company and did all of the field training. He played basketball with the men and had become a friend to them, but he knew that the time would come when there would be no time for fun and games. Robert and some of his friends would often go into the town of Ocean Side and sit by the beach and talk about life and death. The ocean waves had a calming effect, but the waves could sometimes turn deadly. It was reported in the news that three sailors who were walking by the beach were swept away by a giant wave and never heard from again. So no matter where you were you had to be careful.

As their training was coming to an end, the corpsmen would have another reality check. After spending five days and nights of training in the mountains, they noticed that their drill sergeant was in tears. They had just finished eating their dinner and were about to head back down the mountains to the base. They asked him what was wrong. He was as tough as he needed to be, but very sentimental as well. He swelled up and told the company of Navy Corpsmen as humbly but as boldly as he could, that the reality was, that a lot of those standing there would not make it back alive. That had a very sobering effect on the men, but he also had one more announcement;

he said that twenty-five volunteers were needed to go overseas with a Marine Unit. All of the fifty plus men volunteered to go. They knew that you couldn't come back until you went. So the men wanted to get it over with one way or another.

Since there were too many volunteers, the sergeant had everyone put their name in his helmet. The first twenty-five names pulled were the ones who would get to go. Knowing what a bad gambler he was, Robert was sure that his name would be pulled right away. As he got closer to the twenty-five names needed, Robert was still hopeful that his name would be called. After all of the twenty- five men were lined up, Robert was left out. He was surprised and disappointed, knowing that he would have to wait it out until the whole division was called over. The whole base was on standby and could be called up at any time. Robert couldn't understand how his luck could be so bad.

The volunteers and the unit were shipped out immediately. It was less than two weeks when news got back to the base that most of the unit that was shipped over was caught in an ambush and almost all of them were killed, including the twenty-five corpsmen who had bravely volunteered to go. Robert quickly understood something: had his name been picked out of the sergeant's helmet that day, he would no longer be alive. He was very sad for his friends that he had trained with for three months, but he was also thankful that it wasn't his time just yet. He was thankful that his gamble with life and death didn't pay off at that particular time.

CHAPTER NINE

GRADUATION FROM FMF SCHOOL & DOC BECOMES A PLATOON MEDIC

After he graduated from field medical school, he and the rest of the graduating class were placed with a platoon of Marines to be their personal medic. They lived, ate and trained with them. They were now legitimate grunts. That would be the final step for the corpsmen before being sent to war. Robert was somewhat welcomed by the Marines and the staff as their new medic. He also would assume the title "Doc"; no first name. no last name. just "Doc".

It would take Robert a little time to adjust to his platoon and the staff, which consisted of two top sergeants and several corporals. He soon learned that even though he was in charge of medical decisions that he had to answer to the super sergeants first. Robert was in trouble in a hurry. The Marines complained that all of their clean clothes would be stinky because they had to put their dirty clothes in the same locker as their clean clothes. Robert was trained to keep them separate because it would present a health problem. He had the men try it the Navy way of putting their dirty clothes in a laundry bag and tie them neatly at the end of their bunk. When morning came, the inspecting sergeant noticed something quite different. He asked the men, "who was responsible for this?" They told him that Doc was. They called Robert into the office, and told him that this was the Marine Corps, and that wouldn't work here. They said that from now on, everything had to run through them first. Robert naively somehow thought that they might be pleased with the change since it was a health issue, but he was still learning that there was a Navy way, and there was a Marine way.

Every day was a new learning experience for Robert. The Marine Corps was not the Navy, and the adjustments had to come quickly. Every day, he had to be with his platoon wherever they went. After breakfast, there was always marching drills, but Robert didn't have to participate. One morning, the drill sergeant decided that he and the rest of the platoon would get a good laugh at Robert's expense. As he watched the Marines drill, the platoon leader took a break, then he told Robert to take over the marching drill. To his surprise, Robert said ok. Everyone laughed and thought he was joking. Robert knew that he could do it because he didn't see them do anything different than he did in Navy boot camp. In fact the drills were simple. Doc stood in front of the platoon and brought them to attention. He started off with simple right and left flank drills.

Then he heard one of the marines shout out, "Is that all you got Doc?" Then Robert turned it up and mixed the regular flanks with double flanks and through in a few others for good measure. They were barely able to keep up with Robert's drill counts. Even though Robert was a part of the Navy drills, he had never led a drill team; this was a first. The platoon leader saw that Robert was more than capable of handling the drill team. He told him to give the well drilled Marines a break. After bringing them back to their starting point, Robert picked up his medical bag that he had to carry everywhere he went. He went back to his spot as if it was no big deal, but to the Marines, it was. They were very impressed. Their Doc earned a big measure of respect from them that morning.

During the early months at Camp Pendleton, Robert was learning more and more about Marine life. The only Naval personnel on the base were the hospital staff that was made up of Navy doctors and Navy hospital corpsmen. He would go in to town on liberty with his Navy friends, but as time went on, he would also go with some of his new Marine friends from his platoon. One weekend, Robert got a chance to fly up the coast to visit his brother who lived in Freemont, California. He wore his Navy uniform and flew free by flying military standby. It was a risk because the airline and the planes were so small. The stewardesses on the flight looked like volunteer grandmothers. The flight was rough, but he made it there and back safely. In the two and a half days, he took Robert to San Francisco, where they visited Fishermen's Warf and China town. They also managed to squeeze in a drive up to Reno, Nevada, a picnic, and a night out at a club in Sunny Vale, where his brother played drums, piano, and guitar. As the weekend came to an end, Robert had to come back down to earth and head back to Camp Pendleton.

There were times when Robert's outfit would spend days, and sometimes weeks in the rugged mountains around the base. There would be company and battalion maneuvers. There also would be war games involving the whole base. All of the training was in preparation for the real war that was raging in Southeast Asia. The war games were very intense and realistic. They used smoke grenades and chemicals. Every one had to know how to put on their gas mask when chemicals were used. Simulated casualties had to be treated and tagged as though they were the real thing. Sometimes there were actual casualties. Some were routine, and some were life threatening. Robert recalls an event involving a Marine in his platoon. They were on an operation in the mountains on a very hot day. It was extra hot since everyone was in full combat gear. Everyone was supposed to make sure that they took care of their own needs. They had to maintain their food and water supply and make sure they took their salt tablets. They would lose a lot of salt from sweating in the heat. The tablets were big and not very tasty, but they had to be taken to avoid any heat related problems.

Robert's unit had just passed through a low area and climbed up the side of a rugged mountain. Robert had made it to the top of the mountain, and was about to take a rest from the exhausting climb. Just as he sat down for a break, he got the call for "corpsman up". When the corpsman heard that call, he had to drop whatever he was doing and take off to where he was needed. In this case, it was corpsman down, because he had to go back down the mountain that he had just climbed to reach his patient. When he got back down, he was taken to a valley where the casualty was lying on the ground. He quickly noticed that it was someone from his platoon that he had a conversation with earlier in the day. Robert had tried to convince him to take his salt tablets because the Marine said that it was nasty and he didn't really need it. So the first thing Robert asked him was if he took his salt tablet as he was told to. He told Robert no, he didn't. He was sweating profusely and about to pass out. Robert began treating him for heat exhaustion. He gave him some of his own water with salt because he had drunk all of his own water. He watered him down and elevated his feet. He got enough fluid and salt in his system before he passed totally out. He came back around, so he didn't have to start an IV on him. He was feeling better and talking before the stretcher bearers came to take him back to the rear. Robert had to now climb back up the mountain that he had just came down to join the rest of his unit. The Marine later thanked Robert and told him that he would take his salt tablet from now on. All of the military operations provided everything that they would use and need in an actual combat situation. Robert also realized that the training operations were also filled with life and death situations

With all of the training being so intense and demanding, free time and liberty was a valuable change of pace. Pay period meant that the men would have a few more options and they would often take full advantage it. Robert and some of his friends wound venture out a little further from the Base, as finances were available. They would go to San Diego or Los Angeles as time permitted.

One evening, Robert and a few of his Marine buddies took a Greyhound bus to Los Angeles on a Saturday evening. It was only an hour or so ride so it wasn't really that far. When they got there, they didn't know where to go, so they just walked around downtown and took in some of the sights. This was the first time that any of them had been to LA. They had just turned a corner when Robert spotted a Brother walking toward them on the sidewalk. He was wearing shades and a black Knox hat that looked somewhat familiar to Robert. Robert still paid him no attention as he was about to walk pass him and his two friends. Robert and the man looked at each other and realized that they knew each other. Robert shouted out "The Monster" while the other guy shouted out "Darby". They both were in total shock as they embraced. It was Robert's friend from St. Louis that he went to O'Fallon Tech Trade School with in the special program. They had played basketball together at the Page Park YMCA before they went to classes. That's where Robert nicknamed him "the monster", for his ruggedness on the backboards. He was a tenacious rebounder despite being just a little bit taller than Robert. He never could pronounce Robert's last name right, so he called him "Darby" instead of "Daugherty". After talking for a few moments, they decided to go somewhere and do some catching up. Robert told him that he was in the service, stationed at Camp Pendleton. Robert was sure that he had to be in the service too, because it had been over two years since he had last seen him, but The Monster told him that he had not too long ago moved to LA and was living in Watts with his play mother and her family. He was just wandering through the city streets and was going nowhere in particular.

Robert told his two buddies that he would see them back at the base while he and his hometown friend got re-acquainted. Neither one of them was familiar with the city, so they just found a restaurant and got something to eat as they talked about old times and what was going on now. Robert told him his situation and said that he probably wouldn't be around much longer because of the dangerous job that he had in the service. The Monster said that he was looking for work because Uncle Sam had no use for him because of his flat feet. Robert told him that he was glad for him, but not to feel badly for him. They both felt that it had to be more than a coincidence for two dudes from St. Louis to meet again two years later while walking the streets of Los Angeles on a Saturday evening. They still had no place to go in particular, so they just walked around the city for a while.

They were not twenty-one yet, so they couldn't get into any bars. They got someone to get them a six pack from a liquor store, and sat on park bench as they relaxed and talked about everything that came to mind. As it started to get dark, they were about to go their separate ways, when they both decided that it was too early to end their day. Furthermore, they were just beginning to enjoy themselves. Robert asked his friend how far they were from Hollywood and the Sunset Strip. The Monster told him that they were a thirty minute bus ride from the Strip. Robert told him that he wanted to make the best of his time, because he didn't have much time left before he had to go to Vietnam. They both agreed to take the city transit to the strip and see what would happen. If nothing else, they could say that they had been on the famous Sunset Strip.

After the thirty- minute ride, they got off the bus and started walking, while checking out the scene. They still had a little daylight left and they figured they would just go back to LA in about an hour. As they were crossing a street, they saw a tall skinny dude pushing a small piano up a hill on the sidewalk. Robert and The Monster offered to help him push his piano to the club where he was going to be playing that night. After they helped him to the club, he told them to come and check him out later on. They said that they would. They came back after walking around for a while and tried to get in to the club, but were turned around by the doorman because they were underage. The piano player at the Classic Cat Club, tried to persuade him to let them in but couldn't do it. Therefore, they moved on and just took in the night sights. It was about nine o'clock when they noticed a long line of people wrapped around the block. They went to the front of the line to see where they were headed. It was the famous Whisky Ago Go. It was one of the hottest dance clubs on the Strip, and that night they had one of the hottest entertainers performing. The line was so long that it would have taken over an hour to get in, and they knew that they didn't have that much time. They had 'til midnight to catch the last bus back to LA, and it was getting late. They saw that the man at the door who was checking in the customers was a Soul Brother. They had nothing to lose, so they ran a sad story to the man with the hope that he might sympathize with them and let them in. He turned them down and they walked away. A few minutes later, they came back and begged and pleaded with the man to let them in. He finally gave in, and let them in ahead of the big crowd that was waiting to get in. He told them that once they left, they couldn't get back in. Robert and his friend agreed and went into the club and made themselves at home. Once in, they were able to get drinks without any ID check. They got to see the entertainer who was performing and grabbed the first available girl and danced on the huge dance floor with strobe lights blasting.

After about an hour in the club, they started talking to a White dude. They told him that they were from Missouri and he said that he was from Illinois. He said that was close enough, and they were practically neighbors. He said that he was in the Army, and had a hotel room on the Strip. He invited Robert and his friend up to his hotel for a few drinks. As they left the building, Robert and his friend told the doorman that they would be back. The doorman told them to take a look at the line. It was still wrapped around the corner, and people were still waiting to get in. Nevertheless, they went on with their newfound friend. They got to the hotel where they ate and drank and talked and talked. He had what he called, "the good stuff to drink." He tried to get Robert and his friend to stay longer, but it was getting later. They felt that they had a good hour before they had to catch the last bus out. They were feeling pretty good when they got back to the club, and were ready for a little more partying. On their way to the front of the line, they tried to get two girls in the club with them. The doorman, who had already broken the rules for them, told them that they could come in, but the girls couldn't. They went in without them and finished their partying. They looked at their watches and realized that it was almost midnight. They left the club and thanked the doorman for his excellent assistance.

They made a dash for the bus stop with hopes that it wasn't too late. Well it was. The last bus was gone and they didn't have enough money for a cab. There was only one thing to do. They started walking down the 105 Freeway, back to LA. They didn't even think about hitchhiking. After all, who was going to pick up two Black dudes-one wearing a black Knox hat in the midnight hours, walking down a California highway? They figured that they might make it back before morning, and Robert could catch the Greyhound bus back to Ocean Side. After a couple of hours of walking, the Monster jokingly stuck his thumb out as a car went by.

To their surprise, the car pulled over and stopped at the side of the highway. They still didn't think that it was for them, but when they got to the car, the driver, who was a middle age White dude, asked them where they were headed. They told him that they were going to downtown LA. He told them to hop in and he would take them as close as he could to where they were going. The man let them out at an exit that was close to where the Monster's play mother lived in Watts. They walked to the house, and no one was home.

No one came home either. Robert and the Monster slept on the porch in two metal lawn chairs. His play mom and dad got back at about sunrise and took Robert to a bus line where he could catch a bus to the Greyhound bus station. It was still early, when he got to the bus stop, and there was no one on the streets. The first transit bus still had over an hour before it would leave. After sitting on a bench for about a half an hour, a car pulled up with two wine heads in it. They asked Robert where he was headed. He told them that he was going to the Greyhound bus station to go back to Camp Pendleton. They told him that they would take him there for five dollars. Robert agreed and got into the car. Sure to their word, they took him straight to the Greyhound bus station. Robert gave them the five dollars and thanked them. He got his ticket that would take him to Ocean Side. The shuttle bus took him to the base, where he walked back to his barracks. Some of the guys were just getting up, and Robert was ready to go to bed. It was Sunday morning, so he thought that he would go to nine o'clock mass before turning in. He felt that the least he could do, was to thank the Lord for taking care of him through a very eventful night. His friends, who had gone with him to LA, asked him how his night was. Robert told them that he would tell them all about it after he got some sleep. He never saw his friend the Monster again, but he felt that it was a night that was meant to be. Maybe not quite the way everything happened, but it was now in the books.

Meanwhile, the training and maneuvers would pick right back up. There was a major convoy of trucks filled with personnel that tracked up to El Toro Air Force Base. There was also time spent on a battleship in preparation for a beach training landing off the coast of Mexico. The five day trip on the Navy battleship would be the only time that Robert would spend on a Navy ship. After the five day trip, the beach assault was set in motion. The Marines left the ship in amphibious tanks about a mile from shore. It was a scary experience for the first timers. Being under water in a big metal tank didn't seem like a good place to be for Robert and some of the others. Robert asked the tank operator if any tank was ever lost in the ocean. He told him no, but there was always a first time. Since water was dripping through the hatch, nobody thought that it was very funny. The landing was well coordinated as ships and tanks made their way to the beach at the same time. They dug in and established a position and the war games were on. The twelve days of training went well. Everyone took the training very seriously. They returned back to the base in a convoy of trucks. After almost two weeks from the comforts of the barracks, everyone was ready for a good shower, a good night's sleep in their own bunk, and a night on the town was very much in order for the next day, Sometimes, a night on the town would have negative effects. One night after a night of drinking and fun, Robert and two of his Marine buddies came in late one night.

One of the Marines picked a fight with a not so popular associate. The beat up Marine reported that the two marines and Doc [Robert], jumped him and beat him up. Even though Robert wasn't involved in the fight, he was put on report as well. After duty hours, Robert and the two Marines were marched to a field in the mountains. The sergeant in charge told them to take out their E tool, [shovel] and start digging the best hole that they could. After about two hours of digging an almost six by four foot square hole, the sergeant told them to cover it back up. He marched them back to their barracks and told them that he understood their problem, but to try to stay out of trouble. They took his advice and it never happened again.

The mountains of Camp Pendleton were a formidable foe within themselves. Along with being big and spacious, they were inhabited with all types of animals and insects. Rattle Snakes were everywhere. Big tarantula spiders often shared the same trail as the troops. Mosquitoes were five times the size of the ones Robert was used to in St. Louis. Insect repellent had little and sometimes no effect on the flying pest. After pulling his knapsack up in the morning, there would be species of bugs that he had never seen before. He was surprised that he had actually slept on the strange looking critters, but sleep outweighed any other problem. So the bugs and everything else had to take a back seat to the tired and sleepy troops.

One day, while on patrol in the mountains, Robert was left behind to rest his knee that was giving him trouble. After a few moments of sitting on the side of the trail, a big deer came from out of nowhere, leaping over Robert's head, just barely missing him. After just missed being run over by a deer, Robert decided it was time to move on and catch up with his patrol. He was almost the first ever casualty to be injured or worse, by the hoofs and antlers of a big buck. In another instance, he was almost the first to be run over by a tank. During a training exercise, Roberts's company had to quickly move out because the mock enemy force was approaching their position. Robert was taking care of some personal business when he heard the weeds behind him moving. He hadn't got the word about the enemy surge, but knew that he had to pick up and get out of the way. He hid out in some bushes until the tanks and soldiers passed. About an hour later, he caught up with his unit, who thought that he had been captured. They laughed and joked after Robert told them of his narrow escape.

He knew that he didn't have much time before he might be shipped out. He tried to take advantage of all the free time he got. One weekend, he and a Marine buddy took a bus and went to Disneyland for the weekend. Neither one of them had ever been to Disneyland. They were excited as they took the bus to Anaheim. They put their money together and got a hotel room at the Disneyland hotel. Here was a Black and a White dude, one Navy and the other a Marine, staying in the famous hotel. After an evening at the park, they went to the lounge area for a drink and some easy listening music that was being played on the piano. After a short time, Robert began feeling homesick. It was late, but Robert decided to call his mom. He thought that she would be glad to hear from him, but he had to wake her from a deep sleep. She thanked him for thinking about her, but told him to wait until morning, the next time if he wanted to talk to her. It was about two o'clock in the morning, St. Louis time, and he had forgotten about the two hour difference in time. He was still glad that he got to talk to her. He knew that she didn't understand how precious his time was since he could be shipped out any day now.

After a weekend of fun at Disneyland, he and his buddy checked out on Sunday morning and headed back to the Base. It didn't take long for reality to set back in. His Corpsmen friends told him that another one of their fellow corpsmen was listed as a KIA. {Killed in action.} Robert was saddened to hear that the corpsman who was killed was his friend from North Carolina. He had been shipped out to Vietnam less than two weeks earlier. All Robert could think about was the picture that he had showed him of his wife and two beautiful children. He thought he had prepared himself for the certainty of bad news, but he was so hurt, that he really didn't know how to handle the news of his friend. Inside he was a wreck, but outside, he appeared normal. Because he was dealing with it in his own way, one of the corpsmen from Boston asked him if he cared about his fallen friend. He knew that they were close friends, and it appeared to him that Robert didn't care. Robert told him that they were raps, and he was dealing with it in his own way. He also questioned the corpsman from Boston in his sincerity, since he said that he wasn't going to 'Nam no matter what. He said that his momma would keep him from going to war. He apologized when he realized that Robert was still grieving over the lost of his friend.

He knew that he couldn't grieve for long, because his time could come any day. Shortly after that, another one of his corpsman friends from Idaho had been killed in action. He and Robert would go to Los Angeles and Anaheim to watch baseball games together. His friend would rent a small sports car with only one real seat. Robert would sit in a space in the back that barely had enough room for him to sit. The Santa Anna winds would almost rip his face off as he struggled to breathe through the strong winds, but his friend wanted to see his favorite player from his hometown. He played with the Minnesota Twins and they came to town to play the Angels. Robert wanted to see his hometown Cardinals play the Dodgers. It was tough going, but they knew that their time on planet Earth could be short lived. They knew that death was almost a certainty, and wanted to have just a little enjoyment with the little free time they had.

When Christmas time came around, Robert didn't have any leave left He used it all, thinking that he would have been shipped out before the holidays. His only chance of going home would be to fly Military standby for the four day break that he had. He decided to give it a try. He got a break and got on the first flight out to St. Louis. There was rain and thunder during most of the flight, but he managed to sleep through most of it. Before he knew it, he was landing at Lambert Field in St. Louis. He called home and got someone to pick him up from the airport. They weren't expecting him, but they were glad that he was home for the holidays.

He considered it to be the last time that he would be at home and see his family and friends, but there was no way he was going to spoil his time at home with any negative news about the danger he would soon be in. He just wanted to enjoy every moment of freedom with his loved ones.

When his time was up, he called the Base and tried to get an extension of his four day pass. He and his family weren't ready for him to leave. The officer in charge of granting the pass extensions was on leave and couldn't be reached. They said they would call him and let him know as soon as possible. It was time to go back to Camp Pendleton, and the phone call everyone was waiting for never came. He had no choice but to head back to California.

When he got back to the Base, his superiors asked him what he was doing back so soon. He told them that his extension was denied, and he had no choice but to come back. They told him that his extension had been granted for an additional five days. He called home, and his mom told him that the call came right after he boarded the plane. It was too late, and all he could do was try and forget it and get back to work.

As the new year came in, the Base was in a slow down pace. Still, there was an eerie calmness among the troops. He took some time to reflect on some of the things that happened while at Camp Pendleton. During some of the good times, he remembers walking along the beaches of Ocean Side. The town of San Clemente which bordered another side of the Base, also had a nice beach.

There were times when he had to get a little sleep while standing in the rain during some of the exercises. He remembers outdoor medical training classes that he would hold in the mountains for the troops. At times, he would have to wake some of the sleepy Marines as the classes in life saving techniques were held. He remembers a young Native American Indian raise his hand and ask a very important question. He said, *"Hey Doc, what happens if you get hit?"* He told the Marine, that was the reason why they were having the classes, so they would know what to do in an emergency.

He recalls another time when he got in trouble for not carrying out an order by two corporals. He didn't have to sweep the floors in the barracks, but he would do it anyway. He had just finished sweeping the deck, when two Marine corporals were sitting on a bench smoking cigarettes. When they finished, they threw their butts on the floor and told Doc to sweep them up. Robert told them to pick them up since they saw that he had just finished sweeping. They wrote him up for disobeying an order. After going into the office to see the first sergeant, he asked him why he didn't carry out a direct order. He told the sergeant what had happened, and that the two corporals were abusing their authority. He told Robert that he had to carry out the order even if it was bogus. He told the sergeant that he would take whatever punishment he had coming, but he still wasn't going to pick up the cigarette butts of the power hungry men. He told Robert that he would talk to the men, but to try and stay out of trouble. What really got to him was that one of the men had just got promoted, and at one time really had a heart. He had even befriended Robert when he was having trouble with one of his knees. He told the Marine that he was disappointed in him, and he should be ashamed of himself for letting a stripe get to him that way. He told Doc, that's the way it is now. He just shook his head and walked away. He saw how a little power could change what used to be a caring sympathetic person.

He also got a chance to see two Marines from his hometown of Kinloch, who had completed their year's tour in Vietnam. They were back in the States, and stationed at Camp Pendleton. They assured him that Vietnam was no picnic, and they did good to make it back alive. One was a point man, and the other was a radioman. Both were very high risk and dangerous jobs. He was glad to see that they had made it back, but it still didn't help his confidence a lot. They knew that Robert's chances of making it back alive were very slim. They would be civilians soon, and he was happy for both of them.

CHAPTER TEN

ROBERT AND THE 5TH MARINE DIVISION HEAD FOR VIETNAM

The emergency standby siren would go off often, but only be a drill, but one night at about midnight, the siren sounded and it was not a drill. The time that everyone knew would come one day was now here. The sergeants came screaming through all of the barracks to get up and get packed. They assured everyone that this was not a drill, but the real thing. This time, all of the troops jumped out of bed with the reality that the time had finally come. After over eight months at the Marine Base, it was now time to move out to meet the ultimate challenge.

All through the night, everyone packed their belongings. They got their weapons ready, but this time they loaded with live ammunition. Robert was given two clips for his 45 automatic pistol, plus some extra ammo. Later, he was given live grenades to strap across his chest. He checked the large medical chest, and made sure that everything that was needed was packed. He also made sure his own personal medical bag was well supplied. After packing their duffle bags with everything that was needed, their personal clothes and belongings were packed in boxes to be sent back home. The whole base was experiencing organized chaos as they prepared to move out by noon. There were a few Marines who exercised their option of crossing the border back to Mexico. Robert had no options, and for a brief second, wondered what he would do if he did.

He had trained and prepared for this very moment. Some of his friends had already bravely and unselfishly given their lives. Even though he knew all of that, he needed an assurance in his heart and mind that everything would be all right if he didn't make it back alive. Once again, he called on the one person who could give him the answer he needed. He heard an inner voice say to him, "Greater love has no man than this, that he lay down his life for his friends." He didn't know at the time that it was John 15-13 in the Bible, where Jesus said that He would lay His life down for his friends. He knew that Jesus laid down His life and rose again. It was from a sermon that he heard one Sunday at church. He knew that as a medic, his job was to lay down his life for his friends. He also knew that since Jesus died for him, that he would be with Him if he were to die in battle. Even though dying wasn't a very pleasant thought, he knew that he would be in a much better place. So with heaven being his other option, he had his answer and his peace.

After getting all of his affairs in order, he spent most of the morning in the dispensary giving shots to the troops. The shot records had to be brought up to date in order to go overseas. After lunch, almost everything was in place. All of the finishing touches were done, and the division movement was ready. It took a lot of discipline and cooperation for the big green machine to come together. The 5th Marine division was now ready for departure. Even though a large amount of troops were leaving, the Base was still in operation.

On this misty and dreary day, the fully dressed, fully armed, and fully aware Marines were ready to board trucks and buses, and take the huge convoy up the highway to El Toro Air Force Base. The huge cargo and troop transport planes would be lined on the runways ready to take tanks, trucks and troops across the ocean to Southeast Asia.

When they got to the Base, all of the troops were assembled in a huge airport hangar. They were expected to board the planes in about an hour after being briefed by the top military Brass. After they finished speaking, they were told that there was one more surprise guest speaker. After a half an hour or so, the entire assembly was brought to attention as the guest speaker and his party entered the hangar .All of the Brass saluted as the speaker was brought to the podium. Everyone could finally see who it was. It was the Commander In Chief. It had been rumored that he might make an appearance, but it was getting late. The engines of the planes could be heard, and the planes were ready to go.

The President of the United States started his speech by saying "I am asking you men to go over there and help in the conflict of the South Vietnam people against the insurgent Viet Cong and the communist regime of North Vietnam. Robert thought about what the president said. He jokingly wondered how he could be asking the men, as if they had a choice to stay or go. The plane engines were roaring, and the troops are dressed for battle, and there were no other options.

After the fifteen or so minute pep speech by the President, he came down and passed through the ranks as the troops saluted him with their rifles. Robert had another silly thought as he hand saluted the President as he passed him by. He thought jokingly, that if he smacked the President as he passed by, he would go to Fort Leavenworth prison and face a court marshal. On the other hand, he wouldn't have to go to 'Nam and face an almost sure death sentence. Even though he had no intention of doing such a thing, he couldn't wait for the President to pass him by just in case the temptation became too great. Of course, he let the President pass by without incident.

It was later in the afternoon when the President and his staff boarded Air Force One, and took off from the base. It was a nice sendoff speech, and in Robert's mind, it was his last and only chance to see the President of the United States up close and personal. However, it still did very little to boost his confidence and morale. The reality was that Robert and the 5th Marine Division was still headed for danger, and only the Marines who were on their second tour of combat could really know what to expect. The time had come for the troops to board the huge transport planes. There were no seats on the planes. But there were tanks and other heavy and light equipment that they would use when they reached their destination. Everyone adapted, and rested the best they could on the long flight across the ocean. They made three stops for refueling on the way to Vietnam. The first stop was one of the Hawaiians islands. However, all that Robert saw of Hawaii were the mountains from the airport windows. Robert took time to send a postcard to his family in St. Louis. They probably thought that he would be having a good time celebrating in Hawaii. It was there that he finally notified them that he was going to Vietnam. The card that he sent told them that by the time they receive the post card, he would be in Vietnam.

The planes left Hawaii after about an hour layover for refueling. The next stop was Wake Island. Robert remembered the name from movies that he saw as a child. The planes left the small island and headed for Okinawa, Japan. The planes landed at the airstrip early in the afternoon. This was the same day, but the timeline had changed. There was about a three hour layover, and the troops were told that they could go into town as long as they were back a half an hour before take off. Robert and some of the other troops decided to take them up on it. They flagged down a cab and headed for town, which was about ten minutes away. It was actually farther, but the cab driver had no speed limit. He weaved in and out of traffic as the riders held on for dear life. He dropped them off at one of the local clubs, then left to pick up some more waiting soldiers. They split the pay as they paid the driver with the foreign currency that they had exchanged at one of the stops that they had made. Robert and the men didn't care about the change in culture. They just wanted to spend what they considered might be their last hours of freedom as enjoyable as they could. They went into the club and took a table. The club was dimly lit, and they could hardly see anything. They figured that they would order a few rounds of drinks and head back to the airstrip after about a half an hour. After their first round of drinks, the live entertainment started. It was an all girl band, and they considered that to be the cue to their exit. They didn't want to be bored by an all girl band that they wouldn't even be able to understand.

 They had almost finished their second round of drinks, and were just about to leave. Then the drums and guitars started to play. It sounded so good that they decided to see what the girl band was about. After a brief intro, the lead singer picked up the microphone and they still didn't know what to expect from the Japanese girls, but didn't expect much. The guitars led the lead singer into a song that they were totally familiar with, and in English. She began to sing, "Chain, chain, chain. Chain, chain, chain". The background singers came in "Chain, chain, chain, chain, chain, chain, chain, chain of fools". They looked at each other with disbelief. To their surprise, they were singing R&B and soul. They quickly ordered another round of drinks and fell right into the mood of the club. The live girl band was so good that they forgot they were in a foreign land, and what they were there for. They were lost in space and time. One of the men looked at his watch and realized that they had been in the relaxed environment for a couple of hours. They had only a half an hour to make it back to the waiting airplanes. They quickly paid for their drinks and went out to catch a cab back to the strip. But the cabs were all gone. They were taking soldiers back to the strip, so they had to wait for an empty cab. After about fifteen minutes, they finally got an empty cab. They told him to hurry so they wouldn't be any later than they already were. He told the men that he was going as fast as he could. After they finally got to the strip, they paid the driver, and dashed into the airport. There was one person standing in the building where the planes were waiting. It was the sergeant who was responsible for having all of the men on board. He told Robert and his buddies to hurry up and get on the plane. Some of the planes had already taken off, and theirs was the last one to leave. He told them that they were the only ones that were unaccounted for, and they were reported as missing a movement. They barely made it back after overstaying their time in the home-like atmosphere at the entertainment club. Their names were taken off of the missing a movement list as they continued the journey to their final destination. After their time of relaxation at the club, they slept hard on their last leg to Vietnam.

CHAPTER ELEVEN

ARRIVAL IN VIET NAM

As they approached the South Vietnam air space, the troops were awakened and told to prepare for landing. Everyone put all of their gear on and gathered all of the equipment they would take with them. As the plane approached the landing strip, Robert remembered what his two friends from Kinloch that he saw at Camp Pendleton who had served their tour of duty in Vietnam had told him. They told him that even though they had served their full year in Vietnam, that you could be injured or killed on the very first day. They said that some planes had been shot down even as they were landing. So, just entering the war zone was a danger in itself. All of the planes in their group had landed safely without being fired upon. As the plane touched down and came to a stop, there was a sigh of relief from everyone. They had flown thousands of miles and had made it safely to their destination. As the plane was descending, Robert could see from the window of the plane, the wooded areas and some of the villages that would soon be his home away from home.

After they departed the plane, the first noticeable thing wasn't the people or the villages, it was a smell that Robert couldn't associate with anything that he had ever smelled before. It was a very unpleasant odor that he would identify later as unsanitary conditions: a combination of animals, and animal manure that was used as fertilizer in the rice paddies. Rice was the number one source of food for the Vietnam people. As they drove their convoy through the villages of Da Nang, to the area that would be their base camp, Robert began to wonder what he was really going to be up against. A deeper reality of the situation began to settle in as he looked around at the scenery and the people that up to then, he had only seen on television. The scenes that use to be time zones, and thousands of miles away, was now a sudden reality of his past, present, and his possible future. He knew that all of the hours, days and months spent in preparation for this very time, were now in effect. However, no amount of preparations could prepare him for the reality of knowing that at any moment, he could enter into eternity. Even though death was a constant reality, there wasn't a lot of time to think about it. There was always something to do to occupy his time. When there was nothing to do, tiredness and sleep would override his thoughts.

After the trucks and tanks reached their base camp, the troops unloaded all of their personal gear and equipment. They then set up their tents with their own personal shelter. The officers set up their command post tent with help of some of the troops. When they finished with the tents, everyone assisted in digging shelters and foxholes. The war games were over, and now they would be expecting live artillery rounds at any time from the wooded area that surrounded the base camp. The whole area where they were set up was filled with Viet Cong soldiers, whom the majority was actually civilians who lived in the surrounding area. They were guerilla fighters who could move about freely in the villages and set up booby traps in the fields and use artillery mortars under the cover of the thick jungle brush. It was no secret that the situation was not very safe.

After everything was set up, Robert was taken to the medical tent where he would meet the medical staff and the senior corpsman who briefed the incoming corpsmen of their duties. He would also be responsible for sending the medics out on patrol with the Marines into hostile and dangerous territory. He had a very difficult job even though he didn't have to go out on patrols himself, but he had to deal with the fact that when he sent the corpsmen out, that they sometimes didn't return back the way they went out. Some would return injured, and some would return in body bags, never to see the light of day again. Even though Robert knew that he could very well be one of those casualties, he didn't envy their senior corpsman. He knew that it had to be hard to be responsible for someone else's fate. Robert went on a day patrol the second day that they were there. The officer who was in command, was leading his very first combat patrol. Robert wasn't really sure what the patrol was for, other than a show of presence in the area. The lieutenant was given a coordinate to follow to a specific area and then return to the base camp. After about an hour of tracking through the jungle, the troops were struck with a frightening revelation. Their leader had lost his direction, and didn't know where he was.

Everyone had a very uneasy feeling about the situation. Here they were, thousands of miles from home, miles from their base camp, lost in the boonies of South Vietnam, on their first patrol, and surrounded by enemy fighters. The lieutenant had the troops sit quietly while the radioman called back to the base for help. As much trouble as they were in, Robert wasn't sure that anyone knew just how much. They were sitting ducks. Their first patrol could have very well been their last. Headquarters told them to stay put until someone could come and find them. The troops laid low and stayed very alert for over an hour, until a rescue team showed up. After that mishap, Robert thought that they would return to the base camp, but to the disappointment of the men, they continued on the patrol. They marched through several villages that were occupied by civilians who probably doubled as soldiers whenever necessary. They returned back to the base camp later that evening. Robert got his first taste of combat duty, and was thankful that the day ended with no casualties for his unit. The troops got a chance to take a break, unload their gear, and get something to eat. Robert's gear consisted of his helmet, flack jacket, [bullet proof vest], his loaded 45 caliber pistol, and six hand grenades strapped across his chest, and of course his medical bag. Even though the medics were armed, their main objective was to aid and treat the wounded and the sick. Their weaponry was mainly for emergencies to protect their patients. According to the Geneva Convention, it was forbidden for snipers to use the Red Cross on the helmets for target practice. The red or white cross was eventually removed from the medic's helmets. However, the medics could still be easily identified. The medical bag that was strapped across their shoulder made them easy targets. All of the corpsmen would alternate going out on patrol and working at the medical station, which was much safer, but when needed, they would go out on back to back patrols depending on how long the patrol was out. Sometimes, they would be out for a couple of days. The night patrols were the most dangerous because night vision was a major problem.

During overnight movements, they would dig fox holes and set up a communication perimeter. The corpsmen would have to stand middle of the night radio watches so that the radioman could get some sleep. Robert recalls one night patrol that had a great potential for danger. All through the night, flares would illuminate the night skies to mark an enemy position. While Robert's patrol was treading along a hillside, their entire position was suddenly lit up with flares. They were once again sitting ducks that were exposed for any would be attacker. The worst part of all was that their own forces had mistaken them for the enemy and launched the flares. The patrol leader immediately had the radioman call in and let them know that the flares were putting them in danger, and to stop them immediately. Everyone had taken cover until the flares stopped. The only problem was that the enemy might have locked in on their location during the barrage of flares that lit up the night skies. They continued and completed the night patrol without further incident. They returned to the base camp the next morning thankful that no damage was done. They didn't encounter the enemy, and the enemy didn't encounter them. Robert quickly understood how some of his fellow corpsmen from Camp Pendleton became casualties so soon after arriving in Vietnam. His first couple of days were not without drama and potentially negative results.

The base camp was always on high alert. It was a known fact that the camp could be attacked at any time by mortar fire from the wooded area that was just beyond the camp. Every time the incoming alarm would sound, all the troops would hurry to their foxholes for cover. During one incoming alert, a marine was injured as he ran into a water buffalo {a big metal water container} in the dark of the night. The night sky was always brightened up by mortar fire and night flares. It looked like the Fourth of July. But the explosions from flares and artillery fire, were real. During the daylight hours, the phantom jet fighters would make strikes at the enemy's position in the wooded area outside of the Base Camp.

The troops in the camp would cheer as the planes dipped below the tree line, drop their bombs, and rose back into the skies. This would go on as long as the enemy troops would be sighted in the area, which was very often. Even though the air strikes would be precise and effective, there would be times when the cheering would turn to sadness. Sometimes, the jets that dipped below the trees wouldn't come back up the same way that they went down. At times, but not often, a jet would be hit by enemy fire and come back up smoking and on fire. The pilot would eject before the plane crashed. If the pilot survived, he would still end up in enemy territory. In addition, if he wasn't rescued or didn't escape, he probably would wind up as a POW. [A prisoner of war] All that anyone could do was to say a prayer for the pilots and hope they would be rescued. Those brave pilots were the main reason that the base camp would have any sense of security.

The troops could purchase a decent meal with their new money at the base Mess Hall when they were not on patrol or on some assignment. Showers could be taken when there was time and opportunity. Every now and then, cold beers were passed out on a first come, first serve basis. A cold beer on a hot evening was a welcomed treat to those who wanted a nice cold one.

No patrol was routine, or ever taken for granted. Everyone knew that if they were going to be injured or killed, that it more than likely would be while they were on patrol. There were mine fields everywhere, and the enemy wasn't easy to identify. Most of them were simple village people, young and old, women and children. One day while on patrol, Robert's unit was passing through an area that was filled with rice patties. Some of the patties were squared off sections of ponds that had four to three to five feet of water. The murky water was filled with animal waste fertilizer that didn't smell good at all.

The patties had paths called, "dikes" around them for crossing over, and access to planting and picking when the rice harvest was ready. The dikes were about three feet wide, just wide enough for walking. While crossing the dikes with his unit, Robert slipped off the narrow dike and wound up in the murky and smelly water. At the time, he didn't know how deep the water was. When his feet touched the bottom of the water, he was up to his chest in the smelly murky pond. He had all of his gear on and he had trouble trying to pull him self, back onto the narrow path. When he realized that he was sinking deeper into the soft bottom of the pond, a brief moment of panic began to set in .He called out for some of the Marines, who didn't see him fall in because he was at the rear of the patrol. They used their rifles to pull him back to safety as he was slipping every time that he tried to climb out. He was thankful for the Marines help, but he was soaked through and through and smelled like he had been swimming in a cesspool. All he could do was to make sure that he did not fall in again, and get to level dry ground and try to dry out. There was no change of clothes, so he had to wear the smelly and wet clothes until he got back to the Base Camp. It was a day and night patrol, so he had to continue on, in his soaked clothes and boots. Even though it was very uncomfortable, that was the least of his worries. They were still in enemy territory, and making it back alive was a greater priority.

When they got back to Base Camp the next morning, Robert showered and washed and hung his filthy clothes in the medical tent. There was limited space to hang clothes, but he was allowed to use the space that was available. Robert had been in Vietnam for over two weeks, but it seemed more like two months or more. A twenty-four hour day seemed to never end, and when it did, it was time to start all over again. He began to understand more and more how some of his friends were killed in such a short time after they arrived in Vietnam. The potential for dying was very high, especially for corpsmen. Even though none of his patrols were involved in a firefight yet, there was an ongoing possibility of enemy engagement in some way or the other. All of the patrols were on foot, but there were times that they got to ride on the back of the tanks that sometimes escorted them on certain missions.

It was late in February, and Robert was approaching his twenty-first birthday. He was starting to wonder if he would live to see it. He realized that each patrol could be his last, and he wasn't very optimistic about his chances. His birthday was on the twenty-fourth and he was scheduled to go out on patrol that day. His family had sent him a birthday cake from St. Louis and hoped that it would be there in time for his birthday. On the twenty-fourth, Robert went on patrol with his unit, very conscience of the fact that he could be killed on his birthday. He wasn't being negative, but realistic. Just because it was his birthday, made no difference to the people involved in the art of war. With every step he took that day, he tried to be a little more careful. As he went through some of the villages, he had to even be on watch for the children. They would come up to the soldiers and ask them for candy bars and cigarettes. The troops would give them gifts as a gesture of good will. They would see Doc, [Robert] with his medical bag and ask him for band-aids for their sores. Robert would put ointment and band-aids on the sores of the children and any one else who needed them. He also made sure that he had extra candy bars to pass out to the people. They would be more helpful with information about the Vietcong soldiers after they got what they wanted. On the other hand, those same people could walk up to the soldiers with an explosive device that could do much damage. They also could give false information that could lead into a trap. So everything had to be heavily weighed before their word could be taken as truth. Some of the children, as young as ten years old, were soldiers and were very effective. Even though the day was filled with anxiety for Robert, it had a safe ending. He was thankful that at least he got through his birthday alive and well, even though his cake had not made it from St. Louis. He knew that it would have to go through many stages before it reached its destination.

He had the next day off, and took some time to relax in his tent and get a nice meal from the mess hall. There were still other duties, but not having to go on patrol was a rest in itself. After eating beans and frankfurters from his mess kit while on patrol, no matter what was on the menu from the Mess Hall was a feast. And even though the base was always under a threat of being over run at any time, it still was a safe haven compared to being out in the boonies.

After a day off, Robert went back out on patrol again. It was a good patrol because there wasn't any conflict with the enemy. After his day off, he went out on another successful patrol. He had never had to go out on back to back patrols, and wasn't expecting to. Even though his name wasn't on the duty board in the medical tent, the senior corpsman told him that he knew that he was tired and his clothes were not all the way dry from the day before but he was needed to go out on patrol again. It was the twenty-eighth, which was four days after his birthday. He packed his usual gear, which was his flack jacket that he wore, his forty five pistol with extra clips, the grenades that were strapped across his chest, and his helmet and medical bag.

It was the last day in the month of February when they headed out on patrol early that morning. The patrol leader told Robert to follow in the footsteps of whoever was in front of him because they were going on a mine sweep. The Vietcong had planted mines and booby traps in an area where the soldiers patrolled and outside some of the town villages. Their job was to locate the mines with a mine detector and blow them up. After finding the anti personnel and anti tank mines, they would shout out "fire in the hole" as everyone hid for cover. As they passed through some of the villages, Robert once again passed out candy bars and put band-aids on some of the people. They would come up to the soldiers and Doc and say, "give me band-aid, or a candy bar or a cigarette." That was the only English that they could really speak. The villagers called Robert "Doc" because they knew who he was because of the medical bag that he carried. When they got back on the trail, Robert would continue to follow in the footsteps of the person in front of him.

CHAPTER TWELVE

ROBERT IS INJURED BY A LAND MINE

As noontime came around, it was time to take a break for lunch. The minesweepers had cleared an area and everyone picked what seemed to be a safe spot to set up for lunch. Robert made a fire for his lunch from his mess kit. He put his favorite meal: beans and frankfurters on the fire that he had made with some rocks. He also had a cup of hot chocolate that was almost ready to drink. Suddenly there was another explosion. Robert thought that the team had found another mine and detonated it, but then the call that every corpsman listened for came out. "Corpsman up!"

It was then that Robert knew that they hadn't found another mine, but a mine had found a soldier. Leaving his hot lunch behind, Robert grabbed his medical bag and took off running in the direction of the explosion. After following in footsteps all morning long, now he was on his own. After running through the bushes for a short while, he ran into an officer who was also trying to find the injured Marine. Neither one of them was thinking about the fact that they were in a minefield, but was focusing on trying to find the fallen Marine. They had been searching through the thick brush for about five minutes when Robert lost sight of the officer. He kept running in the direction where the blast came from when he saw a small open area. There was a small hill through the path that led to the clearing. Robert was running as fast as he could with his medical bag on his left shoulder. When he got to the hill in the path, he hit the hill with his left foot, ready to go over it. The second that his foot hit the hill, the very thing that he had been trying to avoid all morning long happened. Robert's foot detonated the mine that was hidden under the ground. The loud explosion instantly told him that he was in trouble. He was in full stride when he hit the mine, when he heard a voice say, "Thrust yourself forward as hard as you can." He didn't have time to speculate or think about anything. He just did what the voice said. After he rolled down the hill, he came to a stop in the field. He was hurt bad, but didn't know how bad it really was. He heard the officer who was trying to help find the injured marine yell out, "Doc's been hit!!" Robert began to feel pain like he never had before. He could still hear the ringing in his ears from the blast that blew up under his feet. His left foot felt like someone had taken a sledge hammer and hit it as hard as they could.

Then, he began to smell something burning. He suddenly realized that his flesh was burning from the hot metal from the booby trap mine that was eating away at his torn up body. The hot and jagged shrapnel had penetrated Robert's flesh and was still burning. His left leg, which detonated the mine, was in so much pain that didn't even know that there were other areas of his body that was hit. He eventually raised his right hand and discovered a big hole in the middle of it that was bleeding profusely. At that moment, something real strange happened. Being in instant shock from the blast and not knowing how bad he really was hurt, he had a momentary pity party. He began to think to himself how he would never be able to run again, play baseball or basketball ever again. Then reality set in once again. He heard the voice that he knew was the same familiar voice that had been with him through out his life. He said, "While you are felling sorry for yourself, you will be dead if you don't do something about it right now." He asked Robert what he wanted to do? Live or die? Robert said that he wanted to live. At that moment, Robert started to pray like he never prayed before. In fact, he didn't even know what he was saying. Nevertheless, he knew that he had to call out to God for help. After a very short time, a calm and a peace came over him. By now, some of the Marines came to where he was laying. There was no other medic there, so they asked Doc what they wanted them to do?

Robert thought back to the classes that he would hold under the trees in the mountains of Camp Pendleton. He thought about the Native American Indian who asked him the question, "What happens if you get hit Doc?" Robert told him that it would be their turn to use what they learned in the classes. They also had practical application lessons. He also remembered how some of them were sleeping or not paying attention when he was teaching them first aid procedures. He knew that he couldn't trust his life in their hands, so he had to stay conscious and alert if he was going to survive. The peace and calm that God had given him allowed him to do what he needed to do. He still didn't know how badly he was hurt, but by the look on the faces of the Marines, he knew that it wasn't a pretty sight. The only wound that he saw was his right hand that was badly injured. When he looked at his right hand, he could see a bloody gapping hole in the palm of his hand. He knew that his left leg was hurt very badly, but he didn't dare look at it. He knew that he would really go into shock if he were to see just how bad his leg was and he wouldn't be of any help at all. It could mean certain death if he were to lose control and go into a panic mode. What he did know was that he was in tremendous pain, his flesh was burning-which he could smell, and that he had lost and was losing a lot of blood. With the calmness that the Lord had given him, he told the Marines to first look in his medical bag, get the morphine, and give him a shot for pain. The morphine came in individual vials, and all they had to do was to break the cap off the top, and inject it into his thigh. Then, he told them to get some gauze pads and wraps and apply pressure to the wounds to try to stop or control the bleeding. Then, he told them to make a splint out of some sticks that were lying around and wrap his limp hand with the gauze and wrap.

They waited for a helicopter to come and take him and the other wounded to the medical station in Da Nang. They had done all they could to help Robert, but after more than a half an hour, there still was no chopper. Robert tried to stay calm as long as he could, but the pain shot was wearing off fast and was having very little effect on the tremendous pain that he was in. Even though it was too early for another shot, the pain was so unbearable that Robert told them to give him another shot after almost an hour. He still didn't know just how much damage had been done, but he was in a land of pain that he never knew existed. Any relief at all was better right then than none at all. Not only that, but he was losing blood at a rapid rate and could go into shock at any moment. Robert kept asking where the med e-vac 'copter was. They finally told him that the choppers couldn't land because the area was still filled with mines. The Marines were working frantically to try and clear an area so the med e-vac 'copters could land and take off safely. The Marines did manage to make a pillow for Robert's head out of his medical bag, but felt helpless as he lay in the hot sun with his body wrecked in tormenting pain. Finally, they got word that an area about a half a mile away had been cleared for the helicopter to land. The Marines made a make shift gurney out of Robert's blanket and their rifles. They made the rough bumpy trip, carrying Robert to the area that was secured for the 'copter. Even though it was rough going, Robert was glad to finally be headed out of the jungle to a place where he could get some help. It was a step by step process of getting out of the area because even though they had cleared an area for the 'copter to land, they were still in hostile territory and in danger of being shot down. It was a risky situation for everyone involved in the operation because land mines were all around, and were very well hidden.

When they finally got Robert to the helicopter, he noticed that it wasn't a med e-vac 'copter, but a large Huey fighter 'copter that was out on patrol. The huge blades were blowing hard on Robert and the Marines who had taken him on the journey. The gunner was in the door with his machine gun ready for any trouble. As they lifted Robert onto the 'copter, he saw that there were two other casualties already aboard the craft that had been injured by mines also. The first casualty he knew as a fellow Missourian who was part of his unit from Camp Pendleton. Just before the 'copter took off, the Marines who had helped him wished him good luck. One of them told Doc not to worry because he was going home now. As the 'copter lifted off, Robert thanked them and said goodbye to his comrades.

After a short time in flight, Robert began to feel another problem come on that he had never felt before. He had used all of his water while lying in the hot sun and losing a lot of blood. Water was valuable, so he knew that he couldn't ask the soldiers on the 'copter for water. Robert was so thirsty and dehydrated, that he couldn't help but ask the gunner for just a sip to wet his lips. He told Robert that he felt sorry for him, but he would be out for two days and he didn't have enough water except for himself. Robert told him that he understood and not to feel bad. After a few minutes, he saw how bad Robert was doing and gave him a swallow of his precious water. Robert never knew how one sip of water could be so precious. He really appreciated the gunner's sacrifice because he knew that he had compassion on him and didn't have to share his water. Robert will never know his name, but he thanks God for him even to this day.

The helicopter landed at the Da Nang medical hospital and the injured troops were taken off the chopper. The gunner and the pilot wished them well as they were taken on stretchers into the medical facility. They would go back into the battlefield and continue their mission. The injured soldiers were taken to the triage area where they were evaluated individually. As Robert was lifted onto the examination table, all the pain that was in his body seemed to come crashing down all at once. He was in so much pain that all he wanted to do was to be put to sleep so that he couldn't feel the pain any more. The doctors began to cut off his bloody, tattered clothes to examine his wounds. As they did, the pain began to intensify, especially the boot on his right foot that had absorbed the brunt of the explosion. Every movement that the doctors made seemed to have its own pattern of pain. At that point, Robert lost every sense of emotional calm that he had. He just kept saying that he wanted to be put to sleep. They told Robert that they needed to take X rays to determine the extent of his injuries. He remembers the doctors raising his leg to be X rayed and the tremendous amount of extra pain that he felt. They asked Robert when he last had something for pain. Robert told them that he had two shots of morphine shots while he was waiting to be airlifted out of the field. Robert heard them tell each other that no wonder he was delirious. They said the two shot of morphine were too close together. They said that they couldn't give him anything else for a couple of hours. In fact, they had to give him a dose of atropine to counteract the overdose of morphine that was in his system. Robert had to endure the painful examination without any further medication for pain. After over two hours of careful diagnosis, he was finally sedated and put to sleep. He was taken into the operating room where he spent four to five hours of intense treatment for the many wounds that he received from the mine that exploded underneath him. There were broken and blown out bones. There was severe muscle, artery, and nerve damage as well. Before he went into surgery, he didn't know the full extent of his injuries. As far as he knew, the only injuries he had were his left foot and right hand that he had seen. However, he still didn't know the extent of those injuries. He knew that his left leg was hurt, because he had directed the marines to put a make shift splint on it.

    As Robert looked over his heavily bandaged body, he made a startling revelation; he thought that he had only two sets of wounds- his left leg and his right hand, but as he looked down at his legs, he saw that his entire right leg was heavily wrapped as well. He asked the nurse why his right leg was bandaged. She told him that his right leg was hit as well and the doctors would tell him more about it when they made their rounds. The doctors made their rounds and told him that his right leg was severely injured, but not as bad as the left. They said that they would be able to tell him more after they conferred with each other. When they left, Robert got a surprise visitor-it was the officer who was with him as they searched for the fallen Marine. One of his feet was wrapped and he was using a cane. He said that he had been injured by an explosion from someone else, but was expected to return to duty. He told Robert that one of his men had been killed by a booby trapped gate that had exploded as he opened it to enter the village; he was hit in the heart by flying shrapnel, killing him instantly. He also told Robert the name of the fallen Marine; it was the young Native American Indian that was part of his unit from Camp Pendleton. He was the one who asked Robert what would happen if the Doc. got hit. Robert was very sad and sorry to hear that his friend had been killed. That day turned out to be the deadliest and bloodiest day for Robert and his unit. The realization of the war had been driven home in a very unkind way. Robert was alive and going home. He knew that he had a very long way to go for whatever type of recovery he would be in store for.

The officer also told Robert that the Marines who had assisted him when he got injured, wished him well and to get well. He told Robert that they considered him to be a hero. Robert couldn't understand why they would think of him as a hero because he was only doing his job. Besides, he never even reached the Marine who he was trying to find. All he could do was to try and save his own life. He thought that maybe they were impressed with the way that he handled himself in such a critical condition. When he was first injured, he had no idea what bad shape that he was really in. The Marines who could see how badly that he was hurt, probably couldn't understand how Robert could so calmly tell them what to do, as they ministered first aid to him. Robert was reacting as if he had just stumbled and fell, or just twisted an ankle. What they didn't know was that God had given him supernatural assistance, and gave him a peace that was beyond human reasoning. Robert was under that peace even before the morphine was given to him, so he knew that God was there to help him in his time of need. Later in the afternoon, the doctors came back to take him into the OR to change his dressings and for further examination and treatment of his wounds. Before they took him in, they gave him a realistic picture of what he might be facing. They told him that his left leg was in such bad shape, that they might have to amputate from the knee on down.

He was still in a lot of pain and his head was still ringing from the magnitude of the explosion of the land mine. He was just glad to be alive, knowing that the flying hot metal from the blast could have hit him in the heart or face or some other vital area and killed him instantly. He also realized the voice that he heard, telling him to thrust himself forward as hard as he could, more than likely could have saved his life. By that spontaneous action, it probably helped him from being hit by the flying metal in more areas of his body than it already had. It could have indeed been a deadly ordeal. Not only that, he could have very well bled to death from the amount of blood that he had lost, and was continually losing while he was on the battlefield. There were multiple opportunities for him to have checked out at that point. Being alive and staying alive was now his major priority. He told the doctors that he understood the situation, and to do whatever they had to do. They gave him a good dose of pain medication knowing that the pain would be very intense as they examined him and gave him further treatment.

After they got into the ER, they treated his hand wound first. They unwrapped his hand and flushed out the open wound with a small water hose. There was still a tremendous amount of pain, especially since there was a lot of nerve damage. They removed some of the metal that had become embedded in his hand. However, as painful as that treatment was, it would pale in comparison to the pain that he would feel from the treatment of his legs. After rewrapping his hand, they unwrapped his right leg that he didn't even know was hurt until hours before. They removed the bloody gauze that was packed deep into his thigh and cleaned it with some sterile solution. They also removed as much metal as they could from the open wound before repacking and wrapping it heavily with bandages. Now the time of truth had come. After what seemed like the preliminary treatments, the injury that was the worst of all had to be examined. There would be no need for a lot of treatment if the leg would have to be cut off. Robert could still sense the smell of his burned out flesh as the doctors' slowly took the wrappings off of his badly injured leg. They looked over the wounded leg very carefully while checking and double checking the X rays. Besides being a mangled mess, about a foot of the tibia bone in his leg was blown completely out. Robert wasn't in any emotional shape to look at the severity of his wounds. He could only take the doctors advice and counsel, and accept whatever decision they would make.

They would look at the leg, and talk back and forth to each other. There was no sign of life in Robert's mangled leg, and they made the decision to amputate. They asked Robert if he was okay with the decision. He told them to go ahead with the procedure. They had all of the equipment ready to go ahead with the amputation. Before they started the procedure, one of the doctors came up with one more idea. He told Robert that it was a long shot and no guarantee that it would work, but to try and move his foot. He did as the doctor said, but there was no movement. He told him to try again, but still there was no response. He told Robert to try one more thing. He told him to see if he could move his toes. Robert strained and strained, but there was still no movement. He told him to try harder. He was tired, and he had no more tries in him. So he just relaxed and tried once again to move his toes. The doctors didn't see any movement at first. Then, one of the doctors noticed that his big toe had moved ever so slightly that they had to look real close to make sure that it indeed moved. There was very little muscle tissue left and hardly any nerves and arteries that were still intact. The slight movement convinced the doctors to at least give the leg a little more time to see if there would be any improvement. They assured Robert that he had bought a little time, but there was still a chance that he could lose his leg. He understood the situation, but was in so much pain that at the time, he had hoped that they would cut it off. Once again, he relied on the judgment of the Navy doctors. He couldn't even feel his toes because of the intense pain. He would try to make the best of the doctor's decision. They cleaned the wounded leg and packed and wrapped it, and took him back to the hospital ward. This would be a daily routine since that would be all they could do at the medical facility.

Robert was wired up with IVs in his neck and both arms. He was given a blood transfusion since he had lost so much blood. He was on antibiotics to fight off infection, and fluids to keep his body functioning as well as it could. Of course he took his pain medication every four hours even though they did good to last for three hours. He was in an ongoing state of pain that could have led to a state of shock. The medical staff was on top of the situation and giving him the best possible care. After the doctors made their rounds that afternoon, the Red Cross workers came by to offer their assistance. They offered to call home for the wounded soldiers to let their families know their status. Robert told the Red Cross worker who was assisting him, that he didn't want to call home because he didn't want them to worry. He asked her to write a short letter to them that he would dictate. He told her to tell them that he had a little accident and would be all right and that he would be home, but didn't know when. He told them that he loved them and to pray for him. Robert tried to write the letter by himself with his left hand but his nerves were shot and he couldn't do it. He later wrote some of his buddies at Camp Pendleton to let them know what had happened. It wasn't pretty, but it could be read and understood. He would have to rely on his left hand for a long time to come. He just had to get use to using it.

His friend from Chicago who was still at Camp Pendleton, told him that he would be back home in St. Louis eating White Castles in no time. He said that the staff wished him well.

CHAPTER THIRTEEN

ROBERT IS FLOWN TO A HOSPITAL IN JAPAN

After about four days of spinal taps and cleansing of his wounds, Robert and the other wounded soldiers were airlifted from Da Nang to the Naval hospital at Yokosuka, Japan. The flight took off with a plane load of wounded soldiers late in the afternoon. It was later that night that the plane landed on friendly soil in Japan. The wounded troops were taken to the Naval hospital on buses that were waiting for them. Some were on stretchers, while others who were not hurt as bad, walked. They were taken to a staging area where each wounded soldier was evaluated. There were Army, Navy, Air Force and Marine patients in the triage area. All of the patients had their medical charts with them that the doctors read and treated accordingly. There was a lot of moaning and groaning from the more seriously wounded patients. It had been over six hours since Robert last had any medication, and he was in some very serious pain. They were calling out the names of the patients in alphabetical order but there were so many that it was over an hour before his name was called. He was sure that he would be able to get some pain relief as soon as he was able to finally see a doctor. He was holding out the best he could knowing that relief was just a name call way.

The doctor checked Robert's chart and read where his wounds needed to be changed and cleaned, but there was no order for any pain medication. The doctors had forgotten to write an order for any pain medication so the doctor couldn't give him any until he was examined on the hospital ward. He said that his wounds would still have to be changed and cleansed because of danger of infection. Robert, knowing how much pain that he was already in, and how much more painful it would be without any medication, pleaded with the triage doctor to wait until he could get an order written for pain. He said that it would be morning until he could get anything, and his bandages needed to be changed immediately before infection set in and would have a more serious problem. He had no choice but to accept it and prepare for some extra major pain. The doctor told the nurse to get the necessary tools and wrappings needed for the procedure. As Robert lay on his stretcher with his IV bottles dangling at his side, the doctor began to cut away at the bloody soiled bandages from his wounds. He started by doing the smallest wound, which was his right hand. Robert gritted his teeth and held his breath until the painful change had been made. He knew that the worse was yet to come, so he braced himself as best he could. The doctor asked him which leg would he like him to work on first. Knowing that the left leg was the worst off, and would be the most painful, he told him to start on that leg. The doctor cut the bandages away and began the painful process. He had never felt more pain, than when the doctor poured on a solution and cleaned the fresh open wound as best he could. The nurse assisted him as he completed the job on Robert's left leg. Figuring that the worst was behind him, he relaxed just a little. Up to then, he didn't know what type of pain he would have to endure. He was always given a spinal tap so that his entire lower extremities would be completely numb when there was major work to be done.

The nurse saw how much pain he was in, so she tried to give him as much comfort as she could. She wet a towel and put it on his forehead and held on to his hand. Robert still didn't know what condition his wounds were in. Only that pain, was the order of the day and night. As the doctor began to cut away the bandages on his right leg, Robert was certain that the worse was over. He did expect pain, but nothing compared to the pain that he had already endured. As the doctor began to dig out the bloody bandages that were packed in his thigh, there was a level of pain that he did not know existed. There were about four to five large gauze packs that had to be pulled out, one at a time. Each one that was pulled out almost put Robert in a state of shock. He screamed and moaned and cried so hard, that he thought it would never end. The nurse squeezed his hand and stroked his head hoping for a little support for her agonizing patient. He could see the pain and helplessness on her face, as she did all that she could to make things a little better. The pain was the worst that he had felt. Even the initial blast wasn't as bad as the pain that he was now feeling. When it was all over, the doctor and nurse apologized for the pain that they had to inflict on him. Robert told them that it was all right because he knew that they were only doing what they had to do. He told them that he was a medic himself, and he knew what they were going through.

That very painful distressing ordeal was over. Even though he was still in a lot of pain, he could at least rest for a while until he was moved to a room. It was over an hour before he finally was taken to a room on the hospital ward. As tired and sleepy as he was, all he could do was toss and turn because of the pain. When he did close his eyes to try and sleep, the pain would wake him up reminding him of his condition. It was hours later when he saw a nurse walking towards him with a syringe in her hand. He knew what it was, but could only hope that it was for him. She assured him that it was, and told him that relief was on the way. She said that they woke up the medication doctor who wasn't scheduled to come in until morning. The staff had convinced him that there was an emergency and they needed a medication order for a patient that was in very much need of some pain medication. He had been praying all night for some relief from the intense pain that he had been enduring. He thanked the nurse and most of all thanked God for helping him get through such a tormenting night. He was finally able to get some much needed sleep and some timely rest.

After half of a goodnight's rest and sleep, Robert woke up the next morning to what would be an ongoing reality check. Even though the nurse checked on his IV hook up and his disposition, he still managed to get some rest and sleep and above all, some relief from the excruciating pain. Waking to another new culture in yet another country had not yet set in. His life had taken such a drastic change in such a short time, that it all seemed like a bad dream that he couldn't wake up from. However, the fact that he was still in the land of the living brought about an immediate consolation. His liquid diet meal was brought in, which he delightfully consumed. He was just glad that he could eat at all. Later, the doctors came in and made their rounds. When they got to Robert, they apologized for the troubles of the night before upon his arrival. They asked him how he was doing, and looked over his medical chart that he had brought with him from Vietnam. They wrote an order for pain medication in his charts after giving him a preliminary examination. They assured him that he would receive the best treatment possible and to try and enjoy his stay. They were combat experienced doctors, and had seen the worst of the worst, and knew what they had to do for their patients.

Robert felt that he had already had his miracle, and anything else that he had to deal with would be gravy. After writing the rest of his orders, they left the ward to see other patients. It would be the same procedure of cleaning and redressing his wounds. The first couple of days, they would give him a spinal tap to deaden his lower extremities, but they said that it could be dangerous to continue injecting painkillers in his spine. They said that the best that they could do was to give him a local anesthetic along with his regular pain medication. The technique worked, but not as well as the spinal tap. He could still feel a lot of what was going on, and it was by no means pleasant. He just had to gut it out, and pray a lot. The pain medication was prescribed for every four hours. PRN [as needed] Even though it was obvious that he was in a lot of pain, he still had to ring his bell and ask the nurse for his shot of morphine.

On the third night, Robert would have a little trouble getting his meds. He would always wait until it was time, and sometimes a little later before he called for his meds. There was a change of nursing staff, which Robert thought might be the reason for the slower than normal response for his pain medication. It was late in the night when his medication had worn off, and he was in tremendous pain. His wounds were still open and fresh, and the pain level was about the same as it was when he was first injured. The new nurse finally came in to see what he wanted. He told her that it was time for his pain shot, and he needed it now. The nurse told him that he should be getting better by now, and denied Robert his request for a pain shot. He told her that he had held out as long as he could, and he needed his meds. She still refused him his meds and left the room. Having administered medication himself to patients, Robert knew that the nurse was out of order. He knew that her job was to follow the doctor's written orders, and carry them out. It was not her duty to diagnose, or use her own judgment to determine whether or not the patient needed their medication.

He kept buzzing the nurse's station looking for some service. The same nurse came in over an hour later, and still didn't have any medication with her. She turned off his buzz light and left the room. It was a couple of hours later when Robert couldn't take it any more. He frantically buzzed and called out as loud as he could to try and get the attention of the nurses. Some of the other patients began to buzz their lights, too because they couldn't get any sleep because of the noise that Robert was making. By the time another nurse came in from another shift, Robert was in tears and close to being in shock from the tremendous amount of pain that he was having. He told the nurse that he had been trying for hours to get his pain medication, but the nurse who was on duty refused to give it to him. She checked his chart and saw that he was well overdue for his meds. She apologized for the inconvenience, and finally gave him his medication. Only then could he and the other patients finally get some sleep.

The next morning when the doctors made their rounds, Robert reported the nurse's negligence to them. The nurse hadn't charted out yet and was still at the nurse's station. The head doctor sent for her and told her to come into the room. He asked her why she denied pain medication to the patient when he requested it. She told the doctor that she didn't think that the patient needed it. The doctor asked her who she thought she was to play God with someone else's life. He told her that the patient could have had a major set back, not to mention the possibility of a stroke. He chewed her up one side, and down the other in front of the whole staff. He wanted to make an example of her so that it wouldn't happen again. Robert knew that she would be chewed out, but thought he it was going to be done in private. They were so furious with her, that they let her have it right there. Robert felt a little sorry for her, but knew that she deserved what she got so that she wouldn't mistreat anyone else. Justice was served but Robert was not pleased that it was at his painful expense.

Over the course of a week, Robert was adjusting and doing a little better. Time and treatment was his ally, since he wasn't going anywhere any time soon. The following week, he ran into a little problem. Even though he was hooked up with three different IV units, a serious infection had set in, and soared his temperature up to 110 degrees from a normal of 98.6 degrees. He was burning with fever. He was already on antibiotics and fluids, so they had to use a very conventional method to try and bring his fever down. The doctor ordered plastic ice bags to be placed in strategic areas of his body in order to cool him down. He wasn't quite sure what was more uncomfortable, the cold ice packs or the constant pain that was tormenting his body. After about a half an hour, the nurse checked Robert's temperature only to find that it was still very high. As the ice packs melted down from his body heat, more ice packs were applied. Finally, after over an hour, his fever began to dwindle down, but the very uncomfortable ice packs were still applied until his temperature started to stabilize. It was a welcome relief for him knowing that his body wasn't burning with fever any more. It was also a relief to finally have the cold ice packs removed from his body. Even though things were very uncomfortable for a while, he knew that it was a priority to get his temperature down so that the medicine in the IV's could be effective.

Robert was bedridden, and needed assistance in everything that he did. The only movement he had was his left hand and arm, which was the only thing that wasn't bandaged up. He was hooked up to a catheter, and had to use a bedpan for his other business. He was in worst shape than he dared to imagine, but he knew that being a cooperative patient would help the medical staff as well as himself. His former duty station at the Navy hospital in Maryland was to take care of patients. He was now on the receiving end of the care himself. When he first arrived at the Naval hospital in Japan, he expected to see only Japanese programs on the television set that was in his room, but to his surprise, there were American programs as well. He was really shocked to see *American Bandstand*.

The American comedy shows and dramas were a welcome sight since he was so far from home. Even though he was going through a traumatic and devastating time in his life, somehow he knew that he was never alone. He would always remind himself of the dream that he had when he was a young boy growing up in his hometown of Kinloch, Missouri. After going through some trying times, he asked God was his life going to always be so hard? After going to sleep, he saw Jesus walking beside him down the main street of Kinloch. He had told him not to worry or be afraid of anything or anybody. He told Robert that he would always be with him. Robert held on to that vision, but most of all, he held on to those inspiring and encouraging words that Jesus spoke to him. What he didn't know at the time, was that God knew everything that he was going to go through for the rest of his life. Even though he had very little knowledge of the Bible when he was a young boy and even as an adult, he had a very strong belief that he could trust in the words of Jesus. He had no idea that what Jesus told him was written in scripture, but he knew in his heart and mind that Jesus was real, and his words were words of life. He knew that he was literally being tried by fire, and if it wasn't for the word of the Lord that he wouldn't even be alive.

Robert's wounds were cleaned and redressed every day. Every time that he would go for treatment, the doctors would dig out more and more of the metal that was in his body. The shrapnel that was deep into his wounds were the primary cause of infection and fever. That's why it was so important for them to remove all of the metal that they could. Some of the metal had to come to the surface on its own and then be removed, but there was a possibility that after all of the digging and probing, that some of the metal would never surface so it could be removed. The doctors worked very hard to try to bring some stability to Robert's legs that seemed beyond repair. The doctors managed to clamp off arteries that were constantly oozing blood from various areas of the injured legs and hand. There hands were full as they had to cut away dead and burned out muscles, tendons, nerves and skin. The doctors always wore mask as they treated Robert's injuries. The smell of his burned out tissue and body parts, and the constant ringing in his head from the blast sometimes were very hard for him to bear, but he knew the hard working heroic doctors were doing everything they possibly could to salvage and restore as much as they could of what was left of his injured body parts.

After a period of time, Robert was put on a regular diet. After living on jell-o and broth, his appetite was ready for some real food. His first meal consisted of roast beef, mashed potatoes, vegetables, and juice. His bed was raised upward and the food tray was put across his bed. It took a while for him to finish his meal because he only had the use of one hand. Nevertheless, he took his time and enjoyed every bit of his first real meal in well over a month. Having had a nice supper, he now could look forward to a good breakfast in the morning. After a couple of weeks of feasting on hamburgers and fries, cake and milk, and all of the other good food that was on the menu, Robert had a price to pay. All of the good food that he was eating was being digested all right, but it wasn't leaving his body. His bowels were locked, and he had indigestion, as well as gas. They gave him citrate of magnesia for a couple of days, but nothing happened. They gave him different kinds of enemas, and that didn't work either. Every time he called for his bed pan, he came up empty. In between trying to get his bowels to move, the doctors were finally able to put the finishing touches on the treatment of his wounds. They had to put large wire stitches in some of the wounds that were too wide for regular sutures. They had gotten all of the shrapnel that they could from his wounds. They had done a masterful job in preparing him to be shipped back to the States. Meanwhile, there was one more chore that was facing the medical team. It had been over two weeks, and Robert still hadn't had a bowel movement. The time had come when he was to be shipped back to the States. He knew as well as the staff that it would be an extra uncomfortable flight for him lying on his back with such a drastic problem. It would be well over ten hours before the flight over the Pacific Ocean would be completed. Robert could not imagine the idea of making the long trip in his condition. He knew that he couldn't even lie on his back in his hospital bed any more. He had to lie on his side to avoid the discomfort of his additional problem.

    They were hours from boarding the plane when Robert came up with a last minute plan. He remembered something from his Navy days that would be worth a try. He was never a real smoker but he remembered how the smoke from the cigarette would nauseate him, helping him to have an easier bowel movement. He had never been out of bed except to be taken into the treatment room. He knew that the dreaded bed pan would be of no use at all. So he got two of the corpsmen to take him out of the bed, and put him on the real stool in the bathroom. He told them to get him a pack of cigarettes and a lighter. They put him in the stall, closed the door, and wished him good luck. Nothing else had worked, so they gave Robert a chance to try it his way. It was very uncomfortable for him, but he was desperate enough to give it a try. Not really being a real smoker, he rarely ever inhaled, but this time, he was going to do whatever it took. He lit up the first cigarette and took his time inhaling and blowing out smoke. Then, he tried to have a movement, but nothing happened. Then he lit up the second cigarette and started to puff and blow out smoke. He tried to totally relax as if he didn't have anywhere to go. After half way through the long cigarette, He had a breakthrough. He put the cigarette down and tried, and tried until, bingo! He had finally hit the jackpot. He was sweaty and tired, but what a relief. He called for the corpsmen and told them that it was mission accomplished. They told him not to flush because they wanted to see the results. After getting him back to his bed, they looked, and were amazed at the size of the two weeks worth of trouble that had the whole medical staff baffled.

Robert was now free to travel, minus the extra load that he would have had to carry with him. That was as big a victory as any he had during his many ordeals and challenges. Before all of the wounded soldiers boarded the plane for the States, they were visited by some of the military Brass. They congratulated the wounded soldiers and passed out purple heart medals to those who were wounded in action. All of them got their medals except one. You guessed it. Robert was the only one not to get his purple heart. The staff apologized to him and told him that his name was mistakenly left off the list. They told him that he would have to get it when he arrived in the United States. It was too late since the plane would be leaving very soon. He took it in stride, and was just glad to be going home.

CHAPTER FOURTEEN

ROBERT RETURNS TO THE STATES
LIFE AT SCOTT AIR FORCE BASE

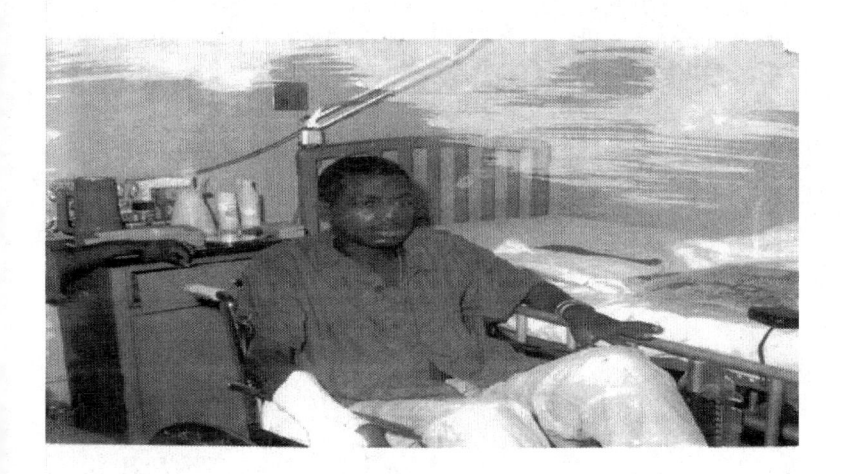

After over a month at the Naval hospital in Japan, Robert and the other wounded soldiers were airlifted back to the United States. Robert would be taken to Scott Air Force Base in Illinois. It was less than an hour from his home in St Louis. It was the MAC [Military Airlift Command] that Robert had chosen because of the closeness of the base to his home. His family wouldn't find out how close he would be to home until he actually arrived. He wanted to surprise them, so he didn't tell them. He also didn't tell them how badly that he was really hurt. That meant that they would be in for another surprise as well.

They were taken to the airstrip in buses and vans, late in the afternoon. Robert couldn't see much as he lay on his back as they drove through the city streets of Yokosuka, Japan. He realized that he was never a visitor to Japan, but only a patient that was passing through on one of his journeys of life. As the flight became airborne, Robert was saying goodbye to Japan and to Southeast Asia. The nurses that were traveling with the troops, checked his IV along with the other patients. After a short while in flight, Robert began to look around the crowded plane and speak to some of the other wounded soldiers. For almost two months his focus was mainly on himself and his own personal injuries. As he was looking around at some of the wounded men, he began to get a different perspective of the war and himself. Some of them had lost one leg, and some had lost both legs. Some had lost one arm and some had lost both arms. There were all types of injuries. Each soldier was carrying their own pains and sufferings back to the States with them. Out of all the wounded troops, there was one Brother that stood out among the rest to Robert. He made eye contact with the man who was lying on his tilted stretcher. He waved at the man with his one good hand in a friendly gesture. Robert thought to himself, how fortunate he was even though he didn't know if he would ever walk again. He couldn't see the extent of the injuries to the soldier's lower body, which was covered with a blanket, but he could see the agony in his face as he was being fed through his nose with a feeding tube. The tube was filled with fluids from an IV bag. Robert felt so bad for him because he knew that he would have to be fed that way for the rest of his life. Robert knew that the soldier would never again be able to eat a hamburger or know the simplicity of eating a normal meal. It really pained Robert then, and even to this day to see the wounded soldier lying there next to him with his entire mouth blown away by an explosive device.

    Robert's heart melted with compassion for the wounded soldier, but at the same time, it gave him a deeper awareness of his possible limitations. There was also a rejoicing in the fact that he would be able to enjoy and taste a regular meal. From that time on, he would look at his own injuries in a different perspective. He would never take for granted something that seems to be simple as eating and enjoying a meal. Whether it was considered good or bad. He also would appreciate something so simple as a sip or drink of water. He would think back to when the gunner on the helicopter gave him a sip of water in his time of need. He would never forget seeing the soldier lying next to him with half of his face blown off. Even though Robert was returning home quite differently than when he left, the long trip across the Pacific gave him a chance to reflect, and try to put his thoughts together. He didn't know what his future would hold, or how he would handle it, but what he did know was that he had to put all of his trust in God if he had any chance at all of making it. How much recovery there would be, he had no way of knowing.

CHAPTER FIFTEEN

ROBERT ARRIVES AT SCOTT AIR FORCE BASE

After the plane arrived in the States hours later, it made several stops at other bases to let other wounded soldiers off that were close to their homes. It was late afternoon when the Military Air Lift plane finally landed at Scott Air Force Base. The base was about ten minutes from Belleville, Illinois, and about forty-five minutes from St Louis where Robert lived. After the plane landed, a crew was waiting with hospital ambulances and stretchers to take the wounded soldiers to the large hospital on the base. As he was put in the ambulance, he was able to once again see American soil. Even the trees and fresh air was a welcomed view and smell to him and the others. He realized that there was another group of casualties that had returned home in body bags and would never again see family and friends again. So, this was a special ride of freedom for him that he was very thankful for.

As they got closer to the hospital, Robert got a look at the large building that was going to be his new home for over a year and a half. He was taken to the staging area where he and the others were evaluated before being taken to their perspective places. Robert was taken to the second floor of the orthopedic ward where there was a room waiting for him. The room had four beds that would be filled with injured soldiers before the day was over.

He was lifted to his bed by two Air Force medics, who were very careful not inflict any more damage than what was already done. His IV's were still hooked up, so that was another thing to be careful with. Nothing was simple, because every time that he was moved, there was always a certain amount of pain and discomfort that went along with the necessary procedure. After he was bedded down and made as comfortable as possible, dinner was brought into his room. Dinner hour was over, but he was glad to finally get a good hot meal. He hadn't had a real meal in over a week. He was put on a liquid diet because of his previous condition at the hospital in Japan. After dinner, the nurses and medics cleaned and changed his bandages. After given some pain medication, he was finally able to get some rest. It was late in the evening, and visiting hours were over.

He purposely waited until visiting hours were over before he called home and let his family know where he was. He knew that if he had called them earlier that they would come to see him right away. He knew that they would have major shock after finally seeing him in such a battered and beat up condition. His family thought that he had only suffered minor injuries as he had told them in a letter that was sent to them by the Red Cross. Furthermore, Robert was dealing with his own thoughts and insecurities. He wasn't at all clear about his own reaction to them after they would see him. It would be a totally different way than from the time he went off to war. Even though he couldn't wait to see them, he wasn't at all sure whether who would be really in for a shock, them or him. There was a part of him that really didn't want to see anyone, and didn't want anyone to see him in such a pitiful and vulnerable condition.

He was given a phone and called home. One of his sisters answered the phone, and was glad to hear from him. He talked to his mother, and told her where he was. Nobody had really heard of Scott Air Force Base, so Robert told them that it was just outside of Belleville, Illinois. They had heard of Belleville, and one of his sisters knew where it was. They wanted to come and see him right away, but he told them that it was too late. He told them to wait until the next day so that they could have more time to visit. They were so glad to hear that he was so close to home and would be able to visit him as often as they could. He told them to tell everyone hello, but still didn't tell them that his little accident wasn't really so little. They said that they would bring his mother to see him the next day, and that they loved him.

The next morning, a group of doctors made their rounds to check the patients' charts, and see how they were doing. They checked Robert's chart and looked over his wounds to see what course of action they would take for his treatment and recovery. After talking with him, they told him that they would continue the treatment that he had been getting all along. Every day, the nurses and medics once again cleaned and redressed his wounds, which they would spend a lot of time doing over the next year.

When visiting hours came around later that evening, all of the apprehension that Robert had stored up was about to finally be released. His mother and other family members came walking into his room with high expectations. As they got closer to him, their joyful disposition started to slowly dwindle as they began to see the painful extent of his injuries. Robert could plainly see their shock and concern, as they looked him over. The IV's were hanging from his neck and arms, and he was heavily bandaged with both legs wrapped as well as his right hand. Even though he didn't know just how much he would really recover, he assured them that he was fine and would be all right. He knew that no matter how things were going to turn out, that he would have to maintain a positive attitude and hoped that they would as well.

Robert could see how uneasy they were because nobody wanted to touch him. They were not sure if they would hurt him or make his situation worse. After all, they had never before seen anyone that was hurt as badly as he was. They had to digest the fact that this was Robert, their loved one, who was lying there in such a drastic and helpless position. He tried to make them more at ease by telling them that they could at least give him a hug. His mom and the others finally came over and gave him a very careful hug. Robert and everyone else were able to adjust to each other and have a good visit. He finally told them what had really happened to him and that he didn't really know just how bad his injuries really were. After he told them that he had stepped on a booby trap land mine, they could finally grasp the seriousness of his condition. They began to understand that he might not ever walk again or could possibly even be wheelchair bound for the rest of his life, but as their visit continued, they also realized they could have lost him altogether. They were thankful that he was alive, and had begun their adjustment process. As they were leaving, Robert could see that they were still a little stunned, but also had a sense of relief. They went back to St Louis and spread the word about what they had seen, and just how serious his injuries were. Nevertheless, it was a good and inspiring reunion for the first visit of many from his family.

The coming days and weeks continued with visits from his family and friends. They all wanted to spend time with him, but scheduled their visits so that they wouldn't tire him out and hinder his recovery. One thing that Robert emphasized to everyone was that he didn't want anyone to feel sorry for him, but he could see that some of his family and friends had a hard time holding and controlling their obvious concerns for him. He knew that it would take some time for them to get used to seeing him in the state that he was in. He was often in a lot of pain, and tried not to let anyone know just how much. They knew that he had to be very uncomfortable because of what had happened and the obvious trauma that he had been through

The medical team of doctors made their rounds and charted their notes as they checked Robert's wounds. They conferred with each other to come up with the best possible treatment for him and the other patients. They came up with a whirlpool treatment, filled with water and antibiotics. Robert would soak in the tub every day for an hour with his wounds totally exposed to the cleansing waters. They removed the stitches from his right thigh, and were surprised to see that they were made of wire. They eventually realized that they had to use wire sutures because the wounds were so deep and wide, but after the danger of infection was no longer an issue, the doctors closed what was left of the opening in the wound with regular sutures. Even as Robert's bandages were being changed, and he had to be put into the whirlpool, he still never looked at his wounds. This wasn't his own idea, but whether instruction that he was following from the familiar inner voice that was leading and guiding him. He knew that it was the Good Shepherd that had told him not to look at his wounds for six months. The medics would always try to get him to look at his wounds before they wrapped them back up, but he would always tell them that it wasn't time. He didn't think that they would understand his reasoning, so he didn't tell them; he would just tell them that when it was time, he would look at all of his wounds. Robert knew that God knew when he would be able to handle seeing his serious injuries and be able to deal with them on a positive level. He knew that it was a very important issue and took it very seriously, even though others might not. Robert continued to receive visitors, but got one visitor that he didn't expect. It was his older brother from California that he visited when he was at Camp Pendleton. He had seen him a little over a year earlier, but his family hadn't seen him in almost ten years since he had moved to California. Robert was pleasantly surprised to see him, as was his family. He only had a few days off from work, but he visited Robert every day that he was there.

Robert had gotten use to the whirlpool treatments. The only thing that wasn't so pleasant was when he had to have the bandages removed. It was always a painful procedure, because the bandages would always stick to his open flesh. Pulling the bandages off was a painful but necessary ordeal. There was no getting around the pain, which still is a vital part of his life to this day.

He would ask the doctors if they thought he would ever walk again? He wanted an honest answer, and they gave him one. They said that they didn't know. They said that all he could do was to take it one day at a time and see what happens, but there was no way that they could guarantee whether he would ever walk again. They told his family the same thing, so they understood the situation and prepared themselves for whatever was in store.

Since Robert wasn't going anywhere anytime soon, time was no issue with him. He knew that it was in his best interest to be the best patient that he could be. He did everything that he could to cooperate with the doctors and the staff, having been on the other side of the fence as a medic himself. He knew the importance of having a good attitude and giving the staff full cooperation. He made up his mind to try to make things easier for them, as well as himself. He would try to go beyond of what they expected from him and what he expected from himself. Days turned to weeks, and weeks turned to months as he made whatever adjustments he needed to make in his new environment of hospital life. As a patient, his second floor room had become his home and place of security. However, the doctors, nurses, Air Force medics, and the other patients had become Robert's family for a time unknown to him or the staff. He was not going to look too far ahead, seeing that his present situation had enough problems of it's own. He tried not to look at the past, but it was so much a part of his present, that it was hard not to look back and realize what brought him to his present condition. Plus, it was always going to be a part of his future that was now being shaped at the Scott Air Force Base hospital.

Robert was weaned off the morphine that he was taking for pain and put on something a little lighter. The doctors didn't want him to get addicted to the potent drug that was known to take over a patient's system. However, the painkiller that they had put him on was by no means a weak drug. It couldn't be weak if Robert was going to get any relief from his ongoing battle with pain. In spite of the pain, he was making progress and decided to take a step of faith. He had never gone anywhere except on a gurney, that he was put on with the help of a medic. He would slowly slide himself onto the gurney that was placed next to the bed as the medic assisted him. He was feeling pretty good one evening, so he asked the nurse if he could use a wheelchair instead of the gurney. He didn't have anywhere to go; he just wanted to get out of the bed. The medic brought him the wheelchair and helped him to get into it. It was a painful experience, but he knew that if he was going to get better, he had to do other things. After getting him into the wheelchair, the medic pushed him out into the hallway where there were other patients just out for a roll. He left Robert at the end of the hallway with them, and told him to call out when he wanted to get back to his room. The other patients had rolled themselves back to their rooms so Robert thought that he might try it too. He only had one hand to use, and really didn't know how to maneuver a wheelchair. One of the other patients gave him some pointers on using and controlling the chair. So Robert slowly made his way back to his room without the aid of the medic. He was proud of himself, as was the medic. He helped him back into his bed where he had a good night's sleep.

    A few days later, Robert got a little more adventurous. He had the medic show him how to set the brakes on the chair so that it wouldn't move while he was getting into the chair. After he fixed the chair, Robert slowly dragged himself from his bed onto the wheelchair. He then wheeled himself out into the hallway where he joined the other patients that were in their chairs. As the days went by, Robert became so confident and adapted, that he could get in and out of the bed and into the wheelchair by himself. He considered that to be his first major step on his road to recovery.

    Even though he was still a long way from his goal, he was still ahead of schedule. He knew that there was a risk factor in what he was doing, but it was a risk worth taking. The staff told him to be careful so he wouldn't have a setback. Since his whole life had been a risk to him, that wasn't even on the same level as the others. He knew that there would be many more risks if he was going to go forward with his recovery. He eventually mastered the wheelchair that he had to use with his one good hand. Before long, he was turning corners, which was the hardest thing to do with one hand. Then, he was able to use the elevator and leave the floor. As the months passed by, he was wheeling himself to the cafeteria for meals.

Robert's new found mode of transportation would give him a new sense of freedom. He could now leave the security of the second floor ward and venture out into new territories. He could now go outdoors to the first floor patio and feel the breezes and sun once again. It had been many months since he had been able to breathe in fresh air and just enjoy being outdoors. Another added treat of being able to leave the floor was that he could now visit with his young nieces and nephews who he could only wave at from his window before. They were too little to visit the ward, and Robert hadn't ever seen some of them before. His adventurous attitude was already paying off in big ways.

Being able to go to the cafeteria that was on the lower level also had some advantages. He could choose from the vast menu and enjoy foods that he hadn't had in a long time. The only disadvantage was that he could only use one hand. It was hard to control his wheel chair and pick the food that he wanted and put it on the tray. It was also hard to cut his meat with one hand. One of the Air Force waves would come to his aid when she saw how much trouble that he was having and cut his meat for him. Sometimes he would just pass up foods that he wanted because he knew he would have trouble trying to get them from the plate to his mouth. He would often be the last one in the cafeteria because it took him so long to finish his meal. Other times he would get something real simple so that it wouldn't take him so long. Even so, all of the positive things that he could now do, far out weighed the negative things. He knew that it would be an uphill battle, but with God and time on his side, there was no hurry. He just did what the doctors said and took it one day at a time.

CHAPTER SIXTEEN

ROBERT FINALLY LOOKS AT HIS WOUNDS

Meanwhile, Robert had reached the six month period that he said that he would finally look at his wounds. During a change of his bandages, Robert told the medic that he wanted to see his wounds before he wrapped them back up. He knew that it was going to be a big moment for him. However, he trusted in the Lord that he knew what he was doing when he gave him that time frame. He had become more confident after being with other patients who were dealing with their injuries and making the necessary adjustments. Some of them had lost one or both legs or arms, and had accepted their status and were looking forward. Even though Robert had accepted his fate, whatever it was going to be, he still had to deal with the reality of seeing his injuries. All he knew was that they were very painful, and that it wasn't going to be a pretty sight. After his six month trial period, he knew that it was time, ready or not. His hand was the first visual test to face. After the medic cleansed the wound, he asked Robert was he sure he wanted to see his wounds. He told him that he was sure. He had only glanced at his hand during the whirlpool treatment, but now he was taking a good look. He saw that the hole in his hand was still there. It was ugly but it was clean. Bones were broken and partly blown out. Tendons, nerves, and muscles had to be repaired in surgery, but there was still progress made. He had taken it pretty good, but decided to let that sink in for a while. He felt that he had seen enough for one day and he would take it slow. He told the medic that he would take things one day at a time to make it a little easier on himself. He wrapped the hand and changed the other two wounds with Robert looking the other way, as he usually did.

The next day, he resumed his visual therapy. He chose to look at each wound according to how bad they were. The right leg was perceived to be the lesser of two wounds, so he started with that one. The medic started with the lower part, which wasn't as bad. He could see the damage done by the explosion, which wasn't severe but still wasn't pretty. After he unwrapped his thigh, he finally got a chance to see the wound that had given him the most pain that he had ever felt when they were changing the dressings on that unforgettable night in Japan. After seeing the wound, he had to hold his breath to keep from passing out. He didn't realize how close he came to losing much more than he had thought. He knew that it was a miracle that the injury stopped where it did. As bad as it looked, it had improved a lot over the months, but still needed more work done on it. Since he had prepared his mind for the worse, he was able to absorb the shock a little better. He had seen two of his serious wounds, and there was one left to see. The next day, he was ready for his final test. He had done well on the first two, and was now ready to face the worst. This was the leg that had been so painful that he didn't even know that the other leg was even hurt. The pain in his left leg, initially over rode all of the other pain in his body. He was clueless about the severity of the wound in his right leg until the night that they changed his bandages without any assistance from pain relievers, but the left leg had always advertised how badly it was hurt with a continuous barrage of ongoing, unlimited throbbing pain. The time had come and he was ready. He waited until the entire leg was unwrapped before he took a look. What he saw was a shell of a leg that at one time was whole and useful. After seeing how it looked then, he knew that there was no way that he could have looked at it months earlier and had the same attitude. As bad as it was, he was somehow encouraged. First, he was thankful that it was still attached to his body, and that it could possibly still be of some use. He was thankful for the words of wisdom from above to help him come to accept what he had seen of himself in a positive way. There was still a level of depression, but it had to be dealt with just like everything else. He could now move on to the next steps in his recovery.

Over the next two months, all of the shrapnel had come to the surface, and the wounds were as healed as they were going to be. A tendon and some nerves were taken out of one of his legs and put in his right hand to replace the ones that were blown out. There was nothing they could do about the bone and the muscle tissue that was missing. After the reconstruction surgery, they sewed the hand up and assigned him to physical therapy. They later built a splint to help him build up strength in the hand.

The right leg was already sewn up and was in an ongoing recover mode. The left leg had no way of being sewn up. There was not enough skin left for the use of sutures on one side of his leg.

Most of the tibia bone was blown out, and the leg had grown new tissue over it. All the doctors could do was to put a skin graft over the soft tissue. They had to cut a layer of skin that was over a foot long and over five inches wide from the top of his right leg to put on the wound. The procedure was simple enough, but had a temporary negative result that Robert didn't expect. The doctors came to Robert's room and explained the procedure to him. In comparison to what he had already been through, the procedure sounded like a piece of cake. They asked him if he wanted a local anesthetic and something else to help him through the process. They told him that the procedure it self wasn't going to be so painful, but there would be a certain amount of discomfort afterwards. Robert told them that the local anesthetic would be fine, but the pain medication that he was on should be enough.

They came to his room and cut away the skin that they needed after giving him the anesthetic. They put ointment on the raw area of his leg and bandaged it up. They left orders to change the bandage every four to six hours. Robert was fine after the first change.

However, later that night, the pain started to override his regular pain medication. It was late in the evening, and it felt like his leg was on fire where they had cut the skin. He called for the medic to see if they could do anything about it. All that he could do was to put some more ointment on the area. He couldn't get any morphine because Robert told the doctor that he wouldn't need any. He had picked the wrong time to try and be brave. He got no sleep, and was in agonizing pain from his leg, which turned out to be a huge open sore on the top of his right thigh. He didn't get any relief until the doctors made their rounds the following morning. After he finally got a shot of some stronger medicine, he was able to get some sleep. He was so worn out from the excruciating pain that he slept through breakfast and lunch. When the shot wore off, he didn't wait. He took his pain medication as needed, and it was needed every four hours for almost three days until the pain was mostly gone. He resumed his usual pain medication that he still needed.

CHAPTER SEVENTEEN

ROBERT IS MOVED TO AN OPEN WARD

    Robert was getting better everyday and was taken out of his room, and put on the open ward with the different group of patients. He would meet some of the patients who had already gone through some of the things that he had. Even though many of the patients were still in recovery as Robert was, it was still a step of progress. On one side of Robert was a patient who seemed to only have a leg injury. He walked with a cane and was in physical therapy. After talking with him, Robert found out that he was a sergeant in the Air Force who had been in a car accident. He was driving back to the base from his home in Kentucky with his wife and young daughter. He survived the accident, but his wife and daughter were both killed. He was very upset with himself and took the blame for their deaths. The car he and his family were traveling in was struck by a truck. He thought that he should have avoided the accident. Robert and some of the other patients did all they could to try and lift up his spirits. He couldn't understand why he survived instead of his family. He wished that he had been the one who was killed instead of them. Even though his circumstances were different from the combat soldiers, he was involved in a tragedy that had changed his life and had an uphill struggle ahead of him. Robert could only tell him of the hope and trust that he had in God to help him in his ongoing struggles. He was sure that God would help him in his time of need. Robert didn't think of himself as spiritual or knowledgeable about the Bible, but what he did know was that he wasn't going anywhere good without acknowledging his heavenly hope on his road to recovery, or after his recovery. Robert listened and talked to the sergeant until he was well enough to be transferred to a hospital closer to his home in Covington, Kentucky.

    As time went by, the visitor's list became smaller. Robert wasn't forgotten about, he was getting better, and his family and friends were supporting him in other ways. He got cards and calls of support from people that he didn't even know. Movies were available for the patients who could make the trip downstairs. Now, he was one of those who could. One afternoon, while Robert was in the first floor movie room, he got some unexpected visitors. Three of his friends from grade school came bouncing in the recreation room looking for him. One of them had moved to Louisville, Kentucky, and was in town for a short visit. After greeting him and giving him a warm smile, they asked the question that he would be asked hundreds of times. *"What happened?"* He gave them a brief description of his mishap, and went on to talk about more pleasant things. He didn't really like talking about his mishap, but tried to give everyone who asked a satisfactory answer. He really enjoyed his friends' visit. They cheered him up and gave him a reason to smile on what had been a pretty dreary day. With people praying for him and a lot work and therapy, Robert was ready for another progressive step. It was getting close to a year when the doctors gave orders for him to use crutches. His bandages were very minimal, and he could get around without much help in his wheelchair. Since he still couldn't use his right hand, a special platform was made onto the right crutch, so that his arm could be strapped onto the device with Velcro tape. His hand was in pain from severe nerve and muscle damage that was done. It was very sensitive to the touch, so he had to be very careful. His left leg was still wrapped up, and he couldn't put any pressure on the still painful foot and leg. It was a challenge, but one that he was ready to meet head on. He would have to learn how to balance himself on the modified crutches. He had to make doubly sure that he didn't fall and cause more damage to his recovering wounds, but nothing was going to stop him from trying and moving up once again on the progress chart. Even pain would have to take a back seat to his efforts on his road to recovery. As his recovery continued, the doctors continued to monitor Robert's progress very closely. As long as he made progress, so would his confidence and privileges. They told him that if he didn't have any setbacks, that he might be able to get weekend liberty and spend some time at home. This was good news to his ears. He had been at the base hospital for almost a year, and hadn't been home in well over a year. He knew that it would be much different this time, but he was up for the challenge.

The following week, he was given a weekend pass to go home. He was ready to leave for home that Friday, but there was a mix up in his files, so he had to wait until the next day. Someone was waiting to pick him up that Friday, but he had to find another ride because of the change in days. That Saturday morning, his brother and a friend of his, showed up at the hospital to take Robert home to St. Louis. He was glad to be finally be going home, but was a little nervous. The closer he got to home, the more apprehensive he became. He wasn't sure how he was going to react, and thought about having his brother turn around, and take him back to the security of the hospital where he had spent so much time. Even though he was thankful to be alive and finally going home, feelings and thoughts began to surface that he never felt before. Little did he know that it was just the beginning of the internal battles that he would have to fight for the rest of his life.

CHAPTER EIGHTEEN

ROBERT'S FIRST TRIP BACK HOME

When they crossed the Mississippi river and the Gateway Arch glittered from the sun, his thoughts suddenly turned to joy. As the forty plus minute drive from Scott Air Force Base was nearing an end, Robert started to relax. The drive ended as they pulled into the driveway of his home in Kinloch. It was a beautiful warm spring day as his family rushed out to greet him and help him out of the back seat of his brother's car. They got his crutches out the trunk of the car and assisted him as he used his modified crutches. After he got into the house, there were hugs and kisses from his mom and the rest of his family. Some of his younger nieces and nephews came up to him, while some of the others kept their distance. They weren't quite sure of what to make of this bandaged up person that some of them had never seen before. He relaxed and talked to everyone who had questions. He had questions of his own, as to who some of his nieces and nephews belonged to. It was a welcome reunion for him and his family, who was preparing a big barbecue feast for him.

After hearing the news that he was home, the crowds began to gather. The crowd became so large that they had to go outdoors to the front yard where there was more room. He was given a lawn chair to sit in, and another chair to prop his leg on a pillow. Everyone tried to make him as comfortable as possible since it was his first time away from the hospital. Friends and neighbors were coming and going, but before long, the whole yard was filled with people who had been passing the house. They had come off the street and joined all of the people who were already there. There were so many people, that it was like a Kinloch reunion. His friends came up to him to say hello and pay their respects. He was very thankful that it wasn't his last respects. His two Marine friends that he saw at Camp Pendleton were civilians now. They had served their tour in Vietnam and had returned home to their community. They were sorry to see him injured and in bad shape, but told him they were glad he made it back alive. They were the only ones to have a clue of what he had been through. The community of Kinloch had its share of problems, but was still a close knit community He hadn't seen that many people in their yard since he was a kid. His sisters had a social club, and would throw a yard party once a month during the summer months. Kinloch was sometimes called *Kinfolk Valley*. Somewhere down the genetic line, a lot of people in the community were blood related.

It was good for the community to see that some of their young men had made it back from the war, alive. Some were injured, but not as seriously as Robert. At least five young men from the community had been killed in action. He could see the genuine concern on the face of everyone who came to wish him well. He could also look beyond the concern, and see the pity they had for him. It was still a fact that he was in bad shape and a shell of what he used to be. At that time, no one knew just how much recovery he would make, if any at all. It had been almost a year, and no one knew what he looked like when he was first injured, but after seeing him in the condition he was in, it was obvious that he had suffered major damage to his body. The damage to his mind hadn't even been considered yet.

Nevertheless it was a very good day. There was good fellowship and good food. Never did he expect to see such a turnout of support. He was very pleased, and couldn't have scripted it any better. Even though it was a very enjoyable day, it was also very tiresome. He had never extended himself that far, and had no way of knowing what his limit really was. What he did know was that he was totally drained at the end of the day. He took his medication and got a good night's sleep. He slept on the couch in the living room because it was the most comfortable place for him.

He was still on hospital wake up time, and woke up early Sunday morning. The only ones who were there was his mom and his youngest sister. It was raining so he was content to just watch television. The rain had stopped earlier than he expected, so he woke his sister up to ask her what time Sunday Mass started. She told him that it started at ten o'clock like always. He thought that she was going to church, but she went back to sleep. He had been going to Mass at the chapel at the hospital, and wanted to go to church. He saw no reason not to go to church even though his mom and sister were still asleep. He got up and cleaned himself up and got dressed. He put his one shoe on and strapped his crutches on his arm. The left leg had a half of a splint that supported his injuries. He hopped out of the kitchen door, and started down the muddy driveway. It was his first time out on his own, and he had less than fifteen minutes to make it to church. Normally, it took about ten minutes to walk to church, but hopping on crutches down the street would take him longer. He figured he could make it for at least part of the service, so he made his mind up to go. There were no sidewalks, so he would have to walk on the edge of the street. When he got a short distance from the house, a friend of his stopped his car, and asked Robert where he thought he was going? He told him that he was going to church. He told Robert that he was going to church too, and he could ride with him. Robert told him that his crutches wouldn't fit in his small car, so he would walk. He told Robert that he could break the crutches down and put them in his trunk. He agreed to take him up on his offer and apologized to him for the inconvenience. When they got to Holy Angels Church, Robert realized that Mass would have been over by the time he got there, if he made it at all. His friend got the crutches out of his trunk, and helped Robert up the steps. He sat on an empty pew in the back, because he needed room to stretch out his leg. During the sermon, the priest acknowledged him and commended him for even being there at all.

After Mass, the people greeted him and told him they had been praying for him. His friend helped him down the steps and back into his car. He took Robert home, and gave him his phone number. He told him to call if he ever needed a ride. Robert thanked his friend as he drove off. Robert realized that the walk would have been harder and more dangerous than he anticipated. He had never been up or down any steps while using his crutches, which would have been a very dangerous feat. He knew that it was foolish, and wasn't going to try it again. When he got into the house, his mom scolded him in her own sweet way. She told him never to do that again even if he was going to church. He told her he would try to find some other way, and not try to walk by himself.

Some of his family came by the house later and helped cook a big dinner, and spend some time with him. Some more of his friends came by later in the day to visit as well. He didn't have to be back at the hospital until the next morning, but had to leave later that evening when a ride was available. His brother and his friend took him to the hospital door, where he went back to his second floor living quarters. He would make many more trips home, as long as he continued to progress. The doctors encouraged the patients to spend as much time with their families as possible. They knew that it was a vital part of their recovery process.

    Meanwhile, he was still getting therapy to help strengthen his injured limbs. He also continued to go home on weekend passes. During one of his home visits, some of his friends took him to the top of the Gateway Arch. It was a challenge because he had to walk a long way on his crutches from the parking lot. They were very patient with him and gave him as much time as he needed. He paced himself so he wouldn't tire himself out as he hopped along the pathway. When they got there, he squeezed into the capsules with his crutches as they ascended to the top of the Arch. It was a very tiring trip, but he wouldn't have traded the enjoyment of being with his friends for anything.

CHAPTER NINETEEN

DEPRESSION SETS IN ON ROBERT

After several months of visiting home, he got an unexpected, unwelcome visitor. Depression had shown up, and he began to look at his situation from a negative point of view. He began to see himself as a burden to his family and friends. He needed help with almost everything he did in some way or another. He couldn't even tie the one shoestring on his right foot. In fact, he couldn't even put his shoe on by himself without taking a lot of time. Cutting his fingernails and toenails was a painful experience with one of his sisters helping him. Even though he had made a lot of progress, there seemed to be more things that he couldn't do than the things he could do. He started to feel out of place with people who had no trouble doing the simplest things. He was in an adjustment state that he didn't expect, and no one had told him about. He didn't quite know how to deal with it, so he didn't come home for a while. He decided to spend some time at the hospital and try to make some sense out of what he was going through.

One day while he was sitting in the recreation room, one of the nurses asked him why he wasn't going home any more? He told her that he felt out of place, and didn't want to see anyone for awhile. What he didn't know was that the nurse was taking notes on everything he said. It was her job to report to the doctors anything that the patients would say that was self destructive or negative statements that could possibly lead to suicide. Robert wasn't thinking about suicide after coming such a long way. He was just voicing his frustrations over something that he didn't understand. He looked at the nurse as a concerned friend, and really felt better after talking with her. He was in for a rude awakening when he got back to the second floor ward. The medics, whom he looked upon as friends, took him to a room where they took his watch, a medal that he was wearing around his neck, and the shoestrings from his shoe. They didn't tell him anything, but it didn't take him long to realize that he was on suicide watch. He felt that by expressing himself to the nurse, a lot of pressure and frustration had been lifted, but she was trained to turn over all negative reactions to the doctors. For four days, he was locked in a room with padded walls all by himself. He felt like he was in prison whether than a hospital. He felt betrayed by everyone and didn't understand what the doctors were trying to really do. The questions they asked him had nothing to do with the problems he was really having. Since he had already said the wrong things to the nurse, he tried to be careful not to say anything else that would keep him locked up any longer than they had already planned for him. He answered the questions they asked as simply and direct as possible. He was finally released after four days, and put on an antidepressant medicine. They told him that he would be all right as long as he stayed on the medicine. He didn't know how deep his depression really went, so he took the medicine as prescribed, but he never again talked to anyone about his innermost feelings. He just couldn't trust anyone with his deep thoughts or their ability to deal with them in a positive and healthy way. To this very day, he still guards most of his innermost thoughts and keeps them to himself and God, who already knows all bout them. After not going home for a while, or having any visitors at his own request, he started to come out of his depressive state. The medicine, some mental adjustments, and most of all-prayer, had helped him fight through all the dark clouds that had enveloped him.

Robert had started going home on the weekends again and was trying his best to get back into the swing of things. The more he came home, the more he became like his old self. The only thing that was concerning him, was just how much of his old self did he really want to be like. Before he went to Vietnam, he wrestled with the fact that his life was less meaningful than he would have liked it to be. He was making adjustments, and slowly getting use to civilian life and social living. Before he went off to war, and realizing that he might not make it back, he felt that he wouldn't miss all of the self destructive things that was so much apart of his life and life in general. Even though it wasn't an everyday thing-partying, drinking, and funfair was an acceptable way of life. It was considered a necessary escape from the toils and pressures of life. He somehow knew that the dangers of prescription drugs, and alcohol could be more dangerous than the perils of war.

Since Robert had progressed as much as he was going to at the hospital, the doctors released him to a transient unit. He would wait for orders to be sent to the Great Lakes Naval hospital where he had to be discharged from. The temporary living quarters was a barracks that housed servicemen from every branch who were waiting orders to be sent somewhere else. He no longer needed full medical attention, but would go back to the hospital if he needed any medical care. It had been over a year since he arrived at Scott, and he had made and was still making a tremendous recovery. The therapist had made him a flexible splint to help his right hand. It was still very painful and highly sensitive to the touch. He still couldn't grip anything, and his arm still had to be strapped to his modified platform crutch. His crutches had become his temporary legs, and had become a part of him that he used with skill and confidence.

He didn't know how long he would be at the transient barracks, but was told that it wouldn't be long. The medical staff had to put together his medical records, and coordinate everything with the hospital in Great Lakes. Since he was no longer confined to the hospital, he was practically a free man. He could even leave the base any time he could get a ride. He would sometimes get a ride to and from St Louis with one of the Air Force transients also waiting orders. One of his sisters would sometimes even let him drive her car back to the base. He had come a very long way, and he had adjusted so well that there wasn't much he couldn't do. Whether it was possible or impossible, he was willing to at least give it try.

He would sometimes go out on the town for a night of fun. Drinking was a way of life, and didn't affect the average military person. As long as they reported for duty the next day, it was a non factor, but for Robert it was a factor. He was on medication and mixed with alcohol, could have deadly results one way or another. One weekend while driving his sister's car back to the base, he had a close encounter. He had a few beers and a mixed drink during the evening hours. It wasn't enough to get him drunk, but he also took his medication before leaving for the base. Robert had a big headache from a toothache that he wasn't aware of, so he figured that he would time his medication with the forty- five minute drive to the base. He took off by himself and headed across the river. By the time he reached a railroad track in East St Louis, he had already begun to doze off. He had only been driving for about fifteen minutes, and had almost forty miles to go. The sound of the train horn had alerted him, so he knew he had to do something else in order to stay awake. Robert rolled down all of the windows and turned the radio up a little louder than normal. He continued to drive down the highway intent on staying awake and alive. He thought maybe he had driven another ten minutes when he snapped out of what he thought was another momentary doze as he had done before. The first time it happened, it was daylight. It was now dark when he snapped back from his momentary lapse. Thinking that he was still miles from the base, his headlights caught hold of a big green road sign that read: Scott Air Force Base, two miles. He was shocked to see that he was only two miles from the Air Force Base exit. Then Robert thought to himself, "was he alive?" He knew that there was at least fifteen miles that were unaccounted for. After pinching himself, he realized that he was not dreaming, and was very much alive. Robert began to thank God once again for protecting him, and keeping him alive once again. He made it to the base hospital and got a good night's sleep. He didn't bother telling anyone about his experience, because Robert knew that no one would believe him. Plus, his sister wouldn't have let him drive her car any more.

During a weekend home visit, Robert decided to make yet another step of faith. Robert had a cane that he used when he made short trips around the house. He would use his one good hand to grip the cane and move about the house. His legs were getting stronger, and he was able to wear shoes on both feet. His left foot was still in a lot of pain, and was by no means a comfortable situation. It was a beautiful day, and he was tired of sitting around the house and even more tired of asking people to take him places. Robert grabbed his cane and took off. It was the first time that he had walked anywhere by himself. He was going to go as far as he could with the use of only his cane. Robert slowly walked from the yard and started up the street. He had figured that if he couldn't make it, he would flag someone down and get a ride back home. He had been walking for about fifteen minutes, and had just passed the confectionery where he used to buy the best cheesecakes and donuts on the planet. Robert was going to try and make it to the corner where Holy Angels Church was and start back. He was only a few minutes from his destination, when an old high school classmate was walking towards him. Robert thought he was going to encourage him because he knew what he had been through, but he told Robert to "Put that cane down. You know you don't need it." Robert told him that he most certainly did, and he was doing good to be walking with it at all. Up until then, he was feeling pretty good about himself. Whether his former classmate was joking or not, Robert's spirits were dampened and suddenly all of his energy was gone. Robert hitched a ride back home, and rested from his walk after pondering over the negative remarks he heard from the man. He decided not to let him, or anyone else put a damper on his recovery. It was another lesson that he was learning about the insensitivity of people who just didn't understand what they were saying. That would be an ongoing battle: knowing that he was doing all that he could and even going beyond of what he expected from himself, and people misjudging his efforts. It has always been a hard pill to swallow, but he just takes a big breath and let it pass on.

   Independence and freedom had its advantages and disadvantages. It meant being responsible or irresponsible. There weren't too many things that were out of his reach, but the same self destructive tendencies that Robert had before the war, were even greater now. Happy hour was a major event for some of the men and women on the base. He and some of the others spent a lot of time drinking as much as they could for half price for a full hour, as long as everyone made it to where they were suppose to be.

CHAPTER TWENTY

ROBERT RETURNS TO GREAT LAKES

It was early June when Robert's orders finally came. He and some of the other Naval personnel were flown from Scott to Chanute Air Force Base in Evanston, Illinois. They were driven by bus the rest of the thirty miles to the Naval hospital in Great Lakes. He had come full circle to the place where he had started at Boot Camp and Hospital Corps School. Robert never thought he would have any reason to return to Great Lakes; but he knew that the only reason he was there, even though he was injured, was that he had survived all that he was trained to do. The fact that he was still living meant that the United States Government had to now take care of him.

Robert was taken to a staging area where he would be diagnosed and sent where he was supposed to go. Robert couldn't wait for them to be finished so that he could finally be discharged and sent home for good. After checking his chart, he was sent to a wing of the hospital where he thought he would receive his discharge papers. After a year and a half at the hospital at Scott, he was glad to be at the Naval hospital. Robert knew that it was his last stop on his long journey back home. He was led to a ward where some patients were already there. He would soon find out that he would be there for a long time and was not leaving any time soon. Robert noticed that the door was locked behind him after he entered the room. The first person he met was a patient with a suitcase in his hand. He told Robert that he was going home to Chicago. Robert said good luck to the patient as he passed him by. A patient told Robert that the man wasn't going anywhere. He said the man gets dressed and packs his suitcase everyday, and acts as if he was going home. Robert had a slight suspicion at first, but now he was one hundred percent sure that he was on the psychiatric ward. He didn't know why, but there he was again on lockdown. He tried to tell the staff that he had come to Great Lakes to be discharged, and that he was in the wrong place. All they would tell him was that he had to talk to the doctor.

Robert waited all day and night, and no doctor showed up. He spent a sleepless night wondering what was going on and hoping the doctor would show up any moment and sign him out. Robert hadn't eaten anything and decided not to until he saw a doctor. Robert thought it would be sooner rather than later. He skipped breakfast thinking the doctor would show up. Lunch time came and went and still no doctor. Robert finally started to put things together. Robert remembered the diagnosis as it read on his chart. It read: multiple shrapnel wounds and depressive reaction.

Robert realized they had taken the second diagnosis as the primary one. Robert recalled the lockdown he had while at Scott when he was on suicide watch for four days, but what he didn't understand was that after being free to come and go for over a year, he was now on suicide watch again. Robert knew that mistakes were a part of military life, so he knew what he had to do; he had to prove to them that he didn't belong there. He had to play by their rules if he didn't want to end up like the patient who never made it to Chicago. He became a model patient even though he was in pain because they took his pain medication. He still took the anti depressant medicine they gave him. He began to eat his meals and clean himself up, as well as help keep the ward clean. Robert relaxed and followed every instruction to a tee. He learned from the other patients by watching their attitudes and reaction to the staff. Most of them had been there for a long time and wasn't going anywhere any time soon. One patient told him he had been there going on two years. He made up his mind not to even set a time schedule. He was just going to take it one day at a time. After a week on the psychiatric ward, he finally got to see a doctor. Robert didn't know what the doctor wanted with him, but was just glad to talk to someone who was in charge. He was taken into the office and given a seat. The doctor sat across from him with Robert's chart in his hands. He looked at Robert and told him he didn't think he belonged there, and wondered why it took so long for the staff to realize it. As he signed his release orders, Robert didn't try to explain anything or defend himself. He was just happy to finally be leaving the place where he never should have been in the first place. The doctor apologized to him for the error and inconveniences. He left the office to check on the other patients .Robert was given his clothes and other belongings as he wished the other patients well. He was then taken to a regular ward where patients were waiting to see the review board. The board gave the patients a thorough examination before determining their degree of disability before being discharged. It was a very important review because it would also determine how much money they would receive in disability compensation pay.

Robert was assigned a bed and introduced to some of the other patients who were waiting to face the review board. All of the patients were Navy personnel who had different types of injuries. Robert was the most seriously injured sailor on the ward. One of the patients was a second class petty officer who received a thirty percent disability rating for a back injury he received while unboarding an airplane. He was coming off leave when his injury occurred. He wore his back brace at all times, and did everything he could to impress the review board. It must have worked because he received a permanent thirty percent rating.

After seeing the non combatant sailor get a thirty percent rating for a supposedly chronic back injury, Robert was sure he would get a favorable rating based his medical records and the physical evidence of his wounds. The review board had a large back log of patients, which meant that he would be there longer than he expected. All he could do was to settle in and make the best of the rest of his stay. Robert had a brief encounter with one of the patients on one of the wards that he was temporarily on. The sailor from Chicago had very minor injuries from an accident, and was waiting to be released. For several days, he listened to the sailor rant and rave about everything. He complained about the food, the service he was getting, and the room.

He told Robert of the other ward he was on when he first arrived at the hospital as he paraded around the ward in his long hospital robe. He thought he had it much better than he currently did. Robert kept pretty much to himself, and tried not to bother anybody. After almost a week of putting up with the sailor's complaining and irresponsible antics, he couldn't take it anymore.

Robert was using only a cane to get around, and it seemed as if he was doing just fine to the sailor as well as the other patients. Other than his hand brace, he appeared to have no other injuries. He called the complaining patient to the side, and did something that he really had trouble with, and didn't want to do. He showed the complaining patient all of his wounds to show him that if anyone should be complaining, it should be him. As he did so, the young Brother from Chicago, had a total attitude change. All he could say was, '*wow*!" He told Robert that he never would have known because he never complained about anything. Robert told him how hard it was for him to show him his wounds, but he wanted to teach him a lesson. After his show and tell experience with Robert, the sailor apologized to him and the entire staff who he was constantly harassing. He thanked Robert for helping him see life in a totally different way. He said that he was very thankful, and would never forget the lesson that he learned from him. He was discharged before Robert, but never complained about anything again as long as he was there.

Robert started making weekend trips to Chicago by catching the train. This time his relatives would see him in a totally different way than they use to. His younger cousins bombarded him with question after question about what happened to him and how he was doing. Robert didn't mind talking with them because they were genuinely concerned about him. His relatives on the South side, West side, and Gary, Indiana, gave him the royal treatment whenever he visited them. When he wasn't going to Chicago, he stayed on the base or took the short train ride to Waukegan, which was a small town not too far from the base.

One weekend, he took the train to Chicago and got a ride home to St Louis with his aunt, uncle, and their family. While he was home, he got a friend to take him around to look at some cars. He wasn't quite ready to buy one, but he wanted to see what was available that he could afford. Robert saw one that he liked, and put a minimum down payment on the car. The dealer said he would hold it for him as long as he could. Robert told him that he would try to come back the following week and close the deal. Robert left with his uncle and aunt for Chicago later that weekend. After the three and a half hour drive to Chicago, they dropped him off at Union Station, where he took the train back to the base.

Robert was wearing down from all the walking he had to do while on the base. He knew that having a car available would help him out a lot. The following weekend, he went to Chicago and had his uncle take him to Midway Airport where he got a standby flight to St. Louis, and got there early Friday evening. He met another sailor on the flight who was flying for the very first time. He was sitting in the seat next to him, and was having a hard time adjusting to flying. Robert tried to calm him down, but he threw up all over the seat, as well as Robert and a few other passengers. Robert and the stewardess helped clean up the disgusting mess. Since both of them were going to St Louis, they had a chance to get acquainted on the forty-five minute plane ride. They both had to be back at the base on Monday morning. Since his new acquaintance had a fear of flying, he suggested to him an alternative could be possible if things went well while he was home for the weekend. After arriving in St Louis, they exchanged phone numbers so they could keep in touch. Robert had been saving for a car, and now had enough to finish the deal if things went well.

Robert knew he would have a busy Saturday, so he stayed at home that evening and got plenty of rest. He had a friend take him to the dealership as soon as they opened. The car he wanted was still there and all of the paper work was done within the hour. He was given the keys to the black Chevy Malibu and then drove away. His first stop was the insurance office. The dealer had already contacted a local office, and all Robert had to do was to go and make the first installment and finish the paper work He was on schedule, but he had to be one more place before noon. Robert had his friend drive his car to the driver's license bureau. Robert had to take the written test and driving test, but most of all, he had to pass both of them in order to complete his weekend mission. His permit had expired before he went into the service, but the test was close to the same. After a brief study of the driver's guide, he took the written test and passed. All he had to do was to pass the driving test. He already had driving experience, but taking a test with someone taking notes as he drove, would be a little different. Even though he was still using his cane at times and had his hand brace, he didn't use them. He wanted to appear as normal as possible. Robert didn't want anything to be used against him before he ever got started. His friend pulled his car to the starting point where Robert and the tester got in. After the preliminary tests, he drove off to the route that was mapped out for the drivers. He relaxed and drove with the confidence that he had been driving with all the time. After returning from his test drive, the instructor told him that he had passed the test. All he had to do was to sign the form and go pay for his license. The easiest thing turned out to be the hardest of all. His nerves were shot and signing the form with his left hand wasn't as easy as it should have been. Robert could hardly get his name on the line, and when he finally did, it was barely legible. The clerk told him to take his time. She said that sometimes people get nervous after taking the tests, and she understood. He was glad she understood. Robert thought to himself, if she only knew. Robert drove to the office where he had his picture taken. After giving the clerk all of the necessary papers and paying the license fee, he drove away legally for the first time in his first legal car.

Robert called the sailor who traveled with him so that he could ride back to the base now that he had his car. He told him to be at his house early Sunday evening. He would have had to drive back by himself. Now, the five hour drive to Great Lakes could be split between the two of them. It seemed like a perfect situation for the panicky flyer and Robert, who needed some help driving. Robert didn't want a repeat of what happened when he fell asleep driving back to Scott Air Force Base a short time ago. He had fun driving around with his friends in his own car, but it was soon time to go. The sailor and his parents came to Robert's home in Kinloch. They wanted to meet Robert and his family before they left for Great Lakes. They were thankful that Robert helped him survive his first flight, and were more grateful that their son wouldn't have to get on an airplane with his fear of flying. He had just finished Boot Camp and had to get use to flying. His parents made sandwiches to go along with what Robert's mom had already prepared for their journey. They left early in the evening with a simple plan to make as many stops as necessary and make it to the base on time and alive.

Even though it was only a five hour or so drive, they made frequent stops. Neither one of them had a lot of experience driving on long trips, so they were in no hurry. They stopped at a truck stop restaurant and had a good meal before getting back on the road. They were trying to time it so it would be daylight by the time they got to Chicago. They didn't want to run into rush hour, and wanted to be able to see the exit signs more clearly. They took turns driving after each stop they made, so they wouldn't tire out. It was dawn when Robert reached the Chicago city limits. Robert was looking for the exchange exit that would take them towards the base. He missed his exit, and ended up in the downtown area. The streets were still relatively empty, but they were unfamiliar and a little tricky. Robert lost his bearings and ended up on a short one way street. He was just about to make the turn off the one way street, when the police saw him and pulled him over.

165

Robert told them that he missed their exit to Great Lakes and got lost in the city. One of the policemen asked Robert if he had been drinking. Robert told him he had a beer over four hours ago. They asked him to walk a straight line and to stand on one foot and touch his nose. He tried to do as they asked, but because of his injured legs, he couldn't perform the test very well. The police assumed that he was drunk, and told Robert's newfound friend to drive if he had a license. He was nervous, but took the wheel anyhow. They gave them directions back to the freeway and drove off. He told Robert how nervous he was driving in the big city, so they had planned for Robert to take over the wheel as soon as they got out of sight from the police. Robert could see how nervous he was, and tried to get him to relax for just a little while. He had run a stop sign and almost panicked.

Before long, the morning traffic had started to flow. They were just a couple of blocks from the exit, when his friend ran a red light. Before he could blink, there was a loud thud and glass poured in from the window of the passenger side where Robert was sitting. His car was pushed to the other side of the street and came to rest on a sidewalk. Robert was shaken up as he tried to open his door and get out of the car. The door was stuck and banged up. He had to crawl to the other side to get out of the car. Though shaken and shocked, he and his friend were alright. The car had suffered major damage, but the two passengers hardly had a scratch. The police came and wrote their report. The driver who hit Robert's car was so thankful that no one was injured or killed, that he took the blame so that Robert's friend wouldn't get a ticket. The police called for a tow truck as Robert and his friend waited on the sidewalk. The tow truck arrived about twenty minutes later. When he saw the car, he just shook his head. He couldn't understand how anyone could have come out of the accident not seriously injured or killed. He stated that if there had been more traffic, it would have been much worse. Robert and his friend knew they had dodged a bullet. Robert was still shaken and dejected seeing his car that appeared to be totaled. After hooking up the car to the tow truck, Robert and his friend got into the cab of the truck and headed for Skokie, Illinois. It was half way between the base and Chicago. The tow driver dropped Robert and his friend off at the Skokie police station and made his report. He then took the car to a repair shop that was closest to the base.

While they were waiting to leave, one of the policemen asked Robert what happened, and where they were from. He told the policeman that they were from St. Louis and were in the Navy. He told him they had an accident in Chicago on their way back to the Great Lakes Navy base. The other policeman asked Robert if he was lying. He said that he fit the description of someone they had been looking for in Skokie. Robert showed them his hospital band that he was wearing, and his driver's license. His military ID was lost overseas somewhere, so he told them to call the base hospital if they still didn't believe him. They said that should be enough proof. As they were leaving to catch the train that made a stop in Skokie, one of the policemen told his friend to make sure that Robert stayed out of trouble. His friend just happened to be White. His friend told him that he was sorry for wrecking his car, and being harassed by the police. Robert told him that his insurance would cover his car either way, but as for the policemen, he told him that he was used to it. He said that he hoped he could see the difference how the color of his skin made the difference in how he was treated in Chicago, and now in Skokie.

They arrived at the base and checked in just in time to avoid being listed as AWOL [absent without leave]. Robert quickly showered and shaved, and went to the dental clinic in the hospital. He had a nine o'clock appointment to finally have his nagging tooth pain taken care of. He wanted to finally be free of the migraine headaches he was suffering from. He was on time, in spite of the adventurous morning. He was called into the room and was about to be treated. The dentist noticed that he was shaking like a leaf and asked Robert if he had some other problem. He told the dentist that he had been in a car accident earlier that morning. The dentist told him to come back in a couple of days. He said there was no way he could work on his mouth in the condition he was in. Robert didn't realize what a wreck he was because of the accident. He went back to his hospital room and went to sleep and tried to recover from the shock and trauma of the accident. Robert took his pain medication and rested for the next two days. After two days of rest, he went back to the dental clinic to have the necessary work done on his mouth. His nerves were steady enough to finally have oral surgery. He had the aching tooth removed and fully recovered in a few days. He was now pain free, from the top of his head to his neck .The insurance company called him after about a week. They told him that in spite of the severe body damage, windows, and radiator damage, they would pay to have it fixed. Robert thought for sure they would total the car, and was surprised it could be fixed. Especially since the estimate was over five thousand dollars. It took about three weeks before he could pick his car up from the repair shop in Skokie. His car looked, and drove just as good as it did before the accident.

Robert saw his friend only a couple of times after they got back. Each time, he tried to assure him that everything would be all right. He knew how badly he felt about the accident. Robert also knew that he did everything he could to avoid him because of it.

Robert didn't stray too far from the base since the medical review board could call him in at anytime. By the middle of August, the board finally called him in. The team of doctors had closely looked over his thick medical chart before they examined him. They thoroughly examined and measured every inch of his wounds. They checked the motion range and usage of all the injured areas. The process took almost two hours as the doctors charted and discussed every aspect of his injuries. When they finally finished, he took his cane and slowly limped out of the room. After the sometimes painful and tiring examination, all he could do now was wait to hear the results. While waiting to hear from the board, he did very little. He had worn a path to and from Chicago, and the surrounding area and was tired and weary. Since he knew his time was short, he didn't want to do anything that would keep him from going home when they finished with him. It was almost three weeks before he got his results. He got a one hundred per cent disability rating. That was the maximum rating, and he was pleased with the results. It was another week or so before his final discharge papers came in. Robert was more than ready to go home. He was officially discharged, and retired by reason of physical disability. Robert and some of the other veterans had gone to Belleville to apply for social security benefits at an earlier date. However, it couldn't be finalized until the medical review results were in. They knew that no matter what their disabilities were, they would have to be financially able to take care of themselves. Robert was finally given his Purple Heart Medal, along with his retirement papers.

CHAPTER TWENTY- ONE

ROBERT IS RETIRED FROM THE NAVY AND RETURNS HOME TO ST. LOUIS

The day after he got his retirement orders, he packed his belongings and headed for home in his Chevy Malibu. He stopped in Chicago and spent a little time with some of his relatives. After having dinner with them and chatting with his cousins, he hit the road and headed for St. Louis. He was rested, relaxed and content. He was in no hurry, so he took his time and enjoyed the ride home. For the first time in a long time, he wasn't on anyone's time schedule. He had made many stops on his long journey home. Now it was just Robert, the highway, his Chevy Malibu, and of course, his Lord and Savior Jesus the Christ. He would go back to St Louis to add other chapters to his very interesting life.

Robert would not only have to adjust to being a civilian again, but a beat up, banged up veteran of the Vietnam war as well. Even though he was somewhat adjusted to civilian life, he knew that the unknown challenges wouldn't be easy. What he did know was that he had to take the advice of the doctors to take things one day at a time. No one knew that he was coming home, so he thought he would pull another surprise on his family after his pleasant, uneventful ride home. He pulled up in the driveway at about nine o'clock in the evening and knocked on the kitchen door that everyone used. He then waited for a response. His youngest sister opened the door and greeted him with a hug. He came in and gave his mother a big hug as well. They were surprised, but he was saving the biggest surprise for last. After he told them that he was home for good, the rejoicing really started. After talking with them for a while, he made some calls and let some of his friends and family know that he was home for good. He watched some television with his sister as they snacked and talked about any and everything they could think of. He had already taken his medication, so he drifted off to sleep on his first official night as a civilian. After a good night sleep, he woke up to the smell of pancakes and sausage. His mom prepared breakfast for him, just like old times. He spent some time with his mom, then took his sister to school. She was enrolled in Business college, and he was glad to be of service to her.

He spent his first day as a civilian visiting some of his sisters and looking up some old friends. The day seemed to pass by like a blur, but it felt good for him to finally be free and independent. Having a car meant that could drive himself to church on Sundays. He wasn't about to leave God out of his life, especially since He was the one who was responsible for him still being alive. He was past feeling guilty about missing Mass. Being raised Catholic all of his life was all he knew about church, so he wanted to express his appreciation to God in every way he could. He was especially glad to be able to take his mom shopping, and take his younger sister and her friends places they needed to go. He was enjoying himself and feeling good about helping his family. He still had to deal with the issue of pain, which he kept mostly to himself. He also had to make ongoing mental adjustments to the so called *simple things* of life. His walking was not easy because the peroneal nerve in his left leg was blown out, with a major part of the tibia bone. The nerve controlled the motion in his foot, and since he couldn't lift his foot, he was always tripping over something. His hand was still very sensitive, and he had to be careful to keep it out of the way of unsuspecting well wishers who always wanted to shake his hand. The brace was helping to strengthen it, but it was still very painful. Pain was and always will be a part of his life, but it always had to take a back seat to progress and things he needed and wanted to do. Most of the physical and mental adjustments were trial and error since he never knew what would happen until he actually started doing things that he had never done before in his present condition. He knew that people had to deal with his obvious handicaps, but he tried hard to shield them from the unseen things that would have really made them uncomfortable. When he ran low on his medicine, he went to the Veteran's Administration hospital to seek medical attention. After checking him out, they started a new medical chart on him and prescribed the medication he needed. He was also given information about being evaluated by the VA so his pay would increase. He was receiving Social Security disability compensation and Navy retirement pay based on his pay grade. It was enough to pay his car note and insurance and barely get him through the month. He had to budget very carefully so he wouldn't run out of funds. The VA compensation would triple what he was getting from the Navy, so he applied for a VA medical evaluation. Just like the Navy medical review board examination, it would take a while before he was called in, and even longer before his pay would start. He made the first step in applying for the evaluation. Now all he could do was to wait for them to call him in. Being free from the Navy and going back and forth to hospitals, gave him a tremendous sense of freedom. He could look upon the coming holidays with great anticipation for the first time in a long time.

The coming Thanksgiving holidays would be his first with his family in four years. When the holidays came around, so did all the memories of the past. He had forgotten how the aroma of the turkey baking in the oven would tease his taste buds. His mom's dressing, sweet potato and pumpkin pies were always added treats. She made his favorite: coconut cake to go along with the other desserts. All the other trimmings and dishes made him temporarily forget all his pain and ailments. His house, and every home he visited had a festive atmosphere. There was plenty of food and drink and loads of fun. He was right back in the norm of drinking as much as he wanted, and sometimes more than he should. Christmas was more of the same: food, drinks, gifts, and partying. New Years Eve was also his first at home in four years. Bringing in the New Year meant more drinking and partying. He was once again living the American dream that the military was fighting to preserve: baseball, apple pie, and his Malibu Chevrolet.

After the new year had settled in, Robert received some bad news. One of his childhood friends was missing in action, and presumed dead. His friend joined the Navy shortly after he and his friend had enlisted. They talked about Boot Camp, and what might or might not be open, as far as job classifications. With a couple of years of college behind him, Robert told him he probably could get into any field he wanted. He told him to be careful, so he wouldn't get tricked into getting into a dangerous field as he had done. He told Robert he would be careful, and should be able to get into the field of his choice. Robert had graduated from Hospital Corps School, and was home on leave when his friend finished Boot Camp. He told Robert he had been accepted into Electrical Engineering School. He had attended Washington University in St Louis, and said he would be eligible for officer's candidate school in a short time. Robert was happy for him, but told him to still be careful. They both were confident that he had chosen a safe enough field.

Immediately after hearing about his friend, he drove to his friend's parents' home. They lived in Kinloch, not too far from his house. He didn't know if he would be able to console them because he was feeling pretty bad himself. After entering the house, he offered his condolences. He was hoping that a mistake might have been made because he thought he was in a safe field. After not saying anything for a few minutes, they knew he wanted to know what happened, so they broke the ice and told him. His father said that their son was a Radar Engineer on a special mission. He said the plane that he was on was shot down over a mountainous range in Afghanistan. The plane, and everyone on it was missing, without a clue where it had gone down. Nothing was heard from the plane, or its crew ever again. His parents were trying to be strong for the younger siblings, who were visibly upset and shaken about what had happened to their brother. One of his younger brothers was having a hard time, and was very angry about the loss of his big brother. He saw how Robert was all banged up, and a shadow of what he use to be. He figured Robert had to be bitter and angry about what he was going through. At that time, he was bitter and angry and ready to join in with the young boy in expressing it. He felt that his injuries and near death experience could have been caused by the very people he was giving aid to. He knew that anyone in those villages could have planted the land mines that killed his other friend, as well as the one that blew him up. The young boy asked him if he was angry about what they did to him? He was about to relieve his frustration and tell the boy just how angry he was. Before he could even think about his response, he told the boy something he had not intended to say. He said, "*No.*" He wasn't angry with the Vietnamese people. He told him and the others who were listening, that they were not to blame for what happened to him. He told them that those people were victims of the war just as he was. He told them that they didn't understand what was going on, and was doing what they knew to do in a time of war in their land. The young boy who asked the question said, "*Wow. I never looked at it like that.*" Suddenly, the boy and his family felt a lot better. Robert felt better as well. It felt as if a big weight had lifted from his shoulders. He hadn't realized that he had been harboring so much bitterness since the time of his brush with death in the fields of Vietnam. He had gone to his friend's parents' home to try and console them, which miraculously he did, but they consoled and comforted him in a way that would last for the rest of his life. He hugged and thanked them for helping him before he left their house. The parents also thanked him for helping them and the children in their time of difficulty. After the allotted time, a memorial service was held for their son, and his friend. He attended the service that was held at Holy Angels Church, where they all were members. He continued to visit, and talk to the family as often as he could. The lost of his friend had more of an effect on him than he realized.

As Spring came around, Robert began to have so many negative thoughts that he had a hard time understanding what was happening to him. Every new phase he would go through became more difficult to deal with. Sometimes he would boil over with frustration and depression, and wasn't sure why. He would be sitting in the living room sometimes, and feel the urge to pick something up and throw it through the big window. Other times, he felt like just screaming as loud as he could. Robert sought help at the VA hospital to try and deal with the situation. The clinic put him back on antidepressants, and ordered follow-up visits. He felt a lot better, but still felt he had to make a change before he did or said something he would later regret. The only thing he could think of was to have a change in scenery.

CHAPTER TWENTY- TWO

ROBERT MOVES OUT ON HIS OWN

Robert had been contemplating moving, but he knew that his financial situation wouldn't allow it. One of his sisters suggested he could stay with her for awhile, but he felt he needed to be away from the dependency of his family so he could deal with his frustrations in his own way. After thinking things over for a couple of days, he decided to make a move. He didn't know when, and most of all didn't know how. He would check the *apartment guide* in the newspaper every day to see if there was anything available that came close to matching his income. Several weeks passed without any positive results. Then he got a breakthrough one day. A friend of his told him about an apartment for rent a few houses from where she lived. She gave him the landlord's phone number so he could make contact with him. He called the man the next day, but he wasn't available. He left his mom's phone number with the landlord's wife. He called Robert the next day to set a time so he could look at the apartment that was in the city. Robert and the landlord got together the next day at the site. When he saw the three story building, he was sure he was going to show him the first floor, but as they entered the building, he led Robert up the spiraling steps to the third floor, which had the only vacant apartment in the building. He had already made his mind up. There was no way he was moving there. Climbing three flights of stairs was out of the question, considering how difficult it would be for him to scale those stairs on a modified crutch or a cane. Robert looked the apartment over anyway because he was sure it would be the first and last time he would see it. Just for curiosity sake, he asked the landlord how much the rent would be. He gave Robert a very moderate price. He even said he would lower the price if he were serious about renting the apartment. It was well within his range, and the best offer he could find. As they were leaving the building, he told the landlord that he would get back with him, even though he had no intention of doing so. He told Robert that he really wanted him to have the apartment. So he gave him two days to make up his mind before he rented the apartment to someone else who was waiting to pay the initial price. He left the apartment and went home with nothing seemingly accomplished.

Robert went back home and started to check the apartment guide of the papers once again. He had already been turned down for an apartment because he had no credit. So things were not looking good at all. As he and his helpers continued to search the paper, the results were still negative. The closer he got to his deadline, the more he looked at the apartment on Greer Avenue as a possibility. The third floor apartment was looking like his only alternative. Even though the price was the lowest he could find, it would still be a tight squeeze for him to budget in another bill. He knew he was down to his last and only chance to make the move he so desperately needed to make. He called the landlord and told him he would accept his offer. He told Robert he would need his first and last month's rent up front before he could move in. That was good news, except he didn't have enough up front money to move in. He reluctantly asked his mother for a loan, who reluctantly gave it to him. She knew how important it was to him, so she gave him a little extra. He told her he would be able to pay her back as soon as his VA compensation started, but for now, he knew he would have to stick to a very tight budget. A major plus for the apartment was it was fully furnished with a refrigerator, a bed, a kitchen table and chairs, and a large dresser. Another good thing was not having to sign a year's lease.

Robert could pay on a monthly basis. All he had to do was survive the winding three flights of stairs. He took the rent money to the landlord and signed the contract .He was given the keys to his first apartment and proudly started to move in. He then went back to his mom's house in Kinloch, and picked up the belongings he had accumulated. With the help of two friends who drove their cars, he was able to move into his new residence having to only make one trip. Up until the time he was actually leaving, not too many people were taking him seriously about moving. His mom gave him a big hug, along with bed clothes, towels, and anything else she could grab hold of at the last minute. It took about twenty minutes for the three car convoy to reach their destination. They took their time, and helped him get everything to his third floor apartment. They rested for a while before leaving. Robert hooked up with them later to celebrate his bold move into his apartment. After leaving them later that night, instead of going to his mother's house in Kinloch, he drove to the city where he now resided. He wasn't at all sure just how he was going to make it, but he knew he could always count on his Heavenly Father for help.

Although he was now a city boy, he spent most of his time in Kinloch with his family and friends. It also wasn't too long before his friend who enlisted in the Navy with him was home for good. He had spent his tour of duty sailing the ocean and the Mediterranean on a battleship. He eventually enrolled in X-ray school at Homer G. Phillips Hospital. After graduation, he worked at the VA hospital as an X-ray technician. He later became head of the X-ray department where he retired after many years. They spent a lot of time together catching up on their lives and renewing their friendship. Since the three flights of stairs he had to slowly climb were tiresome and hazardous, he would make sure he made as few trips out of his apartment as possible, but he found out over the course of time that the challenge of the stairs were helping him gain strength and coordination. It was hard and sometimes tricky when the lights in the hallway were sometimes out, but coming down the stairs was even more dangerous and challenging, especially when he had to carry groceries and other items up and down the three flights of stairs. Robert learned to balance himself with his crutches so he wouldn't fall. As time passed by, he would only have to use his cane. He used his crutch only on special occasions. Although he spent a lot of time with his friends, he made sure he visited his mom and family as often as he could.

Robert was more at ease when he came back to his mom's home now that he was no longer living there. He even talked his mom and youngest sister into taking a trip to Chicago to visit their relatives. His car was in good condition, so they could ride with him and stay a week or so. When the time came, they packed a picnic basket and headed north. It was a beautiful day for traveling, and they arrived in Chicago with no trouble at all. His mom got a chance to see one of her sisters whom she hadn't seen in a long time as well as her two brothers.. After a few days in Chicago, they drove to Gary, Indiana to visit with her other brother and his family. It was like a Chicago family reunion when most of the family met in Gary for a couple of days. A week in Chicago was enough for his mom. She was tired and was ready to go back to St Louis. She enjoyed herself and was happy to see her family in Chicago, but was even happier to be going back home.

When he first applied for a VA evaluation, they told him it could be months before he was called because of the tremendous back log and waiting list. Summer had come and gone, and he was still waiting. He had become good at budgeting his funds by always paying his bills before he did anything else.

CHAPTER TWENTY- THREE

ROBERT'S CLOSE CALL WITH DEATH

It was late autumn when he had another close call. His mom called him on the phone while he was at his apartment one afternoon. She told him that his retirement check had come in the mail. He didn't change his mailing address because he didn't know how long he would be at the apartment. He wasn't in any hurry, so he didn't pick his mail up until later that evening. He was going to cash his check the next day, and pay his car note and rent. After picking his check up and chatting a while, he put his check in the inner pocket of his navy peacoat that he was wearing. Robert went to some friend's house, where they had a small party. They sang and drank and partied until a little past midnight. Everyone got their jackets and coats and started for home. Robert got his coat out of the closest where he left it on a hanger. As he headed for the door, he checked to make sure his check was still there. To his dismay, his check was gone and nowhere to be found. Everyone looked all over the house, and couldn't find his check. He could come to only one conclusion: his check had been stolen. He knew who didn't have his check, but had a good idea who did. However, no one else agreed with his observation, nor did they even question whether or not he could have taken Robert's check.

Robert was really disappointed, because he thought he was among friends. Even though he had plenty to drink and was feeling pretty good before the disappearance of his check, he had become suddenly sober. He left the house sad and dejected. He got in his car and went home to his apartment. All he could think about on the way home was how he was going to pay his bills with his check suddenly gone. The closer he got to home, the more he felt betrayed because he got no support from his friends. Even if the person of interest did not take his check, he knew that he didn't lose it as they supposed. He knew who took his check and there was nothing he could do about it.

When he got home, he was feeling really low. He decided to go to sleep and see what he could come up with in the morning. As he was sitting on the edge of his bed, he suddenly heard a voice say, *"nobody cares about you and nobody loves you."* Whether it was an inner voice or outer voice, he agreed with it. Then it said, *"Why don't you end it all, because nobody loves you."* Robert said, *"You're right."* If his friends really cared about him, they wouldn't have done what they did. Robert had already consumed a lot of alcohol that evening, so he took about twelve to fifteen sleeping pills and washed them down with a couple of beers. It would only take one of the potent sleeping pills that had been prescribed for him to knock him out within minutes. A few minutes after he took the overdose, he suddenly realized what he had done. Immediately he went to the phone and called the VA hotline. He talked to a dispatcher and told him what he had done. After he gave the dispatcher his address and location, he told Robert to try and stay awake and someone would be there in about ten minutes. That's how far Robert lived from the VA hospital.

He got up from the bed and opened all the windows, and splashed himself all over with water. He kept pacing the floor, hoping he would hear someone at his door at any time. It was over twenty minutes and still no knock at the door. He knew he had to stay awake, because once he fell asleep, he knew he might not wake up. He remembered when he was in Maryland when he was on a drug overdose call. The patient had overdosed on a bottle of aspirin, and was already losing color when they arrived. Her stomach was pumped out and she was given an antidote just in time. He didn't want to die, so he fought hard to stay awake until help came. After waiting and waiting, the next thing he remembers was waking up the next morning. Not in the hospital, but still in his apartment. His windows were still open and the sun was shining through the front window. He closed it and drew the curtains that had been blowing in the breeze. Then it dawned on him what had happened the night before. He began to wonder, was he still alive. After pinching himself and feeling his pulse, he realized he was alive. Not only alive, but he felt better than he had felt in a long time. He didn't have a hangover nor feel any effects of the alcohol and drugs he had ingested the night before. Then he was puzzled why no ambulance or support came from the VA hospital. It was about nine o'clock in the morning and he was so thankful to be alive that he didn't even care why nobody showed up, but what he did know was that doctor Jesus showed up and he was right on time. He was so grateful, that he thanked God over and over again. He told God that he knew he should have been dead or at least sick, and He was there for him once again. He said that he knew God wasn't saving his life over and over again for no reason. So he promised he would find out what he wanted him to do, and try his best to do it.

He was so filled with joy and relief that he couldn't wait to get out so he could tell anyone who would listen what had happened to him. He showered and cleaned himself up, and headed down the flight of stairs. At about noon, he stopped by White Castles, which was just a few blocks from his apartment and bought some burgers, fries, and a shake. He ate them before he got to his mom's house because he was so hungry. When he got to her house, he was just about to tell her what happened to him. Suddenly he changed his mind and decided not to tell anyone what he had gone through just yet. He didn't think anyone would believe him anyhow, so he just kept it to himself and pursued God, and tried to find out what he was suppose to do. He did tell her that his check was lost, and he would need another loan to help pay his bills. She helped him as she usually did, and his bills would be paid. Now that he knew his bills would be taken care of, he could relax and concentrate on more important things. Staying alive would prove to be the number one priority.

Robert realized he could not put his trust in too many people. Whether they were friend or foe. He knew there was sometimes no distinction, after his recent and almost disastrous incident. He realized he had to be more effective guarding his mind and his money. It was still fresh on his mind how close he came to death, or the possibility of never recovering from the ordeal. He realized that even had the ambulance showed up to help him, his life would have never been the same. He would have been taken to the hospital and had his stomach pumped if it wasn't too late. Had he recovered, he would have been taken to Jefferson Barracks, VA hospital and put on suicide watch on the psychiatric ward. He would have stayed there indefinitely with a possibility of a long recovery, or none at all. Even though his situation was out of control, and out of his hands, he thanks God that He had the situation under control. God had a time schedule for his life, and he wasn't going to let the deadly spirit of suicide interfere with it. With all the pain and suffering he had gone through, he had never once thought about killing himself. Even when he was on suicide watch when he was at the hospital at Scott Air Force Base. In fact, it was his first introduction to the thought of suicide. Once again, Robert was visited by the grim reaper when he was at one of the lowest points in his life. The valuable lesson taught him to recognize the evil spirit and to be very aware of its deadly intentions. He was learning throughout his life that the deceitful spirit would come in many different ways and forms. He would find out later that the Bible says that the thief comes but to kill, steal, and destroy, but Jesus came that we might have fullness of life. (John 10-10). His life always had its share of doing stupid and foolish things that could have ended in disaster. Some way and somehow, his Heavenly Father had a way of helping him through, and out of them all. He seemed to always offer him a way of escape as he promised in his word.

CHAPTER TWENTY-FOUR

THE VA FINALLY COMES THROUGH

Robert finally got some good news by the spring of the following year. The VA scheduled him to come in for his medical evaluation on a specific date. It was the first step on his way to a bigger paycheck, which he really needed. He knew the medical board wasn't going to do special favors, but didn't worry about it once again. He was aware that his medical records and the physical facts would speak for themselves. During the examination, all of the doctors conferred and agreed that his left leg was so bad, that it was not worth keeping. They told him the leg would be nothing but trouble for the rest of his life. They suggested the leg should be amputated from the knee joint, and he be replaced with an artificial leg. Robert was somewhat surprised at their radical suggestion, but he knew they were as serious as they could be. He knew he could always change his mind, but for now the decision was to keep his leg and live with the pain and inconvenience he would have. He felt the decision was already made when he was at the hospital while he was still in Vietnam. It was at the Da Nang facility, where the doctors made the decision not to cut his leg off based on the slightest of movement in his big toe. He knew that God had allowed him to keep his leg for a reason, and wasn't about to let them cut it off. No matter what the VA doctors thought about it, he knew they wouldn't understand his reasoning for keeping his leg, so he didn't bother boring them with the details. He simply thanked them for the advice, and told them he was keeping his leg for as long as he could. The doctors also suggested he move to a warmer climate to escape the effects of the winter cold on his battered and sensitive wounds. Robert didn't rule out the possibility of moving out West, but he said he would wait to see how his body would hold up under the pressure of the bitter cold that he would have to put up with over the course of time.

After his examination was completed, he left the hospital believing he would get a favorable rating. The next month, he was notified of his one hundred percent temporary rating. The rating was to be changed to eighty percent in the near future. He didn't understand why, but sure enough, his rating was changed after six months. He exercised his right to appeal the decision immediately.

He took the letter they sent him to the Veteran Of Foreign Wars Affairs office, and started his appeal process. Robert gave them the information they needed to help his appeal. As he gave them the information, they typed his complaint word for word. He told them he was not being compensated for his nervous condition, which was ongoing. He also told them that since his right hand was injured, and it was his major hand, he should be compensated for it. After finishing his report, they finalized it and sent it to the appropriate department. Within a few weeks, he was notified that his hundred percent rating was reinstated, and it would be permanent. Robert was very happy to receive the news, since it meant a major change in his pay, as well as his status. He sent a letter, thanking the organization for their prompt response and support.

    Since he would be getting more money, he knew he would have to be very careful with his check. He learned his lesson from his experience when his Navy retirement check came up missing sometime ago. He later found out that the check had indeed been stolen. His bank notified him that his check showed up at the bank with a forged signature. The check was confiscated because the signed check wasn't even close to looking like Robert's signature. His signature was signed with his left hand because of the injury to his right hand, and there was no way his signature could be duplicated. The Navy eventually issued him another check to replace the one that had been stolen.

    Summer was here, and so was his first VA check. He was happy to finally have more finances available. The first thing he did was to pay his mom what he owed her, plus a bonus for being so supportive. His Chevy Malibu was in need of work and had served it's purpose very well. He traded it in for an Oldsmobile Delmont '88. It was bigger and had a little more class than his first car. When he first spotted the red and white car, he knew it was what he wanted.

Robert also started going to a Catholic church closer to where he lived. Going fishing was also new on his agenda. Some of his friends talked him into going fishing with them that turned out to be an enjoyable outlet for him. It took a lot of adjusting, since he didn't even know how to bait a hook when he first started going. He also couldn't cast the fishing rod with his left hand. They did everything for him until he adjusted enough to cast their fishing pole without tearing it up. They were very patient with him as he kept learning new ways of doing things. As time went by, he was able to bait the hook, and cast the line into the water. It was hard reeling in a catch with his off hand, but he eventually got the hang of it. Trying new things like fishing was enjoyable and therapeutic. Fighting through pain and aggravation of not being able to do things in a normal way was a vital and healthy situation for him. It gave him an opportunity to use, and exercise his wounded parts, and also gave him a degree of confidence. In fact, almost everything he did was a part of his ongoing recovery process. With practice and time, he became so confident that he bought his own fishing tackle, and would go fishing by himself. It reminded him of the fishing trip that he didn't get to go on with his father when he was small. His father died before he would ever have a chance to go fishing with him, or do much of anything. Fishing turned out to be a peaceful and relaxing experience for him. Another plus for him was he learned to catch a lot of fish every so often. When he first started catching fish, he would always give them away. He didn't bother cleaning, or eating them. The thrill of reeling in a big fish was enough for him.

CHAPTER TWENTY- FIVE

THE CHICAGO INCIDENT

Fishing was good for him, but he couldn't stay on the fishing bank all the time. Partying seemed to be a necessary alternative, since it was what he and his friends had always done. One particular night of partying would bring about an event that he and his friends would talk about for a long time. They called it the *Chicago incident*. One Friday night, he and some of his friends went to a house party in the city. A friend of one of his partners invited them for a night of folly and fun. The party was jumping, and was fun indeed. The only thing wrong was that it ended at eleven thirty. It was too early for the group he was with. Plus, it was a Friday night, the beginning of the weekend. They gathered on the porch of the house to have a few more beers, and discuss their next strategy. It was still early and they didn't want to waste a good high. They talked about going to another party they had heard about. Everyone was in favor of going to the party, when one of his friends, who is now an accomplished actor, shouted, *"Let's go to Chicago and party all night."* They were all a little toasted, but going to Chicago was not an option. After a few more drinks, they convinced each other to make the spontaneous trip. They knew that Robert had made the trip many times, and talked him into leading the way. The seven foolish young men jumped into two cars and started their journey to Chicago. They were going to party all night, and then return to St Louis the next day. They left at about midnight, and figured to get there by three thirty. After finding some place to party, they would crash at some of Robert's relatives house, then return to St. Louis.

After driving for about an hour, Robert told one of his friends to drive, while he took a little nap. He told him to just stay on the highway and he would be fine. Two of the passengers in his car were his Navy buddy, and his friend since grade school that later became an actor. The latter was the one who suggested they go to Chicago. Everyone had taken a snooze while the designated driver had the wheel. The second car was following them because they didn't know the way. After driving for a while, the driver woke Robert up and told him they were lost. After stopping, he got out of the car and looked around. All he could see were stars, a black sky, and a field of corn. It was pitch black, and they could barely see each other. Robert asked him why he turned off the main highway. He said he became a little confused and took an exit ramp by mistake. He asked the driver in the second car why he continued to follow them into the middle of nowhere. He said he thought the lead car was taking a short cut. There they were, a smart bunch of fellas, in the middle of a cornfield, not even knowing which direction they were going.

The only thing they could do was turn around in the cornfield and go back the direction they came from. Robert was hoping to see a familiar setting that would help take them back to the main highway. It was a good thing they had gassed up because they drove for several hours and didn't even see a farm house. It was like they were in the twilight zone because there was no sign of lights or life anywhere. After driving for hours, they finally found something that seemed to be a major street. It wasn't a heavily traveled road, but compared to the road they had been on for hours, this road at least showed a twinkle of life. They kept driving in the darkness, hoping they would run into anyone who could point them in the right direction. It was about four o 'clock in the morning and their chances of seeing anybody were very slim. Suddenly they saw headlights coming towards them from the opposite direction. They flashed their lights, hoping that whoever it was would stop and give them some assistance.

As the lights got closer, they saw a pickup truck that just passed them by. They were so dejected, that they just pulled to the side of the road not knowing what to do. Then they noticed the truck was turning around and coming back. This was their only chance for help, and they didn't want to blow it. They figured that once the truck driver saw that it was seven black dudes in the middle of nowhere, in the darkness of the night, he would drive off as fast as he could. They decided to send the one who had the lightest skin to go to the truck when he got to where they were. It was a stretch, but they figured it was the only way to keep from scaring the driver off. They were so desperate to get out of the maze they were in. They had to make it work when the driver got to their cars. When he got to their cars, the truck driver talked to Robert's friend, who told him about their situation. The truck driver gave them directions back to the highway, then turned around and went on his way. They thanked the friendly stranger, as he passed them by.

It was almost daylight by the time they reached the main highway. Instead of heading back to St Louis, they continued on to Chicago. It was fully daylight when it started to rain. It only lasted for a short time, but the highway was wet. Robert tried to wake up anyone who could give him a break from driving. Everyone was knocked out, and he was tired. He had been driving almost all night long on their trip that should have taken only three and a half hours. They were still half way from Chicago when Robert hit a skid in a curve in the highway. He quickly adjusted on the wet pavement and continued on. After traveling several more miles on the rain soaked highway, he hit another skid. Only this skid was bigger than the one he had before. He was in the far left lane, when his Oldsmobile started to skid out of control. He saw that it was too late to try and straighten up the car, so he could only do one thing. He remembered that the driver's manual said to go with the skid in an emergency situation. He was going at least fifty-five miles per hour when he checked his rear view mirror, then skidded across the highway. He firmly held the steering wheel as the car continued skidding. The car didn't stop until it had torn down over a hundred yards of fence. It then went down an embankment, crossed a small creek, and stopped just short of a cornfield. He got out of the car and looked up the embankment in amazement of what had just happened. He woke up his weary passengers who had slept through the whole ordeal. As they woke up and saw that they were down an embankment in a cornfield, they asked Robert what happened, and how did they get down there? He told them they had just run off the road a little bit. As they were rubbing their eyes from their sleep; it began to dawn on them what had really happened. Everyone crossed the small creek, and climbed back to the side of the road. The riders in the second car were there to help pull them to the side of the street. They said they saw the car when it went off the highway, and thought for sure nobody had survived. A trucker who had also seen the car disappear off the highway, had called for help on his CB radio. Within a few minutes, the County sheriff showed up to help assist in what he thought would be injuries or casualties.

 The sheriff was glad to write in his report that no one was killed or even hurt. He called for a tow truck and tried to get a clearer idea of what caused the accident, other than the street being wet. All he could see was the possibility of the tires being a little low on treads. He suggested Robert get some new tires as soon as possible. A tow truck arrived to pull the car up the hill, but had a little problem. His tow cable wasn't long enough to reach the car. He had to go back and get an extension to put on the cable he already had. He didn't expect the car to be such a long way from the street. After he pulled the car up the hill, he was surprised to see that it only had one dent near one of the tail lights. He was even more surprised to see the car in perfect driving condition. They thanked everyone who helped them, then continued on their journey after paying the tow truck driver.

They were still over an hour away from the windy city as Robert finally got some sleep while someone else drove. Robert was still asleep when they pulled into a service station to get some gas just outside the city limits. He was sleep on the passenger side, while everyone else went inside the station for refreshments. The gas station attendant knocked on the window, and told him that the car needed to be backed up so he could reach the gas tank He was so sleepy and groggy that when he started the car, he put it in drive, instead of reverse. He hit the gas pedal real hard, and the car took off. Everybody started screaming after seeing what was going on. He quickly hit the brakes before it hit a wall in front of him.

After almost nine hours, the two cars finally arrived in downtown Chicago. They drove around the city for a while, then found a restaurant and got some breakfast. They sat on some park benches just talking and relaxing. Robert made a few phone calls and let his relatives know he was in town. He told them he didn't know how long he would be there, but would let them know. It was almost noon when they got together to see what they would do next. After feeling each other out, they all agreed what they should do next. They were happy they had made it to Chicago, but everyone agreed to turn around and go back to St Louis. Everyone was so tired, they just wanted to go home and get some real rest. They didn't care if they saw anything else in Chicago. They were ready to hit the highway again. So about a nine hour, overly adventurous trip through the night and morning hours, those smart young men spent about two hours in Chicago, and then left for home. Robert was somehow refreshed, and drove all the way home. This time, they were back in St. Louis and in their beds within four and a half hours. One thing all of them were convinced of, was that

God was with them during every minute of what they called, the *Chicago Incident.*

CHAPTER TWENTY- SIX

ROBERT MOVES IN WITH HIS SISTER

Life for Robert sometimes proved to be a little more interesting than he wanted it to be. In the process of trying to live a normal life, things sometimes got turned around and his life was anything but normal. In order to get a little more exercise, he bought a basketball. He would go to a park within walking distance from his apartment and shoot hoops by himself or with whoever was at the basketball court. He didn't want to be treated any differently, so he didn't bother telling anyone about his injuries unless they asked. Sometimes it was apparent that there was something wrong with his leg because of the noticeable limp. Overcoming his limitations meant focusing on what he could do, and not on the negative things. Pain was a product of his injuries, so he just had to live with it, even though it wasn't and still isn't easy. To others, it may appear not to be a problem, which is just how he wants it to be.

Even though his life was improving, he was still an accident or wreck waiting to happen. Because of life's challenges, and sometimes his own foolishness, he knew he would have to depend on God's help. God had brought him through many trials and perils already, and he knew there would be more. He tried to keep himself aware of the fact that life on planet earth wasn't going to be a picnic. After some intense bible studies, later on in his life, he would begin to understand why.

Depression would sometimes get the best of him, and he would sometimes talk about it with friends. One day he was talking very negative about some things he thought he might not be able to do. She quickly jolted him back to reality with a simple point blank statement. She reinforced what he already knew, when she said, if he focused of what he had left, he could live a normal family life just like anyone else. He was looking for a little sympathy, but she gave him a good positive dose of reality. He never wanted to burden his mom with his problems, but just visiting and being with her helped him out a lot.

At times, Robert would write poetry to express his thoughts, and to help him deal with some of his feelings. Here's his first poem:

"The Confused Mind"

Who am I? What am I doing here? Why is it warm this time of year? I'll go for a walk. No, I think I'll run. What's that shining? Oh, it's the sun. Who are those people? What do they do? Oh I feel just fine, how about you? Can you tell me the time? How's the weather? Oh anyway, it really doesn't matter. What will I do, and where did I go wrong? Where do I fit in, or do I belong? Where did it start, and where does it end? Where am I going, and where have I been? Do I look depressed? Oh, how can you tell? Do I look like the Living Hell?

    He didn't really know how long he was going to stay in his apartment, but he was thinking and talking about moving. One of his sisters suggested that he move in with her and her husband, and her kids until he decided what he wanted to do. After thinking it over, he decided to accept her offer. He had always gotten along with her husband and the kids. They were eager to have him move in, and helped prepare a room in the basement for him. He enjoyed playing games with the three boys and two girls whenever he got the chance. They were so close to him; he was more like their big brother, than their uncle. The boys could be bad sometimes, but he had a way to help keep them in order. One morning, her husband died of a heart attack from a tragic accident he had on a previous job. Since then, a nephew and the two girls have passed away. Even though they were grown when they died, it still hurt him very much. He was especially close to his nieces, and still has a lot of trouble dealing with their deaths. He did a lot of growing up during his stay with his sister and her family.

    He would meet more people during the year that would help influence his life. He was still going through the ongoing process of weeding out certain people from his life, but he was still a party animal, which meant indulging and sometimes over indulging in his favorite alcoholic beverages. Mixing drinks was one problem, but when he sometimes mixed alcohol with religion, he became a different kind of animal. Even though everyone was toasted, he would bring up the subject of Jesus and God. He knew what God had done for him, and he sometimes had a hard time suppressing the topic when no one wanted to hear it. He still went to Mass and paid his respects on Sunday morning, even after a night of partying. He kind of felt that if the priest was glad to see him, God would be, too. He knew he had to do better than he was doing, so he went out and bought himself a Bible. There was a lot he didn't understand, but there were some things that were plain and simple. Regardless of his ongoing struggles, life had become one big party, but inside, he knew he was going to have to pay a price for all the partying and fun he was having. He went straight to the part that dealt with what he was doing. The main reason it took him so long to get a Bible was because he knew he would find out what he already knew. There were no instant revelations or changes, but it was a step in the right direction.

Even though he went to church all his life, he was still illiterate when it came to the Bible. He always made good grades in religion courses in grade school and high school. In fact he made straight A's in religion his freshman year at Aquinas High. It was time for some serious searching. He had bought books about religion and religions from the Mall book stores. He even bought science fiction books and books on occultism. Since he knew very little about the bible, he got some of the best comfort and revelations from some of the poems he would write. He wrote about experiences and questions he had about his life, and life in general. His answer would come in his final writings in his book of poetry. After all the questions and analyzing, it came down to one name: *Jesus*. It was always Him, but somehow he got lost in the confusion and politics of religion and struggles of life. He titled his poem, *"You Are My King"*. Now it was up to him to find out all he could about his King, and His kingdom. He knew it would take some time, but because of the King, he would be given the time he needed.

CHAPTER TWENTY- SEVEN

ROBERT BUYS HIS FIRST HOUSE

He thanked his sister for giving him some time to regroup and letting him stay with her. It was time to make his next move. They had helped each other during their times of pain and struggles. The children were a blessing for him as he was for them. It wasn't goodbye, it was just farewell for a while. They would always be a part of each other's lives in the years ahead. Finding another place to live wouldn't be so easy. He had bought two cars, but his credit status still wasn't up to par. He took out another loan to pay for a television set for his mom to help establish his credit.

He didn't want to wait for a long period of time to make his move, so he looked for another apartment. Since he didn't have to sign a lease, his first apartment couldn't be used on his credit statement. Meanwhile, he put in an application for a VA loan as a back up plan. They eventually called him into their office to let him know how it was progressing. They told him that things looked pretty good, except for one thing. Since it was his first time trying to buy a house, he needed a determining factor to make the loan more acceptable. He asked the processor what kind of factor would be acceptable. He asked Robert if he was considering getting married. He told them he was not. They said it would show stability and stand a better chance of going through if he were married, or considering it. He was dating a girl at the time, but marriage was nowhere in the picture. The processors ran the application through to see what would happen. The loan department sent the application back with the same suggestion of being married or at least getting married in the near future. He and his friend talked it over and agreed to have the intention of marriage put on the application for the good of the house. After a couple of weeks, the application came back approved. He was going to try and live a better life, but marriage still wasn't a part of it yet. In order to get his loan, he put things in motion and waited to see what would happen later on. His primary focus for the time being was a place to live. After his approval, he began to look for a house.

. All of the apartments that he applied for had turned him down, but a house would be much better. After an all out hunt for a house in his price range, he eventually found one. It was in an area in the city called, *Walnut Park*. He moved into the house with his small list of assets. He had to start from scratch, but he gradually furnished his house with new furniture. He was thankful that God had closed other doors when he tried to get into another apartment. God in His wisdom opened bigger and better doors that would be an investment for his future.

He settled into his house and began to experience the responsibility of owning a home, but he still didn't know what his future would hold. Before he moved into his house, the girl he was with decided she wanted to see a fortune teller she had seen before. She wanted to know whether or not she and Robert would get married. He didn't think one way or the other about fortune tellers, so he went across the river to East St. Louis to see the lady fortune teller. When they got to the lady's house, his friend got out of the car. As he grabbed the door handle to get out, he suddenly changed his mind about going in. Without knowing why, he told her he wasn't going in and they should just leave. She said she didn't want to waste the trip there, so she went in by herself. He told her to be out in ten minutes, or he was coming in to get her. She came back out after paying the lady fifteen dollars. He asked her how her visit with the lady went. She said the lady told her some things no one could have known about her. She also said some things about Robert no one could have known. He didn't know how the lady did it, but he wasn't impressed. He asked her what else she had to say. She said the lady told her they wouldn't get married. His present wife has her to thank for being so foolish as to follow the advice of a fortune teller. He told his friend that the lady couldn't predict the future, but only suggest it. He told her the lady might have been right about some things, but it was up to her to make up her own mind about such an important thing. As time went by, he and his friend drifted apart. It wasn't because he believed the fortune teller, but he wasn't going to wait around for her to get permission from a psychic to tell her what to do. He knew he had a lot to learn about life, but something within him wouldn't let him resort to getting information from someone who claimed to know the future, and charge money for her services. He had seen God working and directing his life as far back as he could remember. His life was sometimes filled with pain and suffering, and a lot of uncertainty, but he knew he could trust in God. He knew there was no lady luck, or crystal ball that could do for him what the almighty God of the universe had done, and was going to continue to do by the grace of his Son.

He had become use to a life of unexpected twist and turns and deal with them one at a time. All he could do was to try and make the best of every situation. He didn't know when, where, or how his life was going to go. What he did know was he didn't need any more mystery or adventure for a while, but as his life had been scripted, he never had to wait very long to enter the realm of the unexpected. Right on cue, one of his friends would reintroduce him to a girl he hadn't seen in about nine years. The meeting was quite odd since he never really was supposed to meet her at all. One of her little girls had told her someone wanted to see her. He was just waiting in his car for his friend to return from a house near by. She came out looking as if her peace had been disturbed and asked what he wanted. He recognized her as someone he had grown up with. He told her hi, and he didn't ask to see her. In fact, he didn't even know she lived in the house she came out of. She went back in the house and Robert figured that would be the end of that. Robert's friend told him that his friend was a friend of hers and she was in the process of getting a divorce. That was as much information as he cared to know. He figured that would be the end of that meeting as they drove away.

CHAPTER TWENTY - EIGHT
ROBERT GETS MARRIED

Robert never asked his friend anymore about her, nor did he want to know anymore, but his friend would continue to provide information on his own. The information he was giving, made it cut and clear that there would be no more contact with her. The fact that she had four young children was as much as he needed to know, but somehow, her and her friend managed to invite Robert and his friend to a dinner they had cooked for them. That dinner somehow became the beginning of the end, or the beginning of his beginning. He was still open to the idea that he would get married, but the idea was far away from his mind; and having an instant family had in no form or fashion ever entered his mind. He had learned a little fishing language from his friends. Such as, if a fish hangs around the bank long enough, he's sure to get caught. True to form, he didn't follow his own advice. He hung around the bank too long and eventually got caught. Robert not only got caught, he's been gutted, filleted, and had a fork stuck in him. After over thirty years of marriage, he's very well done.

    God truly does work in mysterious ways-his wonders to perform, for Robert didn't know squat about being married and raising a family. He knew he was really stretching his faith and trust in God. This time, he had to have enough faith for a family of five and eventually seven people.

    Opening the door to marriage was a big step for Robert, but entering into the door was an even bigger step. The only clue he had about the subject was what he had seen with some of his family members and other people he knew. He knew his only chance of surviving and thriving in marriage was going to be with major assistance from the only Father he really ever knew. If God wasn't going to be there for him, he knew he might as well not get married at all. From the start, he was pretty much on his own. Family members on both sides understandably had their misgivings and doubts. There he was in such an obvious fragile condition and position. With no clear chance of making the marriage work, he and his new wife were in the minority of people who thought they could. The priest couldn't even perform the ceremony because of the rules in the Catholic Church about marriage and divorce. The justice of the peace was their only option. They entered into their marriage with the belief that all things were possible with God. With the odds already against them, they figured the worst that could happen would be that it failed, but how would they know unless they gave it a try. Well they have been trying for over thirty years and are still going on. There have been troubles, trials and the thoughts of giving up. There have been mistakes and bad decisions and stubbornness on both parts. Those are some of the things people thought would surely bring an end to their marriage at any time, but through the grace of God and faith in that grace, they have managed to overcome their shortcomings, and continue to bond because of the love and patience of God. They know it will continue to take spiritual growth and guidance for them to stay with the plan that God has for their lives and their children's lives.

For seven years, he and his family lived in the house on Arlington Avenue in Walnut Park. During that time, two more boys were born into the family. Six children would now share the house that he initially bought for himself. They met more good friends and neighbors during their stay in the neighborhood. Some of them would become lifetime friends. He would sometimes take some of the neighborhood kids on fishing trips with him. He also coached a neighbor baseball team that was sponsored by the church he attended. His wife made snacks and drinks for the kids who would somehow end up on their front porch. She also had a Brownie girl scout troop in the neighborhood. Their children would always bring friends home with them where they made themselves right at home. Their house was known as the neighborhood kool-aid house because everyone was welcome as long as they respected them and their property. The neighborhood had a few trouble makers that had to be dealt with in a way that wouldn't lead to bigger trouble.

With all of the children growing and developing their own identities, life in the Daugherty household would sometimes get quite hectic. With school, doctor appointments, grocery and clothes shopping, his world had changed dramatically. No longer was he just focused on his needs, but had to focus quickly and often on the needs and wants of his family. Things were happening so fast, he didn't have time to evaluate himself as a father. Even to this day, the adjustments are constant with adult children and grandchildren. The band just keeps on playing. He and his family were involved in a lot of activities at the Catholic church they attended. He and two of the girls sang in the choir, while the others were involved in other programs

His family was involved in the neighborhood block unit, which helped with keeping the block they lived on clean, and other helpful projects. He would often take on personal neighborhood problems.

There was an instance when the neighborhood kids and adults got together and cleaned up a vacant lot for use as a playground for the kids. After a week of hard work, one of the residents took the lot over, and turned it into a salvage yard for junk cars. He even burned tires on the lot that filled the whole block with thick black smoke. None of the residents in the neighborhood challenged him because he had a reputation of hurting, or cutting people who crossed him. Robert took it upon himself to do something about the problem. He called the Alderperson for their ward and set up a meeting with her. He convinced her to come and take a look at what was going on in her ward. Within a few days, she drove down the block to see for herself. The next day, she showed up with the Mayor and they surveyed the problem area. Shortly after the Mayor's visit, the man was given a citation, and a week to have the lot cleaned up. Not having a choice, the man cleaned up the mess he made.

One day, he saw Robert walking down the street and told him that he knew he was the one who called the city officials on him. Robert told the man that he indeed did call the city officials and he would do it again if he had to. He told the man how wrong he was for turning the lot into a junkyard after all the hard work the kids and adults did. He told Robert he knew he was wrong, and it was against the law, but no one had ever challenged his actions. He told Robert he respected him for what he did, and would try to be a better neighbor and person. He said he use to work in law enforcement, but his life took some bad turns. He said he had been taking it out on everyone else, including his wife and kids. Robert shared with the man some of the bad experiences he had been through. He told him that if it hadn't been for God helping him through, he never would have made it, and he still couldn't make it through. The man agreed with him and said he believed God was real. He said that he had been close to God at one time, and could get back on track if he really tried. After talking with the man on his front steps, they shook hands, and Robert went home to his family. He told his wife where he had been, and she thought he might have been in some danger. He told her that the man wasn't really dangerous, but just needed someone to talk to. The man did become a better neighbor, and no one had any more problems with him.

There were some good times at the Daugherty's house on Arlington. There were family gatherings and picnics with some of their close friends. The kids spent one summer in Northport, Alabama with one of their aunts. Robert's mom spent almost a year with them, and really enjoyed being with the kids. Their red brick house withstood winter storms and the hot summer heat, without having central air conditioning. One thing that was hard to get use to was the slow deterioration of the neighborhood. There were always problems that could be solved one way or another, but when the drugs began to infiltrate the neighborhood, it didn't take long for other problems to spring up. Home burglary became a common thing and property damage was becoming widespread.

Gun shots could be heard in the late night hours, as well as early evenings. One evening, he was sitting in his backyard relaxing, when he felt a sudden urge to call his children in. They were playing on the front sidewalk with some of their friends. It had just turned dark, but it was still early. He told them to come in the house right away. They asked him what for, since it was still early? He told them he really didn't know, but to just come in the house right away. They were in the house less than five minutes when shots rang out on the front sidewalk area where they had been playing. All the other kids had scattered as someone ran down the sidewalk, shooting at another person that he had been arguing with. His kids thanked him for calling them in the house before the shooting started. He told them he was glad they were obedient, even though there seemed to be no reason for them to have to come in the house so early.

One afternoon, while his wife was at work and he had gone to pick the kids up from school, their home was broken into. Things were thrown all over the place as they made their way out with an entire stereo system. They made their way out the back door with two large speakers and the system. Other small items were taken as they took what they could with the time they knew they had. Before Robert left to pick up the kids, he moved his check that had just came in the mail. He just put it in a place where no one would think to look, just in case his house was broken into.

The entire neighborhood was at the mercy of the burglars, who would even tear iron bars from the windows of some homes. The really sad thing was that, nobody ever seemed to see or hear anything. All they could do was report it to the police and the insurance company, and hope it wouldn't happen again. The thought of moving was out of the question, since their finances wouldn't allow it.

The kids were getting older, and more space was very much needed. With the limited property space available, the only place they could build was up. He and his wife talked about the possibility of adding another floor to the house that had a basement and a main floor. That seemed to be the only option, until they had another serious incident take place at their home. One night when Robert was at a high school gym with his boys and some of the neighborhood boys, something happened at their home that changed everything. He was responsible for the gym, as well as what went on in the gym. There was a group who were known for trouble that he wouldn't allow in the gym because of a sure night of trouble. The small group of boys left peacefully and the rest of the boys had a good time playing basketball and other games. He took his boys home after dropping a couple of the other boys at their home. When he got into his house, his wife was waiting at the door. She told him to go and look in the room of their youngest son, who was three years old at the time. He didn't think it would be anything serious since she didn't seem particularly upset. He went into the room and saw broken glass all over the bed of his son. He still didn't get the full picture of what happened until he asked his wife. She told him that someone had thrown a brick through the window. After looking again, he saw the brick lying in the midst of all the broken glass. He franticly asked her why she didn't tell him what happened when he first came home. She told him that she didn't want him to explode and do something stupid. She knew how angry he would be, so she gave him time to slowly let it sink in. She was right on, because he immediately put together who had done it, and had grabbed a baseball bat and was on his way out the door. He knew that the boys he had turned away from the gym were responsible for the brick in the window. All he could think about was what if his baby boy had been in the bed when the brick was thrown through the window. She asked him where he was going? Before he could think about anything else, he just paused and looked at her and said, *"It's time."* She knew exactly what he meant. They went into the room and cleaned up the glass, and put a board over the broken window. After putting everyone to bed, they talked about the option that they didn't think they had.

Since he was still angry and very upset about what had taken place in their home, he talked for a very short time. They waited until morning before they could do some real serious talking. When morning came, they didn't just talk about the possibility of moving, they started making plans to put their home on Arlington in the past. They looked very hard at their budget, and just like before, there was a very narrow gap between income and outgoing. It was going to be a very tight squeeze, but they were left with no other options. They knew they had to vacate the premises before someone was seriously hurt or killed. Even when he was in the war, he didn't have to kill anyone, even though he was very well equipped to do so. Since the war, the thought of killing someone had never entered his mind, but when he saw his kids as being a target for unruly and stupid people, he felt he could and might have to hurt someone real bad. Physically he knew he wasn't capable of doing much damage, if any damage, but he certainly knew how to even the odds and was prepared to do so. Rather than do anything irrational, he and his wife agreed. It was indeed time to move on.

CHAPTER TWENTY- NINE

ROBERT AND THE FAMILY MOVE TO NORH COUNTY

They put their house on the market in early spring. A lady from their church who worked in real estate helped them sell their house, while a broker helped them find another house. By early summer, everything came together right on time. School was out, and they had time to get things together. The financial situation was the biggest obstacle for them to hurdle. In order to meet the price range of the houses they were looking at, every dollar had to be accounted for. Their mortgage payment would be three times the amount they had been paying. They eventually settled on a house in North County that would meet their needs. The final decision would rest in the hands of the loan department. They had prayed that everything would come out in their favor, so they were not worried. Since they had found a buyer for their house who was in the process of working out a loan, all they had to do was convince the lenders that they would be able to meet their mortgage payments. When they got down to the final papers, the loan officer asked them what they were going to do for fun, since they wouldn't have much money left over after their house note was paid. They told the loan officer not to worry because they would eat popcorn and watch a lot of television for entertainment if they had to.

Things were really going well. Their house was sold in time for them to use some of the money for the down payment. They closed on the house in time for the buyers of their house to move in. They rented a large U-Haul truck, and moved everything out. With the help of some able bodied relatives and friends, they made the move to Old Halls Ferry Road in North County. It was only about a fifteen- minute drive, but it seemed like they were moving miles away from their old neighborhood. The four bedroom, ranch style house was a major improvement from their house in the city. The space was a welcome and needed addition to their growing household. A large room in the finished walk out basement was perfect for an additional bedroom. The big bonus for Robert and the kids was a big above ground swimming pool, with a seven feet deep end. Robert thought the pool would be a big help for him as a therapeutic aid for his battle wounded body.

He and the kids were ready for a summer of fun in the sun. His wife didn't care much for the water, so she would just be a spectator. Initially, it looked like they all would be only spectators. Even though they had seen the next door neighbors swimming in the pool before they moved in, they still didn't know how deep the water was. They assumed it wasn't so deep as to be a problem. He ran a test to get a better idea of how deep the pool was. The older boy, who was eleven, had been going swimming with some friends at Fairgrounds Park when they lived in the city. He told everyone he could swim, and nobody had any reason to doubt he could or not. Robert held the long safety pole as his son went into the water. He told his son not to go but a few feet out just to be on the safe side. His son held on to the pole, and his feet were no longer touching the bottom of the pool. Robert was satisfied that the water was deeper than he first thought. He told his son to come back to the edge and come out of the water. When he got closer to the edge, he decided to let go of the pole and take the last couple of strokes by himself. After the second stroke, he began to sink under the water. Robert didn't think he was in much trouble because all he had to do was grab the pole. It was apparent that he was in a little more trouble than he should have been. The youngest boy, who was three years old, saw the water splashing as his son was struggling to make it to the edge. He grabbed Robert by the leg and said, "*Knuckle drowning.*" It was then when Robert was about to panic. He told him to just grab the pole so he could pull him out of the pool. He had to practically hit him with the pole so he could feel where it was. He finally grabbed the pole and was pulled to safety. Robert scolded him for letting go of the pole. He asked him why did he lie and say he could swim in the first place. He said he thought he could until he started going under. He began to realize that he had a big, deep problem, and the problem wasn't with the water.

The problem was that no one in the family could do any serious swimming, not even Robert. He had passed his NQS [none qualified swimmer] class when he was in Navy Boot Camp, but had only learned a personal survivor course. He could hold his breath for a long time and only swim underwater. He knew that if he had to jump in the deep water and try to save his son, there would have been two drowned people. His blessing was looking more like a curse. The more he thought about it, he was thinking about having the pool taken out before somebody drowned. Before he made any rash decisions, it was time to dive to his knees again. He asked his Heavenly Father what he should do about what he thought was a water problem. His answer came quicker than he thought it would. He heard clearly, *"not to be foolish, but to learn how to swim, then teach his family."* He went to work on the sound advice the very next day. Since he wasn't afraid of the water, he started on what he already knew how to do. He could swim under water and float on his back, but he couldn't take two strokes without going under. The first thing he did was to practice taking strokes in the shallow water. After half an hour or so, he got pretty good on going from one side to the other. His next step was to try the deep end of the pool. He wasn't afraid to try it the same way he had been doing it in the shallow, but since he was the only one in the pool, he put a floating donut on his leg. He practiced with the donut for about ten minutes before he tried to swim on his own. He remembered what he learned in the NQS classes in Boot Camp. He knew he had to totally relax in order to be effective in his quest to become a real qualified swimmer. He started in the deep end, and stroked across the pool and back until he was comfortable with his strokes. After he completed his stroking, he knew he had to learn how to tread, in case he got in trouble in the deep water. He pushed off from the deep end and took a couple of strokes, then he turned around and came back He did it over and over until he could go out further each time. Eventually, he was treading water, and swimming back to the edge whenever he got ready. His final test was to jump into the deep end and go to the bottom of the pool, and come up swimming. He knew he could hold his breath underwater for well over twenty seconds, and it would take less than ten seconds to get to any side of the pool whether he swam underwater or on top. He practiced that exercise until he was satisfied with his progress. In a little over an hour, he was swimming as if he had been doing it all his life. Thanks to his Heavenly Father and his perseverance, he had qualified himself as a swimmer.

The next step was to teach the kids. As the plan was written, he used the same pattern for them that he used for himself. In less than two hours, he had successfully taught four of the kids how to swim. One of the girls practiced by her self, and passed the test when she was ready. The three year old just got comfortable being in the water, and Robert gave him a test when he was ready. He said he was tired of swimming with water wings. He took them off his arms and jumped from a high plank on the deck, into the deep water. He went to the bottom and came up swimming like a pro. Everyone kept an eye on him, but he was swimming better than some of the others. The twenty eight thousand gallons of water would get major use throughout the summer by the family and host of friends who came over to cool off. He would go on to teach over fifty people to swim in the pool over the years. The pool would also be used for several sessions of baptisms. He well understood, and was very thankful that father really did know best. Even though his pool needs a major upgrade, he maintains it enough to be used every summer. It takes a lot of work, but the enjoyment and relief it provides makes it all worth while. The pool is a major improvement on the small wading pool he dug in his back yard on Arlington. He even cemented it, and made a sitting ledge on the sides of the very small wading pond.

CHAPTER THIRTY

ROBERT'S MOTHER PASSES AWAY

Just before the thanksgiving holidays, he got a phone call from one of his sisters with some very disturbing news. It was an ordinary Monday evening, until he got word that his mother had died. He was heart broken and stunned, knowing he would never see and talk to his mother ever again. He knew it had to be true, but he wasn't quite sure of how to handle the reality that his mom was dead. It was even harder for him, since he had just seen her alive the day before. He and his family were on their way home from the city where they still attended church. He was taking the usual route home, when suddenly he changed directions. He told his family that they were going to visit his mother before they went home. They got to her home in Kinloch and surprised her with the sudden visit. It had not been so long ago when she was living with his family when they lived on Arlington. She had grown very fond of all of the kids and was really glad to see them. They all gave his mom a great big hug, and talked with her for awhile. He could see a faraway look in her eyes, and it was obvious to him that she wasn't feeling well. He tried to cheer her up and encourage her any way he could. He reminded her that everyone would see her at his house for Thanksgiving dinner, which was only four days a way. She seemed to perk up a little bit, but that look in her eyes was still there. After a very good impromptu visit, everyone gave her a kiss and a hug, except Robert. He was preoccupied with trying to convince her that everything was going to be okay. As they waved goodbye, he told her he would pick her up Thursday morning, which was Thanksgiving Day; little did he know, he would never see his mom alive again. He was very glad he followed his heart and visited her, not really knowing the significance of the visit. His one big regret though was that he didn't give her a hug and a kiss, like the rest of his family had done. That's the reason he makes it a point to give people a hug whether they want one or not.

He realizes now, that he shouldn't wait, or put off doing something so simple as hugging, and giving someone a kiss on the face. That was the last lesson he learned from his mother, which he takes very seriously. You never know when it might be the last time you'll see the ones you love.

So why should anyone waste so much time assuming that they'll see someone the next day or week, or month, or even year. It wasn't until later that night he was able to really weep for his mom. He was talking on the phone to a friend who had called to offer his condolences, when he started weeping and crying uncontrollably. His wife had to take the phone and let his friend know what was happening. Robert called him back later to apologize to his friend who understood the situation. He felt a lot better and was finally able to try and regroup and be a support for the rest of the family. He was doing a lot better as preparations were being made for his mom's funeral. He was feeling as well as could be expected on the day of the funeral, but things would take on a different look later that morning. Most of the family rode in the limousines that left from the house that all of the family was raised in. He didn't want to ride in the limo, so he and his family drove to the church in his car. When they got to the church, his family went inside while he found a place to park. When he got to the door of the church, the usher told him he would have to go downstairs to the overflow room in the basement. He told the usher that he was family, figuring that seats were reserved for the immediate family. The usher told him that everyone was saying they were family, and there were no more seats in the church. That's when he totally lost it. He ran down the steps of the church in total disbelief and anger. He was shouting, *"He couldn't even get in his own mother's funeral!"* He went back to his car and began pounding on the car saying words he didn't normally have in his vocabulary. A friend of the family came to his aid and tried to calm him down. He was so out of control, he even thought about knocking the usher out. The family friend went to the door and explained the situation to the head usher. The usher finally found him a seat towards the back, next to one of his uncles. It wasn't where he should have been, or expected to be at his mother's going home service, but at least he felt better by being in the church. After his blood pressure went down, he was able to relax and absorb what he was there for in the first place. He was glad to see the large number of people who had turned out to support the family. He realized that the usher was right. There was a lot of family in the church, as well as the basement; and even the friends and onlookers were considered family as well. As the service went on, he was honored that his mom was so well known and loved. He was really proud to be Miss Vinnie's son, and even prouder of her because of the legacy she left behind. She had touched more people than even those who were there.

He had been thrown a lot of curves in his life, but this one was a bitter pill to swallow at first. He had missed almost half of his mother's funeral, and she was still teaching him about self control, patience, love and forgiveness. Towards the end of the service, he noticed a bird flying out one of the windows in the church. He didn't know what it meant, but he had a peace that took him to another level of calmness. Friends and relatives greeted briefly outside the church, before going to Washington Park cemetery for the burial. Everyone went to Holy Angel's church, where the re-pass was held in the auditorium of the church.

There was a large gathering of people there that couldn't get in the church for the funeral. In fact, they couldn't even get close to the church because of all he traffic. The volunteers had everything in place, and was ready to serve the food. The people had brought enough food to the church to feed over half the people in Kinloch. His family was very thankful for the entire community of Kinloch who went more than the extra mile with the Daugherty family. There was also support from people in the city, as well as family and friends from all over the country who came to pay their respects. Family and friends met at Robert and his wife's home later in the evening for a reunion and social gathering. His mom didn't get to come to Thanksgiving dinner. Instead she got to go home to a place where there is no more crying or pain. She got to go home to be with her Heavenly Father where there will be another reunion of many brothers and sisters, who have had their sins washed in the blood of the Lamb. One of her favorite songs was, *A Highway to Heaven*. He remembers her singing that song with him on her lap when he was a small boy. Now she's waiting to see her children, as they travel the narrow highway that leads to eternal life.

CHAPTER THIRTY - ONE

ROBERT'S SEARCH FOR KNOWLEDGE AND TRUTH

The physical chapter of both of his parent's lives was over, but the flame of their spirits and memory could never be put out. He never got to meet any of his grandparents, so the Daugherty legacy will live on in their children and their children's children. He had to focus on trying to be the best father he could be to his children, which he knew would be an ongoing experience. Life had brought him to the point and time in life where he and his heavenly father knew he needed something more than he already had if he was going to be more effective on the highway of life. He really didn't know what it was, so he wasn't looking for anything in particular. His spiritual life consisted of going to Mass with his family, and saying grace over his food. He would always call on God when he needed something, and believed He was with him all the time.

Based on his teachings about the Bible, he was as spiritual as he was going to be. He read his own bible from time to time, but he could understand very little about what some of the writings really meant. Sometimes he would talk to a friend he grew up with in Kinloch, who had become a preacher. They use to party and run together, so he was glad for him. He would tease Robert about a Catholic medal he wore around his neck. Robert would brush him off because he believed the medal had some power in it. He would constantly tell Robert what the bible said about certain things hoping he would get a clue. He was becoming weary of his friend, and started to avoid him. He was getting on whatever nerves he had left. He was thoroughly indoctrinated in Catholicism, and didn't want to become confused and lose the little faith he thought he had.

He had already been introduced to the possibility of reincarnation while he was in the hospital at Scott Air Force Base. His physical therapy nurse was complimenting him on his projects that he had to do with one hand. He had to cut hundreds of strips of string, and glue them to a board. The art creation would turn out to be exotic birds, whales, and seahorses. It was very time consuming and took a lot of patience. The nurse struck up a conversation asking him if he believed in ESP [extra sensory perception]. He told her that he didn't know what it was called, but he knew he had experienced some strange things over the years. They shared some of their experiences with each other as he continued working on his projects. She was very friendly and he enjoyed talking with her. After a short time, the subject got a little deeper. She asked him if he believed in reincarnation. He believed that Jesus was incarnated miraculously and didn't have an earthly father, but as far as a person being born over and over again, he couldn't accept that belief. When he was at camp Pendleton, he had a debate with a Marine who believed one of his uncles came back as a roach. The Marine was so convinced that he called his mom in Muncie, Indiana to have her confirm it. Robert still didn't believe her, nor did he believe the nurse. She left him alone for a while sensing that she had stuck a negative nerve in her patient. She was right. He didn't want to talk to her anymore. He still thought she was nice, but also a little crazy.

After laying low for awhile, she came to Robert and gave him a small paper back book. The cover had a picture of a man wearing thin glasses, who was called the *sleeping prophet*. She said he could go into a sleep-like trance, and tell people about their past lives. He told her he still didn't believe, but would read the book when he got some time. He took the book, but had no intention of reading it. Everyday he came to therapy and she would ask him what he thought about the book. He would tell her it was a good book but he didn't believe it. He didn't tell her that he never read a page from the book. After about a week, she told him about a meeting that the organization behind the teachings of the sleeping prophet was having. She thought he might be interested in going to the meeting since it was being held at a hotel in St. Louis where he lived. He told her he would let her know if he would go with her. He decided to finally read the book since he saw how serious she and a lot of other people were about the clairvoyant. It took him a few days to finish reading the book from his hospital bed. He finally told her that the book was interesting, but he wouldn't be able to make the meeting. When she realized he wasn't going any further, she asked for the book so she could pass it on to someone else. They never talked about the subject again, but she had already planted her deceptive seeds.

After he bought his first bible, he still looked other places trying to find the true meaning of life and death. Even though he didn't believe or understand the theory behind reincarnation, the nurse had planted the seed in his mind. He went to the book store to seek out more information on the sleeping prophet. The first place he looked was in the religious section of the store. He couldn't find any of his books and didn't understand why. He asked the clerk, who told him to try the science fiction section. He looked and was surprised to find a series of books on the sleeping prophet. After eventually reading about every subject the man talked about, Robert was hooked. The man seemed to have an answer for every topic and mystery there was. He even talked about God, Jesus, and the Bible. His sincerity about not being a false prophet seemed to be a priority for him. He was quoted as asking God to reveal to him whether or not what he was doing was of the devil or not. He said he was walking in the woods by himself one day when an angel appeared to him and told him to keep using his gift as long as he was using it for good. He would prescribe simple remedies for sickness and diseases while being in his sleeping state. Everything he was doing and saying seemed to be for good, but as Robert would later find out, was contrary to the scriptures.(2 Corinthians 11-14 says that even Satan can disguise him self as an Angel of Light.) Even though the man had read the whole bible sixty six times for each year of his adult life, he still couldn't grasp the spiritual truth and revelation of the written word. As for the belief or teaching on reincarnation, Hebrews 9-27 says, *"It is appointed for man to die once, and then be judged."* For awhile, the sleeping prophet was all he had to give him insight and answers about some very deep subjects, but he would soon be exposed to something that he hadn't seen since he was a kid in Kinloch. He would peek in on some revival tent meetings that were held on a lot, not too far from his home. He would tell some of his family members what he heard and saw and they told him to stay away from those sanctified folks. In spite of their advice, he would go back every night and sit on the hill to see what they were doing. He was more curious about what he saw and heard than he was impressed. He figured there was nothing wrong with them, since they were church people. His number one question was: *'Why his church didn't do what those church people were doing?'* They were praising the Lord, and having fun doing it.

    Robert was still somewhat confused as far as religious doctrine and teachings were concerned, but he had come a long way in establishing some mental stability. One of the last chapters of poetry that he wrote had given him all the assurance he needed in knowing who was in charge.

"You Are My King!"

'You help me see when I have no light. And when I'm blind, you give me sight. And when I'm down and feeling low, you give me strength and help me grow. You lead me Lord from every danger. You help me to know the total stranger. You help me make it through the day, and follow Lord your loving way. Sometimes it seems that I don't care, but every day your cross I bear. Good Christian love has a special glow. For all of their deeds, and works will show. I cannot live but for myself, for I worship not, the golden calf. You give me patience, and lots of grace to carry me over 'til I see your face. Faith, you said, can move a mountain. And faith I have in your Life giving fountain. Our daily tasks are sometimes hard, but fitting for you just reward. You give me courage to speak the truth. For you are the soil, the tree, and the root. You listen Lord, to my every cry. You'll touch me Lord, when it's time to die!'

As for as what he saw at the tent revival when he was a kid, he would be exposed to the same thing years later at a very unlikely place. It would be in the auditorium of a Catholic church. He was introduced to a Catholic Charismatic group in a very peculiar way. He was relaxing in the pool one evening, when he was interrupted by a phone call. His oldest son was at the home of a family friend where he got into a squabble with a girl in the neighborhood where she lived. The girl's mother called him and said her daughter, who was about the same age as his son, had been beaten up by him. He got out of the pool and told his wife he was going to see what kind of trouble their son was in. He asked God to help him to stay calm, in what seemed to be a big problem he was about to face. His son had given her his phone number and she sounded very upset on the phone. When he got to the lady's house, his son and his friend were waiting in front of the house. The lady came out of the house and appeared to be ready for battle. Her face was red, and all he could see was trouble. He apologized to the lady, and asked what he could do to help the situation. He had his son apologize to the lady and explain what had happened. After he told his side, the lady told her daughter to come out of the house and explain her part in the squabble. After she told what happened, it was obvious that little Polly was just as much to blame as his son. Her mother made her apologize to everyone as well. All the apologies were accepted, and everyone hugged and all was well. As he was getting ready to leave, he told the lady he had prayed for a peaceful solution to the problem as he drove over to her house. It wasn't long before they were talking about Jesus, and a lot of good spiritual stuff. She told him that she was trying to grow as a Christian and was attending a Wednesday night prayer group at St. Christopher's Catholic Church. She said he would enjoy it if he checked it out. He said he would check it out since it was right up the street from his house. He had come to the lady's house expecting the worse, but left in a mutual agreement of friendship. He took his son and his friend back to his parent's home with the warning to stay out of trouble.

The next Wednesday that came around, he showed up to see what she was so encouraged about. He went with an open mind, not knowing what to expect. He saw the lady who had invited him and she was pleased to see him there. The singing was very good and inspiring. The testimonies were also inspiring and uplifting, but when they started speaking in tongues and prophesying, that was a first for him. He didn't know how they did it, but he was impressed to see what was going on with the Catholic brethren. He had never done it, nor could he do it, but he felt right at home with the group. He would return and enjoy the refreshing atmosphere and uplifting service

CHAPTER THIRTY - TWO

ROBERT GETS BAPTIZED IN THE HOLY SPIRIT

God had a way of taking what seemed to be a sure disaster, and making something good out of it. All God needed was a little cooperation from him to make it happen. His preacher friend from Kinloch still wasn't finish with him. He told Robert about a special service he was having at his church, and asked him to be there. Robert told him to remind him when it was time, and he would try to make it. He was actually going to try, but wasn't going to try very hard. Since the service was on a Friday evening, he really might not try at all since Friday was one of his evenings to relax and enjoy a nice cold beer. When Friday evening came around, he was sitting on his couch watching a Cardinal baseball game while sipping on a cold one. His friend called him to remind him of the service. He told him to come to the service because this could be it. Robert asked him what was, *IT*? He told him to just come and see for himself. He told his friend he might not be able to make it, so don't look for him. The service started at seven o'clock, and it was seven fifteen. It was officially too late to go. He figured that by the time he got there, the service would be almost over. Just as he settled back, and opened another beer, he was suddenly jolted with a burst of energy. He put his beer down, and jumped to his feet. He had not planned on doing anything except sit on his couch and watch the ball game.

All of a sudden he was getting ready to head for the YMCA building in Kinloch where the service was being held. It was a little cool so he grabbed his jacket and started out the door. Just then, his youngest daughter was going down the hallway when he told her to get her jacket and go with him She asked where they were going. He told her she would see when they got there. He told his wife he was going to Kinloch, and would be back soon. He was being driven by a force, and couldn't have changed his mind if he had wanted to. They got to the church and couldn't find a parking spot. He figured that was a sign to turn around and go back home. After he went up the street and turned around, he saw an empty parking spot that seemed to have his name on it. He parked the car, and he and his daughter went up the steps into the building. It was jammed packed, but the usher somehow found two seats close to the front for him and his daughter. He was there, but he still wasn't going to fall for something that was going to be out of whack. He listened to the preacher very intently to try and find a reason to get out of the place, but to his surprise, he found himself agreeing with everything he was saying. He had never heard preaching like that before and was very impressed. Robert was sure it was time to leave when the next sign came. All the lights went out in the building, and it was completely dark. They told everyone to stay seated, and the lights would be back on shortly. Sure enough, the lights came back on and the service continued. After the preacher finished his message, he asked if anyone wanted to receive Jesus. A lot of people went to the front and got saved. Robert figured that the service was over, and they could go home. Then the preacher made another call. He said now who wants to receive the Holy Ghost? He didn't know what the preacher was talking about, so he just sat there while some people went up front and got in line. He turned around and looked at his preacher friend and pastor of the church. He looked at Robert and gave him an affirmative nod. He knew that was his cue to get in the prayer line. He waited until the line was as full as it was going to get before he grabbed his daughter and got into the line. It was the first time he had been in a service like that, and didn't know what to do. He told his daughter to just do like everybody else when the preacher got to her.

 He came down the line, putting his hands on the people's heads and praying for them. Some of them were falling to the floor and speaking in tongues. He looked down the line and saw one lady shout, and run around the church. He said to himself that whatever they were getting, he wasn't going to get it because he wasn't going to be able to do what he saw the lady doing. As the preacher got closer to him, he just relaxed and told God that he was just going to receive whatever he wanted him to have. When the preacher got to him, he already had his eyes closed and his hands raised. All he remembered was the preacher putting his hands on his forehead, then moving down to someone else.

 After he finished, he told the counselors to take everyone who got filled with the Holy Ghost into a room. Robert was about to go sit down, when they ushered him and his daughter towards the room with some of the others. Robert told one of the workers that he didn't get anything, and he needed to go back so they could pray for

216

him some more. The worker told him that he was in the right line and didn't need to be prayed for again. He still couldn't understand why he was in the line since he didn't feel any different than he did before, and certainly didn't remember speaking in any foreign language. Being completely puzzled, he asked his young daughter if she got it. She said yes. He told her to let him see. She started to speak in tongues just like the others had done. When he saw her speaking in tongues, he said that if she got it, as bad as she was, he knew God wouldn't leave him out. He opened his mouth, and out came a language he never spoke before. Once he started, he didn't want to stop, and he hasn't to this day. He realized that he had it all the time, but it wasn't like everybody else. He didn't feel anything because he was lost in the Spirit, who was giving him what his friend knew he needed all along. He had received the same baptism that the disciples received on the day of Pentecost in the book of Acts and 1 Corinthians, Chapter 12, verse 28. It is also called one of the gifts of the Spirit. As he continues to cultivate the precious gift, it gives him something he didn't have before. His Spirit gives wisdom, more understanding of the Word, and of his savior, Jesus the Messiah. The Son of God not only is with him, but he knows that He lives in him, giving him hope for the future glory to be revealed in him. He realizes that the Holy Spirit is bringing to his remembrance all the things he has written about, starting at the age of two. In the Gospel of John, he is called, *the helper*. He and his daughter went home that night with a precious gift that didn't cost them anything. His prayer for her is that she allows that gift to grow and mature, so she can be a better witness for the Lord Jesus Christ.

Even though he has the baptism of the Holy Spirit, he still has a lot of growing and maturing to do. He was invited to give his testimony at some of the Full Gospel Businessmen meetings, and now had the confidence and boldness to do it. He would gain more experience every time he spoke, and become more knowledgeable about how to be used in the ministry. Some of the women from St. Christopher's prayer group were at one of the Full Gospel Businessmen meetings where he was giving his testimony and ministering to the people. They arranged a special service for the prayer group with him as the surprise guest speaker. Only the leaders knew who the surprise speaker was going to be, so he kept quiet and continued to come to the Wednesday night services. On the night of the service, they had food and fellowship before he was introduced. Everyone was asking each other who the surprise speaker was going to be. When he was finally introduced as the speaker, everyone was totally surprised. They didn't know what to expect since they were expecting someone who was important. He took the podium and gave his testimony. Afterwards, he ministered salvation and many received the baptism in the Holy Spirit. He knew that God was no respecter of people, and would pour out his Spirit on those who were open to receive him. The people were filled with natural and spiritual food that night, and he was glad to be a part of the blessings. His wife would receive the Baptism of the Holy Spirit in her prayer closet, shortly after a large conference by one of the top evangelistic ministries.

CHAPTER THIRTY - THREE

ROBERT'S STRUGGLES AND VICTORIES, AND GROWING AS A CHRISTIAN

He made gradual improvements in some things he knew he had to change in his life. He knew there was no way he could ever come close to being perfect, but he set some goals for himself in order to try and please his heavenly father and feel better about himself. He knew that the only person to live a perfect life was Jesus, and by trying to follow in his footsteps would be the best he could do. Drinking was a pastime in his life, and would take some awareness and time to kick the habit. The awareness came when he took one of his daughters to a doctor's appointment at the Federal building. While he was waiting for her to come out, he decided to have his blood pressure taken by a portable unit that was set up in the building. After the nurse took his pressure, she asked him was he all right? He told her he felt fine. She took his pressure again to make sure the reading was correct. When the reading came out the same, she became very concerned. She franticly told him he needed to see a doctor right away. His pressure was so high that she thought he would have a stroke right in front of her. He told the nurse he would have it checked out as soon as he could. His daughter finished her check up, and he drove home feeling a little concerned but not to the point of panicking.

When he got home, he called the clinic at the VA hospital to see if he could come in and be checked out. They gave him an appointment to come in the next day. He kept his appointment and saw the doctor. They diagnosed him as having high blood pressure, and said he had it for quite some time. He couldn't understand how the many visits to the hospital hadn't discovered something so important. They gave him a follow up appointment where he was put on blood pressure medication. Even though he was never diagnosed with high blood pressure before, he was sure that alcohol was playing a major role in his out of control blood pressure.

He decided he needed to quit drinking if he wanted to stay alive for a little while longer. He knew it wasn't going to be easy because everywhere he went there was going to be drinks available. He failed the test the very first time he visited relatives. He turned down the first offer for a mixed drink, but he eventually gave in and got stoned as usual. After he got home, he knew he had to do something different if he was going to quit drinking. After a night of drinking, he asked God to help him to quit. He was tired of waking up with hangovers and waste half of the day trying to recuperate from it. After a few days, he no longer had a taste for alcohol, but in order to avoid the temptation of drinking, he had to stay away from people and places that would provide the opportunity for him to drink. He had to stay away until he was strong enough to resist the urge to join in on the partying. It meant staying away from some family members for a while. They didn't understand at first, but he had to do what he knew was best for him. His messed up gall bladder had already been removed, and the doctors told him he was a walking time bomb before he came in for treatment. He didn't need any more incentive to stay off the sauce. Some of his people thought he might be trying to be better than everybody else because he didn't indulge anymore. Not only did he save a lot of money by not drinking, he more than likely saved his life.

He continued going to Mass on Sundays, as well as attending the prayer group on Wednesday evenings. He also was going to bible studies, and learning more about the scriptures. Even though he didn't know what God had in store for him, he stayed in the Catholic Church until he got the green light to leave. He wanted his family to learn more about God and the bible, so he wanted to make sure the timing was right. He left the Catholic Church after he felt the time was right. For a short while, he felt like a man without a country. His family visited some other Catholic churches until they found out where they would be going. He didn't have to look for a church for very long. It was obvious he was going to be at his friend's church in Kinloch. The change wasn't easy for everyone since they had grown up in the Catholic Church. The move wasn't as easy for Robert either. He had been a part of the Catholic Church since the first grade, and had a lot of good memories, but his life was on a course that was charted by God, and he wasn't about to miss out on what he had in store for him and his family. He knew the decisions he had to make wouldn't be favorable by everyone, but since God was leading him, he didn't mind being unpopular for a while.

CHAPTER THIRTY - FOUR

A NEW CHURCH ENVIRONMENT

Sunday service would never be the same again. The music, spirit, and the preached word was full of life. He had never heard and understood the bible the way he did at his friend's church. He had been raised in the Catholic Church and everything was new to him and his family. His pastor friend grew up in the Catholic Church, and knew the change he was going through. In the years he was at Miracle Temple Fellowship, he learned a lot about the bible and He also a lot of positive and negative things about the power and use of God's word. One of the main things he learned was to be *a doer of the word, not just a hearer*, according to James, 1-22. Even though he felt relaxed and was learning a lot, he was always mindful not to be lured into a false sense of security. He was very thankful to his friend for giving him and his family a chance to grow in the Word. He also exposed him to different ministries, while giving him an opportunity to minister in the word and the music ministry. His wife served as an usher and worked in the children's church. Some of his kids sung in the children's choir and played for the church baseball team. Everyone gained a wealth of experience, which they were able to use later on in life.

After he spent a number of years at the church in Kinloch, he moved on to Hope Church, which was closer to his home. He was part of the praise and worship team, which he enjoyed very much. His friend had helped him find his place in ministry so he was comfortable being able to fit right in without any trouble. God performed another miracle for him during his stay at Hope Church. While he was on his way home after a midweek evening service, his car was hit by a pickup truck. It wasn't an ordinary accident because if it had been, he and his nieces and nephew would have been hurt real bad, or killed. He was driving through a town called, Baden. It was a rainy night, when the pick up truck rammed him from behind. His small station wagon had just come to a stop at a red light, just as he was about to exit the town. There were four or five cars directly in front of him waiting for the light to change. He was almost bumper to bumper to the car in front of him when he looked in his rear view mirror and saw the yellow truck getting closer and closer to him. He suddenly realized that the truck was not going to stop.

Just before the truck made impact, he could see the driver's eyes get real big, and his face in a state of shock as he was about to slam into the back of Robert's car. By the time the truck driver saw that the traffic had stopped, it was too late when he finally hit his brakes. Robert didn't have time to do anything. He was too close to the car in front of him to even attempt to move out of the way. He didn't even have time to warn his passengers of the impending danger. All he could do was to hold his steering wheel as tight as he could, and call the name of Jesus as loud as he could. As soon as the truck hit his car, glass from the rear and side windows came flying through the car hitting the two kids who were in the back seat. The glass continued to the front seat, hitting him and his niece all over their bodies. At that point, he thought they were about to die. He was waiting to be crushed between the truck and the car in front of him, when suddenly his car was miraculously taken out of the line of traffic, and into the oncoming traffic in the left hand lane. His car hit the front end of a cab that was coming up the street, then went across the sidewalk. His car stopped a few feet in front of an apartment building. What should have been a five car, chain reaction pile up, turned out to be only a three car accident. The cab that stopped his car from slamming into the apartment building only had the side of the front fender damaged. The truck that hit his car had minor bumper damage, but Robert's car was crushed in like an accordion and totaled. His nieces and nephew were taken by ambulance to the hospital and released after the glass was removed from their body. Robert stayed on the scene and traded insurance information and waited for his son to come and pick him up. What had just taken place was systematically impossible, but with the angels of God and His mercy, he had escaped the hands of the destroyer once again. He gives God all the praise and honor for who He is and what He's done and is continually doing for him. The only thing he suffered from was delayed whiplash and minor shock, which he was compensated for. His niece's family also received compensation for their involvement in the accident. He knew that God had sparred his life so many times, so he continued trying to find out what else he had to do. He and some of his children had been involved in the nursing home ministry. They would visit with the people and pray with them. They also would sing songs with them to lift up their spirits. He was part of a prison ministry team that went twice a month to minister to the prisoners. He has been ministering to homeless and street people at a downtown shelter for over thirty years. He has seen many souls come to know the Lord Jesus Christ as their personal savior. He now attends Jubilee Worship Center in Florissant, Mo. He leads Praise & Worship, and does other chores around the church. Pastor Aubrey Kishna, and his wife Vimla originally from Guyana, pastors the Assembly Of God Church.

Robert has used his kids and relatives in the ministry over the years, and now is constantly praying for someone to minister to them. He also spends a lot of time helping family and friends in their times of difficulty and need. One of the hardest things for him to deal with is people who bring out all of the negative things when things don't go right sometimes. He realizes that the more you do, the chances of error increases. Since most of the criticism comes from people who do very little or nothing at all, he calls on God's grace and love. Even though life is sometimes hard, he knows that God's grace is indeed sufficient enough for him, as it was for the apostle Paul.

Over the years, he has developed a love for writing and composing songs. He took some basic piano lessons so he could compose the songs he writes. Since he has only partial us of some of his fingers on his right hand, he has to make some adjustments in order to play some of the chords. He hopes to be able to put his songs on a CD, which he plans to be one of his future projects. He still ministers at the homeless shelter on Locust Street in the city. He will continue to do so as long as the doors are open and he is allowed to go in.

He and his wife Rosemary (Tracy} have been married for over thirty years, and have a host of grandchildren. His sole desire is that everyone in his family would come to know the Lord Jesus Christ in a very personal way as their Savior and Lord, and live for him as best they can. He also prays that everyone who reads his story would be inspired to do whatever God has in store, with the time they have left on planet earth.

His prayers go out to every soldier, male and female and their families. He would like to encourage them to look to Jesus and call on his name as they face the dangers and perils of war. For the book of Acts, chapter 4, verse 12 says, *there is no other name under heaven by which man can be saved, but the name of Jesus.* Robert is so thankful to have the opportunity to share his life testimony. When he looks back on his life, he can see clearly that he has been under a death sentence, but time and time again, his sentence has been put on hold. When he was on the combat fields of Vietnam, his death sentence was commuted. His heavenly father has done a masterful job of steering him from the snares of death, and giving him a chance to live; but he is more thankful for the fact that through His son Jesus, He has given him the ultimate Life sentence. Jesus own words tells him that, *"He that believes in my Words, and on Him that sent me, has everlasting Life, and shall not come into condemnation, but has passed from Death Unto Life.*

(The Gospel of John, 5th chapter, and the 24th Verse.

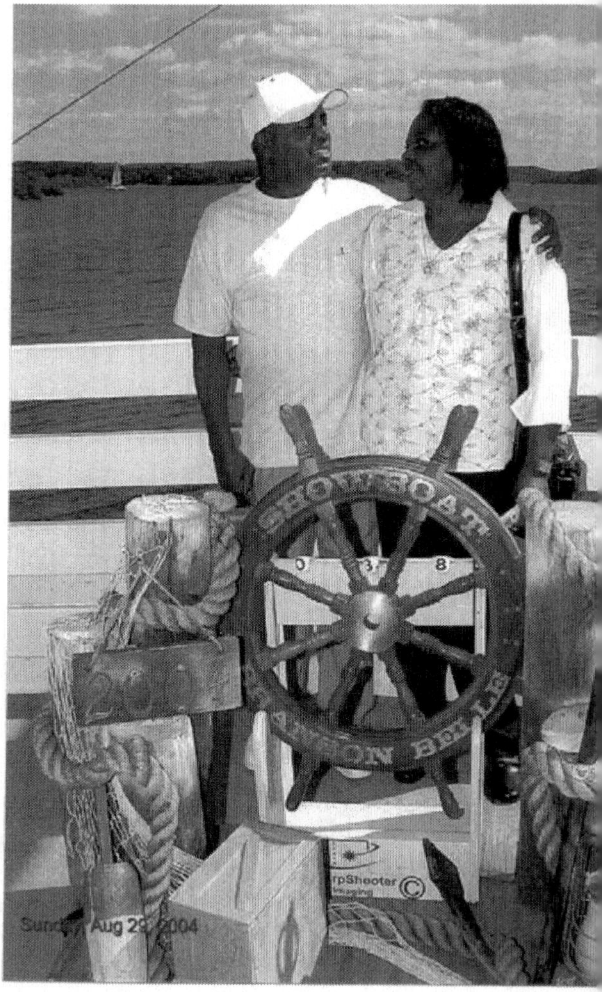

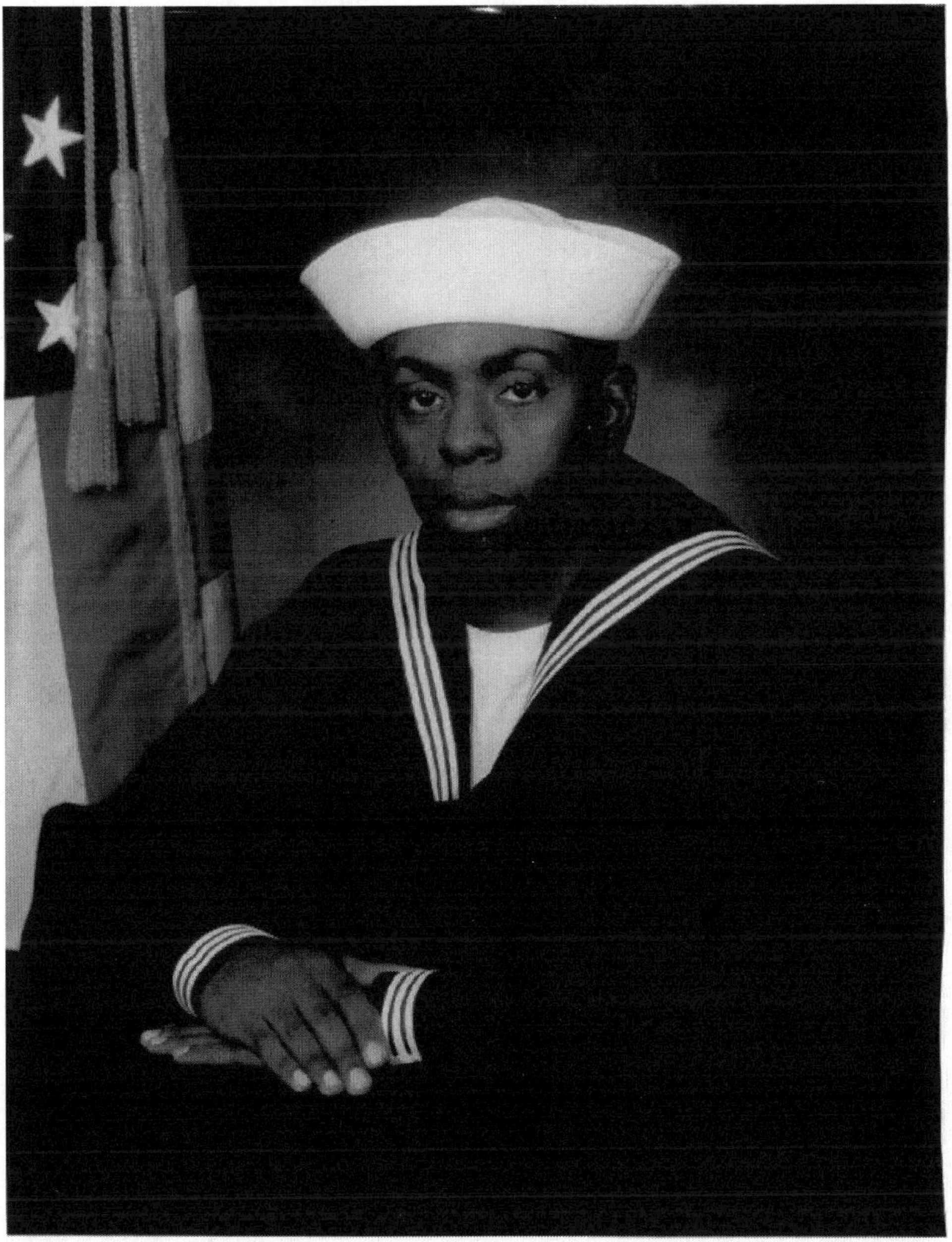

Johnny

may 73

229

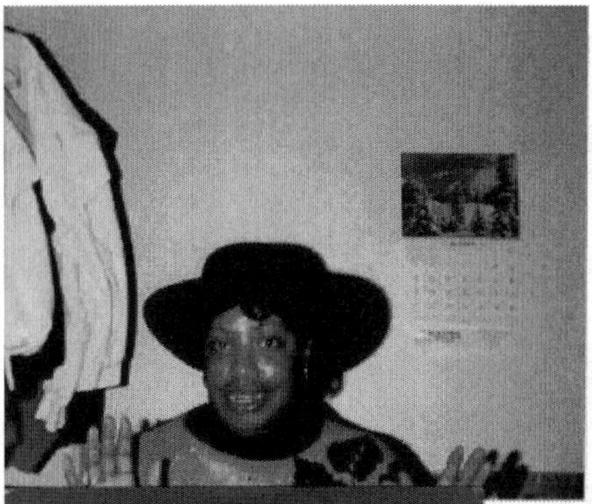
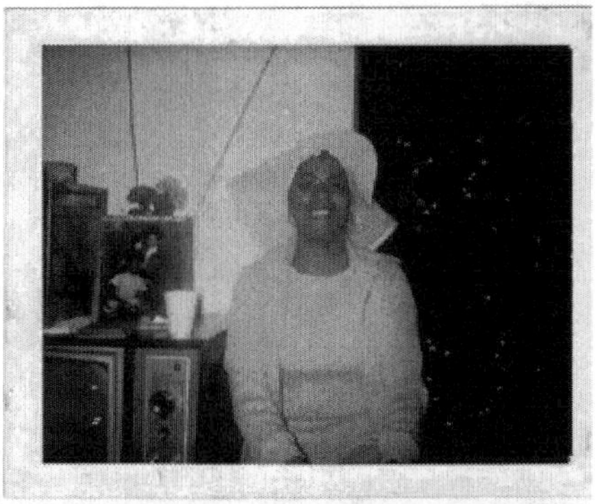
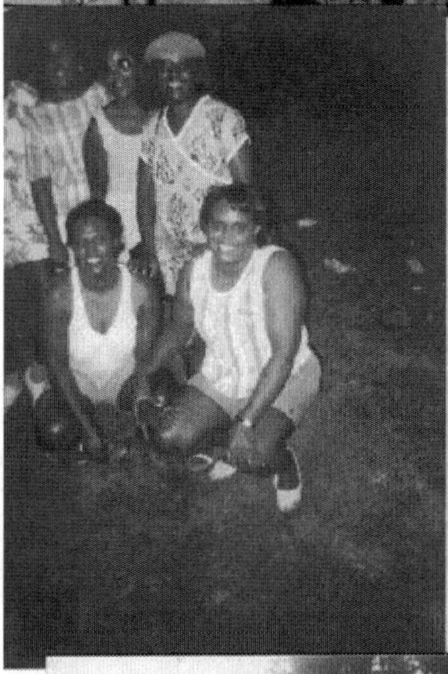
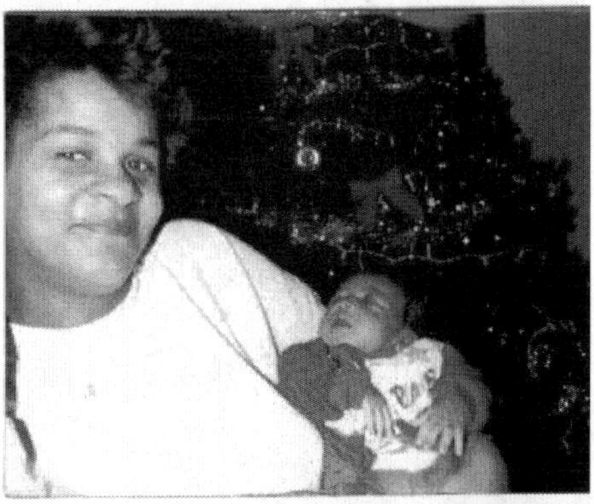
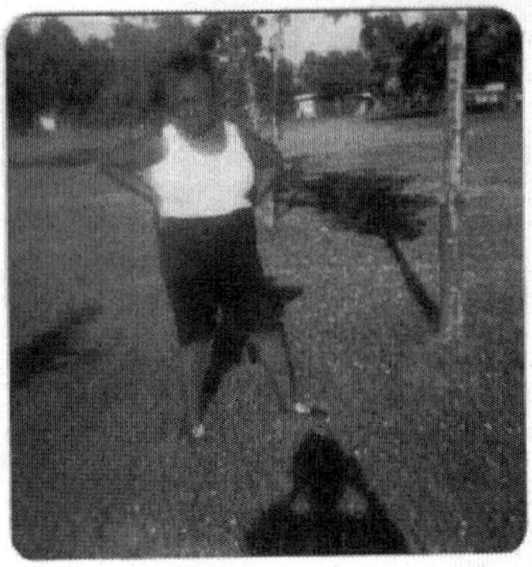
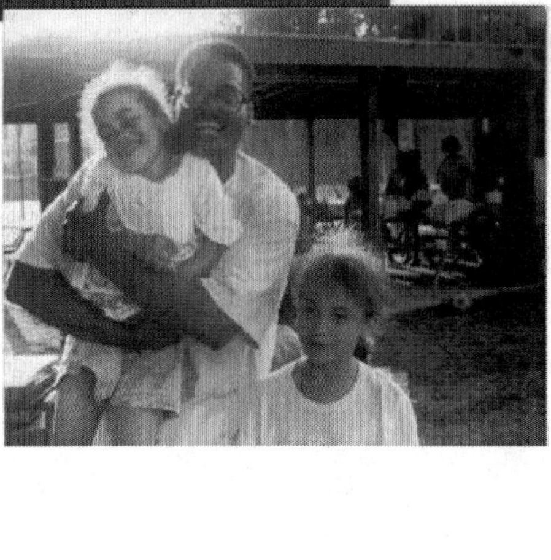

231

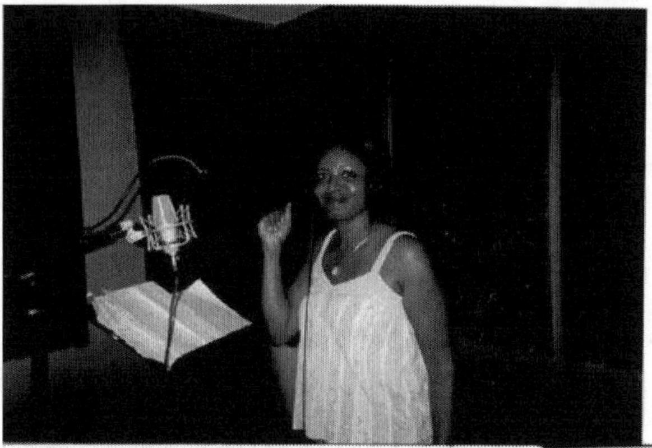

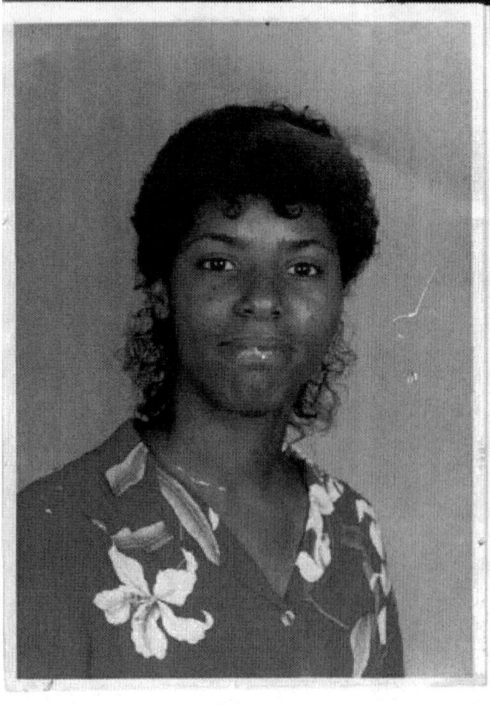

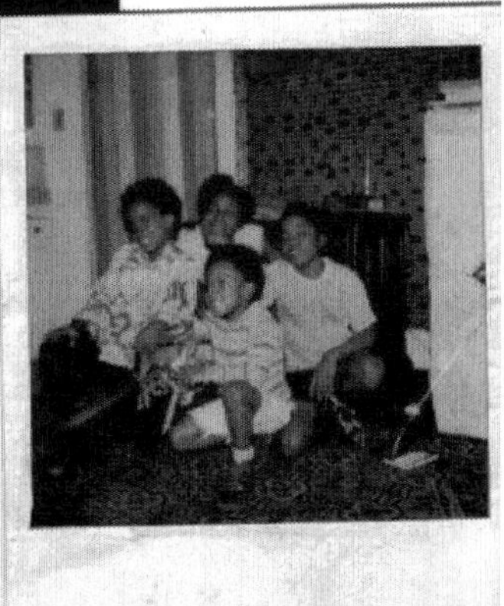

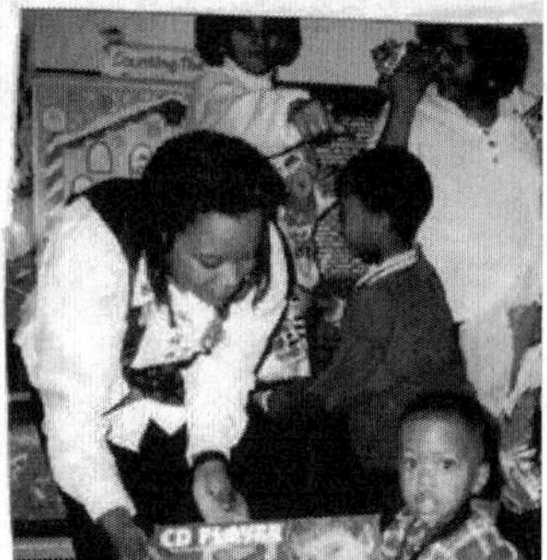
CD PLAYER

233